Dynamic Structure of Reality

Hispanisms

Series Editor

Anne J. Cruz

*A list of books in the series appears
at the back of this book.*

Dynamic Structure
of Reality

Xavier Zubiri

Translated from the Spanish and Annotated
by Nelson R. Orringer

University of Illinois Press
Urbana and Chicago

Publication of this work was supported by the Program for Cultural Cooperation between Spain's Ministry of Education and Culture and United States Universities.

First published in 1989 as *Estructura dinámica de la realidad.*
Library of Congress Cataloging-in-Publication Data
Zubiri, Xavier.
[Estructura dinámica de la realidad. English]
Dynamic structure of reality / Xavier Zubiri ; translated from the Spanish and annotated by Nelson R. Orringer.
p.   cm. — (Hispanisms)
ISBN 0-252-02822-8 (cloth : alk. paper)
1. Ontology. 2. Becoming (Philosophy) I. Orringer, Nelson R. II. Title.
III. Series.
B4568.Z83E7713   2003
111—dc21   2002151759

Contents

Acknowledgments

The present translation owes much to Thomas B. Fowler, president of the Xavier Zubiri Foundation of North America and translator of Zubiri's first book, *Naturaleza, Historia, Dios* (*Nature, History, God*); and to Gary M. Gurtler, member of the philosophy department of Boston College, who made an extensive critical reading of the present manuscript, as he did for the English translation of *Naturaleza, Historia, Dios*. From Fowler have come valuable suggestions on translating scientific and metaphysical terms in Zubiri; from Gurtler, inestimable hints on rendering terms from Aristotle and Scholastic philosophy. The translator cannot adequately express his gratitude to these two outstanding Zubiri scholars, who have made this translation the product of a dialogue of three minds. Nor can he underestimate the contribution of Diego Gracia Guillén, director of the Xavier Zubiri Foundation of Madrid and foremost critic of Zubiri, for granting permission in the name of the foundation to publish the present translation.

Translator's Introduction

Late in 1968, Xavier Zubiri Apalategui (1898–1983), one of the greatest twentieth-century Spanish philosophers, offered a public course on the problem of becoming: acorns become oaks, human beings grow old, the color white fades to nonwhite. An authority in history of philosophy, Zubiri knew of many earlier philosophical studies on the theme. Yet he too needed to make his unique contribution, and he invited his students to edit and publish his course as an organic whole. Why this problem in particular? What distinguishes Zubiri's approach from others? How did he set about to do justice to an apparently inexhaustible area of inquiry?

Many answers lie in his biography. Zubiri studied philosophy and theology in the Seminario de Madrid between 1915 and 1919. He would always display a Scholastic precision in handling concepts, would adapt to his own thinking many terms borrowed from Scholasticism, and would take into account Scholastic philosophy from Aquinas to Suárez to Maritain.[1] In 1919, he met the philosopher José Ortega y Gasset, professor of metaphysics at the Universidad Central de Madrid.[2] This relationship cannot be overestimated in measuring Zubiri's intellectual development. Antonio Pintor Ramos, one of Zubiri's most penetrating exegetes, has written, "The intellectual authority of his teacher Ortega is the condition of the possibility of Zubiri's philosophy."[3] Zubiri defined Ortega as a resonator, a propeller, a sensitizer, and a creator of a philosophical ambiance.[4] Ortega let the voices of all fruitful Western intellects be heard through him in Spain. He introduced into his nation philosophers and scientists with impact on the present book: the biologists Hans Driesch and David Katz, the physicist Albert Einstein, the founders of quantum mechanics Werner Heisenberg and Erwin Schrödinger, and the philosophers Edmund Husserl and Martin Heidegger.[5] To discipline Spaniards, Ortega needed to transmit to them a high quantity of information of elevated quality. The transmission required the creation of an ambiance adequate for philosophizing in freedom. The importation of new philosophies implied recreating them, not accepting them docilely. Hence, in Zubiri's as in Ortega's pages, venerated Scholastic philosophers as well as the forward-looking quantum physicists undergo criticism. Zubiri recognized the submissiveness of nineteenth-century philosophy to sects or parties. He tried his entire life to keep himself and his philosophy as nonpartisan and universal as Ortega had recommended.

Zubiri found Ortega's philosophizing so "liberating" because Ortega taught the need to live philosophy from within as the personal drama of the philosopher. He was quick to detect valuable ideas. Hence, he quickly opened Zubiri's mind to the value of Husserl's *Logical Investigations* as well as to Heidegger's *Being and Time,* two works very influential on the pages here translated. Ortega contributed to fine-tuning Zubiri's own sensitivity. Zubiri has written that Ortega was able to "feel intellectually" all great human problems. Zubiri, whose greatest work is perhaps the trilogy *Inteligencia sentiente* [Sentient intelligence] (1980–83), could hardly have asked more of a teacher. He praises Ortega for making philosophy a constant way of coping with problems. For that purpose, Ortega offered a "home" to his students, cozy and warm for the best, cool for the mediocre. He set aside a space for philosophizing, be it the informal discussion table over coffee, the column of the cultural journal, the classroom, or the theater for public philosophy lectures. Zubiri, out of necessity, would have to follow Ortega's example. Zubiri spent much of his life—from 1942 until 1983—earning his living by giving extrauniversity courses to the Madrid public. *Estructura dinámica de la realidad (Dynamic Structure of Reality)* (1968) exemplifies such a course.

Understanding this work requires taking into account not only Ortega's impact on Zubiri but also Zubiri's education beyond the Pyrenees. In 1920 and 1921 he studied philosophy at the Institut Superieur de Philosophie in the University of Louvain, from which he received a master's in philosophy after submitting a formal study on Husserl. In 1921 he also received his doctorate in philosophy at the Universidad Central de Madrid with a thesis, directed by Ortega, on Husserl. After publishing his dissertation in 1923, and after winning by state examination a chair of history of philosophy at the Universidad Central de Madrid, Zubiri spent three years in Germany. Between 1928 and 1930 he did postdoctoral philosophy studies with Husserl and Heidegger at Freiburg. The following two years he resided in Berlin, where he saw or met Einstein, Schrödinger, Heisenberg, and the mathematician Zermelo.[6] In *Dynamic Structure of Reality* Zubiri recalls a personal meeting with Heisenberg (either in 1930 or 1931), whom he asked a question in quantum mechanics yet received no clear response. The question, on the reversal of time among elementary particles, would remain open in Zubiri's mind over thirty years later, when penning *Dynamic Structure of Reality*.

While Zubiri stretched and deepened his mind in philosophy and the material sciences, he attended to the exploration, often difficult, of his own religious faith. God appears in the pages of *Dynamic Structure of Reality* despite Zubiri's announced aim of making intramundane philosophy. In 1920, Zubiri received his doctorate in theology at the theological college of the University of Rome. The following year, he was ordained a priest in Pamplona. The academic pursuits that occupied him almost exclusively over the next fifteen years would make him change course in life.

In 1935 he returned to Rome to arrange his own secularization. In March 1936, he married in Rome Carmen Castro Madinaveitia, daughter of the Spanish historian and philologist Américo Castro Quesada. During the Spanish Civil War (1936–39), the couple resided abroad. When they returned to Madrid in the fall of 1939, Bishop Eijo y Garay obliged Zubiri to leave the city because of his status as a secularized priest. It did not help that Zubiri's new father-in-law, Castro, living in exile in the United States, had been an avid supporter of the Second Spanish Republic, which had fought Franco in the war. After resuming his teaching in Barcelona, Zubiri decided to go on administrative leave in 1942, thereby forsaking the Spanish university system forever.[7] Ever after, he would earn his living from his public lectures.

Zubiri fared considerably better than his teacher Ortega in fascist Spain. Although remaining steadfastly apolitical—he had learned Ortega's lesson better than Ortega himself—Zubiri had the fortune to win through his personal charisma and intelligence the warm friendship and intellectual respect of Pedro Laín Entralgo, Xavier Conde, Antonio Tovar, and other gifted members of the centrist wing of the Falange, the only political party allowed by the Franco dictatorship. Not only did Zubiri contribute intellectual stimulation and ideas to Laín's philosophy of medicine from 1941 on, but in an impoverished postwar Spain, it was Laín who arranged for Zubiri to receive compensation, first for philosophy courses imparted in private to him, Conde, and their friends, and afterward, to the general public.[8] Laín also introduced Zubiri to Diego Gracia Guillén, future president of the Xavier Zubiri foundation of Madrid, an exemplary editor of Zubiri's works and a rigorous interpreter of his writings. Thus, within a potentially stifling atmosphere of Francoist Spain, Zubiri found a small island of philosophical freedom. Laín, a significant historian of medicine, has confessed that from a private course taken with Zubiri in the early 1940s, he himself derived a basic premise: Greek medicine regards sin as a sickness, while Semitic medicine sees sickness as a sin, with lasting consequences in Western medicine.[9] Zubiri owes to Laín insights on the notion of becoming in eighteenth-century French vitalistic medicine, examined in this book (see chapter 8).

By 1968, Zubiri had gained acclaim for having published three major works: his first and most frequently reprinted book, *Naturaleza, Historia, Dios* (*Nature, History, God*) (1944), comprised of articles on varied philosophical themes; a systematic treatise in metaphysics, *Sobre la esencia* (*On Essence*) (1962), concerning the science of reality as reality; and *Cinco lecciones de filosofía* [Five lessons of philosophy] (1963), a compilation of course lectures on how six major philosophers view philosophy—Aristotle, Kant, Comte, Bergson, Husserl, and Heidegger.[10] All three books, especially the second, have contributed numerous ideas to *Dynamic Structure of Reality*. Still, many conceptions from *Cinco lecciones de filosofía* on Aristotle, Kant, Bergson, and Heidegger prove useful to Zubiri's 1968 course on the metaphysics of becoming: Aristotle found philosophy an activity that renews its own potency—the knower never ceases to learn—and the contrast between potency and actuality becomes seminal to Zubiri's thinking on dynamism. Kant raised the scientific notion of causality to a universal principle, and Zubiri seeks to give dynamism to cosmic causality. Bergson envisioned becoming as the chief creative force in the universe, and Zubiri aspires to add structural rigor to Bergson's vision. Heidegger saw our being grounded on our temporality, our historicity, while Zubiri, not finding Heidegger radical enough, grounds our being on our dynamic structure. Husserl, moreover, provided Zubiri a phenomenological method, a road to presupposition-free, immediate knowledge of becoming in its most meaningful aspects. Therefore, when *On Essence* generated enthusiastic reviews with one reservation—namely, that Zubiri had treated being in too static a fashion—he held ample information to correct that misgiving.

Husserl's method allows Zubiri to give a dynamic structure to his work on becoming that is worthy of its title. Husserlian phenomenology calls for eidetic reduction, or suspension of historical presuppositions to solve a problem. The thinker, with spatiotemporal forejudgments put out of play, rises to a self-evident, universal truth encompassing the phenomenon under study. Then he disconnects everything merely having to do with the phenomenon from everything essential to it. He gathers together all its essential notes to present its essence, passing from the most universal to the most particular notes of that essence. Finally, he describes all these notes, one by one, directly and without mediation of extraneous theories. Hence, in his prologue, Zubiri specifies his problem: becoming. He then explains his tripartite division in solving it: in part 1, he aspires to attain its essence by clarifying the meaning of "dynamic structure of reality"; in part 2, he promises a description of its aspects by delineating one by one the dynamic structures comprising reality; finally, in part 3, he offers a brief but intense synthetic vision of reality qua dynamic.

Part 1 advocates suspending three basic forejudgments in the history of philosophy: that the problem of becoming is a problem of being; that the one undergoing the becoming is an underlying subject; and that becoming consists of change. After detaching himself from his book title to gain a direct view of becoming in its raw reality, Zubiri recommends dissolving the traditional linkage between becoming and being. The great Greek philosophers erred. Zubiri carefully examines their errors, word by word. He presents the phrases with which Parmenides of Elea in the fifth century B.C. uncompromisingly presented becoming as a union of being and non-being but dismissed non-being as off-limits to the mind. Next, Zubiri provides the confession of Plato that he was committing an act of parricide against his intellectual father, Parmenides: he struck the older thinker a fatal blow by disregarding his prohibition and theorizing on non-being. He concluded that, in theory, it was other-than-being, and this differs from non-existence. Finally, Plato's pupil Aristotle disagreed with his teacher, whom he thought too theoretical and not practical enough to treat becoming as a physical unit. In making this critique, Aristotle would commit what Zubiri saw as an error with long-range consequences in philosophy and science: he would hypothesize the existence of an underlying subject or being to which to attribute becoming. At the same time, however, he would invent concepts such as potency that would shed light on vast areas of science (potential and kinetic energy) and philosophy (dynamism). Still, Zubiri finds no evidence for Aristotle's and so many others' identification of becoming with changing. Nor can Zubiri concur with Aristotle that it is *being* that becomes. Instead, *reality* becomes.

This conviction causes him to leap to a self-evident truth in chapter 2: that reality differs from being. Reality is prior to being, grounds being, and undergoes all becoming. The priority of reality to being is a main thesis of *On Essence*. In *Dynamic Structure of Reality*, Zubiri replaces the inert Aristotelian notion of substance with the dynamic concept of structure. He suggests as much in an energetic, graphic fashion: taking the example of a bearded man, Zubiri imagines him deprived of all his essential attributes one by one like an artichoke stripped of its leaves. He concludes that realities are not substances, but organized systems of notes and properties, or structures. To show the error of viewing reality as substance, Zubiri locks horns with Aristotle in his *Metaphysics* as well as with nineteenth-century science (see chapter 4). In the process, Zubiri reasons that becoming differs from change.

Having set becoming apart from everything relevant to it but non-essential, he finally defines it as the "structural dynamism of reality," a formula virtually reproducing the title of his book. To clarify his position, he offers five steps to understanding him, each more universal than the following: "structural" means respective, or referential, as every reality is comprised of notes referred to every other, just as every reality refers to every other reality; respectivity, or referentiality, forms part of reality as such, and the referring is a formal characteristic making reality active, dynamic; this dynamism is the constitution of reality as such, whose structure Zubiri terms its "in its own right," its being something in itself and for itself; merely by virtue of being in its own right, of showing its essential properties, dynamism is comprehensible as a "giving of itself"; and such cosmic generosity distinguishes dynamism from a mere process or change. An orange, by possessing and displaying its essential properties, its symmetry, its bright color, its juiciness, its roundness, engages in no change or process. To synthesize, becoming means (1) respective, (2) dynamic, (3) constitutional, (4) self-giving, (5) distinguished from change, and (6) different from process. In part 2 (chapters 5–10), Zubiri systematically describes the main dynamisms of the universe, showing that they have these six properties while moving once more from the more universal dynamisms to the less. At the same time, Zubiri's rationale describes an ascent from the humblest dynamisms peculiar to all realities to the highest and most self-conscious, wherein dynamisms acquire greatest self-possession.

Chapter 5 lays a foundation by describing causal dynamism, formally underlying the dynamism of the world. The idea of respectivity (referentiality) generates Zubiri's original idea of causality, transcending the notions of Aristotle, of mathematical physics, and of Kant: causality means for Zubiri the functionality of the real qua real. Raw impressions—cold, red, painful—present themselves to human beings as being real, in other words, respective, referred to other realities. Among the different causal dynamisms, Zubiri describes the dynamism of variation as the most basic, and the most basic variations, the spatial ones. These reflections lead to considerations on topology, relativity, and quantum mechanics insofar as displacement in space involves dynamism (see chapter 6). Another causal dynamism is that of alteration, wherein the essences composing a world are active in and for themselves. This structure includes transformations of chemical compounds and high-energy particles; repetition of individuals producing like individuals, such as electrons bombarded by photons and producing new electrons, animals giving rise to clones (although Zubiri did not live long enough to see their production); and genesis of realities belonging to the same phylum, understood in a broader sense than the biological one. Yet a third type of causal dynamism, the dynamism of selfhood, consists of a reality as such being active by itself. Zubiri describes the progress of life from the constitution of living matter to the formalization of the living being through the differentiation of cerebral functions (see chapter 8).

Chapter 9 concerns maximum formalization in the form of the human dynamism of self-possession. Here Zubiri addresses the problem of how the hominid becomes a human being. After reviewing the different evolutionary "strata" of hominids from the archanthropus to the Cro-Magnon, Zubiri decides that a new type of essence is at hand in the universe, one which he calls "open essence" in a discussion with Heidegger. Chapter 10 deals with two results of open essence visible in the "dynamism of living together": society, which both Ortega and Zubiri conceive as "depersonalization";[11] and history as a "dynamism of world-making" meant to enrich the individual human being. An individualist at base, Zubiri thereby responds to Hegel, who views the human being as a servant to history.

Chapter 12, though intended to synthesize all the preceding ones, also carries Zubiri one step beyond. He briefly reviews nearly all the dynamisms he has previously discussed—variation, alteration, transformation, selfhood, self-possession, personalization, depersonalization, and world-making—but he also poses four questions to underscore basic positions already taken: Who is dynamic? What is dynamism? What is the character of this dynamism? What is the dynamic structure of reality? We need only recall the title and theme of Zubiri's book to provide answers: the "subject" of dynamism is each reality as such, a universal, not a particular. I immediately recognize this cat as a cat when receiving my raw impressions of this purring mass of tawny and white. Dynamism is the becoming that constitutes reality. The character of this dynamism is universally causal, emerging from the respectivity of its structure, and it is therefore definable as the functionality of the real as such. The dynamic structure is as a whole the respectivity of the universe in its totality. To borrow a favorite example of Zubiri's, the reality of light is its brightness as such; its dynamism, the electromagnetic wave-structure; and the dynamic structure, the universal order into which this light inserts its edifying glow.

Dynamic Structure of Reality has helped inspire Pedro Laín Entralgo's *Cuerpo y alma: Estructura dinámica del cuerpo humano* [Body and soul: Dynamic structure of the human body] (1991). Zubiri, confesses Laín, attracted him for making a philosophy both up-to-date and Christian. He met the challenge of contemporary science and philosophy of science without renouncing his religious convictions.[12] Zubiri, Laín points out,[13] conceived structure as the "spatial, dynamic expression of substantivity" understood as a cyclical, respective set of notes integrating reality. The real object—crystal, organism, star, or galaxy—is the systematic set of its notes.

By substituting the new idea of structure for the ancient one of substance, Zubiri joined not only philosophers but also scientists of his day. Toward the end of his life, Alfred North Whitehead openly rejected substantialism and espoused a view of nature as a set of emergent events, with material objects seen as structures that organize, change, and disappear.[14] Maurice Merleau-Ponty ceased to view the cosmos as matter full of juxtaposed parts, conceiving it instead as a place filled with "behaviors," the "structures" of living organisms.[15] In physics, Einstein broke with absolute, substantialized Newtonian space and lent geometric structure to gravitation, equating it to the curve of the universe. In biology, Ludwig von Bertanffly applied the "theory of systems" to biology.[16] Instead of reducing a being like the human body to its parts or properties, he focused on the arrangement of parts and their relationship to a whole in their openness to their environment. In quantum mechanics, strange bondings began appearing in spectroscopes between atoms, between electrons and nuclei, and between particles within nuclei, displaying or promising to display unsuspected structures to the careful observer.[17]

Zubiri's dynamic structuralism also bears a Christian stamp attractive to Laín. Throughout Zubiri's philosophical development—first as an object-oriented phenomenologist guided by Husserl (1921–28), next as an ontologist following Heidegger's lead (1931–44), finally as a metaphysician of reality (1945–83)[18]—he insists that the universe originated in an act of creation out of nothingness. It emerged from the gratuitous act of a God transcendent to the world. Any intramundane theory limits itself to examining secondary causes. Zubiri finds occasionalism a plausible metaphysics—the notion of divine intervention at every instant, of continuous creation (see chapter 5). It was no less plausible that God granted a potency to cosmic matter at the instant of its initial creation. This potency was actualized billions of years later when humankind emerged. The mutant australopithecine that gave birth to the first *Homo habilis,* according to Laín, somehow lay within the potentialities of matter prior to the Big Bang.[19] The creatures imitate unawares the generosity of a self-giving Creator. Every reality—the starfish, the aster, the asteroid—gives of itself by mobilizing its dynamic structure. Zubiri also gives of himself by systematically raising awareness of main structures in the universe. He modestly accepts his role in history as a secondary cause, a self-effacing system builder. An acknowledged heir to Heraclitus, one of the first philosophers to perceive reality as dynamic, Zubiri most admires the ancient Greek philosopher's fragment 112 for hinting that reality is a latent structure: ἁρμονίη ἀφανὴς φανερῆς κρείττων, usually translated as "The hidden harmony is better than the visible one." Zubiri seeks a more literal translation: "The fastening that is unseen is stronger than the one seen." Where others translate "harmony," Zubiri has substituted a carpenter's work of joining pieces of wood (see chapter 12). In structuring ideas, Zubiri performs an act of intellectual carpentry while aware that his faith links the carpenter's trade to divinity.

Translator's Note

The intellectual challenge of reading Xavier Zubiri pales by comparison with the task of translating him. His philosophical rigor accounts for his reputation as a classic in his own time. Not even most trained minds of his native Spain can meet the lofty demands he makes of his readers. What a formidable undertaking it is, therefore, to try to make his ideas available to English speakers! The translator of Zubiri must proceed basically guided by three ideals: precision, clarity, and linguistic deftness. The imperative of precision stems from Zubiri's chief self-demand as a thinker, because any translator can at once identify Zubiri's most frequently used adverb as "precisely" (in his Spanish, *precisamente* and *justamente*). Still, the translator must balance Zubiri's need for precision with the necessity for clarity. Zubiri himself has found the balancing act precarious, often tempting the conscientious translator to avoid venturing out on the tightrope at all.

For example, the present work, *Estructura dinámica de la realidad* (*Dynamic Structure of Reality*) (1968), has originated as Zubiri's response to reader misinterpretations of his earlier treatise *Sobre la esencia* (*On Essence*) (1962). Hence his frequent recourse to self-repetition here, not always with the desired result of comprehensibility because of the complexity of his terms. To make himself understood in a flash of insight, Zubiri often resorts to inventing words, straining conventional Spanish to the limit through the unusual use of suffixes. For instance, he transforms the traditional notion of essences as substances into his own idea of essences as substantivities. Where a neologism in Zubiri's Spanish has a cognate in English, as is the case with "substantivity," conceived by him as a systematic organization of self-sufficient notes or essential features of an object, I use that cognate in the confidence that it will readily be found in English dictionaries. When Zubiri coins a word, I include it in the text in brackets after my translation of the word. Certain of Zubiri's neologisms lack exact English cognates but have graceful equivalents that are close enough, which I gladly employ. Hence Zubiri invents the word *temporeidad,* meaning the characteristic of time as referred to being. I prefer to use the preexisting English word "temporality" because it is defined in context and adequate to the purpose. Moreover, I follow the same practice in treating Zubiri's rather baroque neologism *coherencial,* where English "cohesive" will do just as well, and his astounding verbal monsters *actuosidad,* for which I use the clear and simple preexisting word "activeness," and *estimulidad,* for which I substitute the acceptable word "stimulation."

Shortly, I will show that he can invent esthetically pleasing neologisms. The example par excellence has to do with the two orders of human access to objects, the particular and the universal. The essence of a thing determines that it is "such-and-such" a thing, a particular "something" different from others. This order of reality is what Zubiri calls the "talitative" [*talitativo*] order, derived from the Latin *tale,* meaning "such." He distinguishes this order from the order of universals, or what he terms the "transcendental" [*transcendental*] order, whereby things present themselves as pure and simple realities. I see thus-and-such an object with a silver hue and four sharp prongs as the reality of a fork. I can never perceive anything concrete or particular without my intelligence operating over it and apprehending it as a universal, a reality as such. Let me, therefore, simply use the word "particular" and sidestep any neologism, because the notion of "particularity" [*talidad*] arises so frequently. On the other hand, I readily borrow a neologism that has sprung in the fertile mind of Gary M. Gurtler while reading the first version of this translation. As graceful a neologism as *talitativo* is *sentiscencia,* a coined word denoting vague, primitive, general sensitivity, eventually to develop into usual sharp sensitivity. This is a word that scarcely appears at all in the present text, yet it signifies something that no one before Zubiri himself has actually discovered. Knowing that my readers will tolerate the inchoative infix -*scence,* as in "luminescence" and "incandescence," I take the liberty of using Gurtler's translation, "sentiscescence." Another Zubirian neologism that offers esthetic enjoyment is *personeidad,* which I translate "personhood," the substantive part of the human being, as distinguished from *personalidad,* "personality," which develops through the assaying of possibilities. Moreover, Zubiri displays maximum skill as a neologizer when he invents *extructo,* a hybrid of the words for "structure" [*estructura*], "extract" [*extracto*], and "construct" [*constructo*]; no translator can resist imitating Zubiri and coining the corresponding English hybrid "extruct."

Another example of a term seeming to demand invention of a cognate is the major concept "respectivity" (in Zubiri, *respectividad*), meaning referentiality of and between the forms and modes of reality; one mode of being real is in respect or reference to another form of reality. The word appears so often that along with its cognate I sometimes place the familiar word "referentiality" in brackets. By analogy, any and every expression I find in Zubiri's text derived from a language other than Spanish appears translated by me in brackets placed immediately after that expression. For instance, the Latin expression *primo et per se* always recurs with my translation: [first and by itself]. I take for granted that many of my readers do not read ancient Greek, and I will provide English equivalents the first time unfamiliar Greek words appear in Zubiri's work without failing to supply the original for the sake of precision.

Finally, there occur with alarming frequency neologisms in Zubiri's text that resist the formation of English cognates. The most amusing example is *suidad,* meaning the quality of being one's own individual—be it a person, place, or thing. If I invented the neologism "suity," I would risk the word becoming too closely associated with the English "suety," "loaded with animal fat." Instead, I prefer paraphrasis to render the word as "self-possession." A related example is the key concept *de suyo;* here Zubiri follows the example of his teacher Ortega in laying hold of a common idiom in Spanish but redefining it in a technical way. In everyday Castilian, it is commonplace to hear, "This matter is *de suyo* complicated," wherein *de suyo* means "of itself." In Zubiri's metaphysics, however, *de suyo* signifies the first transcendental property belonging to a real thing simply because it is real. The property *belongs* to the thing but also lies *within* as something legitimately intrinsic to the thing. Therefore, to express this legitimacy with a common English phrase, following the suggestion of T. Fowler Jr., I prefer to make use of the expression "in its own right" every time Zubiri employs the expression *de suyo.* Once in a while, Zubiri invents a word like *subjetualidad,* or the property of serving as a subject, but he employs the word so seldom and in so limited a context that paraphrasing the word in English rather than neologizing seems sufficient. The same holds true for the neologism *accional,* which I simply render "characteristic of action"; and the odd new noun *enclasamiento,* which I translate as "insertion into classes." Then too, because Zubiri seems reluctant to employ the traditional vague word *psyche,* he provisorily invents the term *psiquismo,* for which I use "psychic makeup."

These, then, constitute some of the tribulations to be faced in translating Zubiri. A translation of *Estructura dinámica de la realidad,* however, is long overdue in English. May the agility of language for which I am striving approach the agility of the thought here unfolding on the printed page.

Dynamic Structure of Reality

Foreword
Diego Gracia Guillén

Dynamic Structure of Reality is the title of the course of eleven lectures given by Xavier Zubiri in Madrid on November 18, 21, 25, and 28 and December 2, 5, 9, 12, 16, 19, and 20 in 1968. The course was organized by the Sociedad de Estudios y Publicaciones. Six years earlier, in December 1962, he had published his book *On Essence,* considered by some critics to be novel and exceptional but excessively "static." It seemed to be written with a focus more on Aristotle than on Hegel.[1] Zubiri attempted to respond to these critics with his 1968 course. Hence its content should be considered as the natural extension of *On Essence.* It is no accident that the text of *Dynamic Structure of Reality* ends with the following paragraph: "Reality as essence is a structure. It is a constitutive structure, though one whose moments and ingredients of constitution are active and dynamic in themselves. Consequently, what has sometimes been said of my book [*On Essence*] is absolutely capricious. It has been said that it is a static book, a book of concepts merely at rest. I am very sorry. Rightly or wrongly, I hold precisely that in an essential and formal way, dynamism concerns essence such as I have described it in my modest, cumbersome book *On Essence.*"

This is the intellectual context in which Zubiri gave his lecture course on the dynamic structure of reality. In this context the general objectives that he set out in the introduction to the course achieve their full sense: "In this study I am going to deal once again with the problem of reality, but from an aspect and an angle to which I have repeatedly alluded, although I have not insisted thematically and systematically on it: the problem of becoming. Reality is not only what it actually is; in some way or other it also involves what we can more or less vaguely call becoming. Things become, reality becomes."

In *On Essence* Zubiri attempted to explain the first of these points, "what reality actually is," and in *Dynamic Structure of Reality* he proposes to study the second one: that reality "becomes." It is best not to lose sight of the fact that for its author this second analysis is inseparable from the first. For this reason the pages of *Dynamic Structure of Reality* presuppose those of *On Essence*. Hence in the general introduction he goes on to say, "Each is the child of his own sins. And in this case my sins are in print. Naturally I cannot take for granted that every reader knows my book *On Essence* (1962), but neither can I explain it formally and extensively. That would mean repeating something which would bore both the reader and myself. Thus I must necessarily follow a middle road, calling to mind some concepts, the ones most directly pertinent to the problem of the dynamic structure of reality."

The general thesis of *On Essence* is that reality is not "in itself," nor "for itself," nor "in me," but it is "in its own right" [*de suyo*].[2] The thesis of *Dynamic Structure of Reality* is complementary to the earlier work and states that reality "gives of itself." The problem of this book is nothing but the way of joining the idea of "in its own right" with the idea of "giving of oneself." Zubiri's answer is that both terms are not in a relationship of what is "constitutive" with what is "operative," but in a much more radical and deeper way, as "substantivity" and "respectivity." Therefore it is not the case that "giving of oneself" follows out of being "in its own right," but rather that being in its own right is constitutively a giving of oneself. It could be said that realities are structures that in their own right give of themselves.[3]

Probably the reader will discover in this book a new Zubiri, though only relatively new. In *On Essence* he seemed to address mainly Aristotle and Scholasticism;[4] in *Inteligencia sentiente*, Kant, Husserl, and phenomenology,[5] and in *El hombre y Dios*, Saint Augustine and theology.[6] But here in *Dynamic Structure of Reality* the reader will discover an unsuspected Zubiri, who with enormous intellectual discipline and equal energy retraces the path of a Hegel and proposes an extremely convincing alternative both to the latter's *Phenomenology of Spirit* and to Engel's *Dialectics of Nature*.[7] The difference lies in the fact that in the present case it is not a question of "nature" or of "spirit," but of "reality," and neither a question of phenomenology nor of dialectic but of dynamic structure. Seldom has a philosopher undertaken so much, and seldom has he acquitted himself in a more rigorous and original fashion.

A few words concerning the editing criteria. The oral course of 1968 was tape-recorded and afterward set down on paper. Zubiri subsequently corrected the transcription by crossing out some things and adding others. The basic text on which we have worked is this one, which incorporates into the original version the corrections made by Zubiri himself.

Starting from there, the criterion of the editors has been that of harmonizing in the best way possible absolute fidelity to the text with the desired flow and gracefulness. It has not always been easy to achieve this grace, since spoken language is filled with many grammatical licenses, slang phrases, repetitions, etc., that written language allows to a much lesser degree. On the contrary the editors realized that it was Zubiri's express wish to have this course edited in the form of an organic, systematic book and not merely as a typed text of lectures. We have suppressed most of the repetitions and slang phrases of the lectures and changed the original structure of lessons to one of chapters. Even so, the reader will soon note, especially if he attended the course or any of the many that Zubiri offered throughout his lifetime, that the extremely unique way in which he gave his oral lessons is still recognizable. This is so true that these readers will find it hard to read many phrases of this book without being carried back to the little seminar room of the Sociedad de Estudios y Publicaciones in the Plaza del Rey in Madrid and hearing Zubiri himself pronouncing them. To such a degree were they unique to his way of thinking and speaking—in short, to his way of doing philosophy.

We have added some footnotes, though not many. A few are Zubiri's own notations, difficult to integrate into the body of the text. The rest are ours and have for their objective the identification of the main explicit and implicit quotes from the text by referring to the appropriate sources.

I will end by setting down some necessary thanks. The first and the main one goes to Carmen Castro, Zubiri's widow, for patiently working to make the text just right. José Antonio Martínez and Antonio Ferraz have helped to improve the editing. It was no easy task, but it has been worthwhile.

Madrid
April 3, 1989

Prologue

In this study I am going to deal once again with the problem of reality, but with one aspect and from an angle to which I have repeatedly alluded, although I have not insisted thematically and systematically on it: the problem of becoming. Reality is not only what it actually is; it is also in some way or other involved in what we can more or less vaguely call "becoming." Things become, reality becomes. It is a question of entering into this problem.

Having said this and nothing more, I have offered only a nominal definition. But I have posed the first problem: How should the phrase be understood which lends a title to this book, *Dynamic Structure of Reality*? In the second place it will be necessary to study what are the dynamic structures that reality offers and has. Finally, I will go back to approaching in a systematic fashion the problem of reality in its dynamism.

The book therefore has three parts, each devoted to the following issues:

1. What does "dynamic structure of reality" mean (going beyond the nominal definition)?
2. What are the dynamic structures of reality?
3. Reality in its dynamism.

Each is the child of his own sins. And in this case, my sins are in print. Naturally I cannot take for granted that every reader knows my book *On Essence* (1962), but neither can I explain it formally and extensively. That would mean repeating something that would bore both the reader and myself. Thus I must necessarily follow a middle road, which is that of calling to mind some concepts, the ones most directly pertinent to the problem of the dynamic structure of reality.

The first issue to be posed is this: What is the dynamic structure of reality from the strictly philosophical point of view? It is not a question of ascertaining in a concrete fashion what is it that the various sciences tell us, for instance, about the physical universe in its becoming, or about organisms in their becoming, or about the evolution of organisms throughout time, or about historical vicissitudes. All these themes somehow have to become evident in these pages, but, rightly understood, they must become so from a strictly and formally philosophical point of view, I insist. What comprises this point of view is precisely what I hope to set out little by little in the first pages of this study.

~ Part 1

What Does "Dynamic Structure of Reality" Mean?

1
Reality and Becoming

To explain the title of this book, *Dynamic Structure of Reality*, I begin by dispensing with it. I will proceed as if such a title did not exist, and I will adhere precisely to what I said at the start of these pages: things, in fact, "are" in a certain way but also "become," have a becoming. What does this becoming mean?

Becoming is from a certain standpoint coming to be something but unavoidably ceasing to be something that was, or adding something that was not to what already is, to what already was.

However that may be, into the idea of becoming there seems to enter at first glance, and in a very thematic and formal way, something that is non-being. Things are, but in the measure that they are-not they may be otherwise or cease to be in the way that they are. If this were so, becoming would evidently imply in a certain way and to a certain degree the passage from non-being to being, or from being to non-being. Becoming would be constituted by a moment of non-being, as distinguished from things that, insofar as they have being, are constituted only by the moment of being.

Even so, this can be understood at the same time from still different angles and from different points of view.

1. Becoming as an Ontological Problem

To say that becoming implies the moment of being and non-being seems to force us to say that the ingredients of becoming, in some way or other, are precisely being and non-being. Hence, clearly, the problem of becoming would be a problem of ontology; it would be the inner, intrinsic joining of what we call "being" to what we call "non-being."

b   This way of focusing the problem of becoming, common and with a long history in philosophy, can be taken at the same time from various points of view.

Parmenides

c   For example, it is possible to think, in that union of being and non-being, that the terms "being" and "non-being" are taken by themselves. Then, clearly, the problem of becoming is the problem of how the moments of being and non-being are intrinsically joined, if we take being and non-being *in and for themselves*. In this case, clearly, since what philosophy is seeking in some form or other is a logos, a reason, and in this case the reason to explain the joining of being with non-being, the problem of becoming might be a problem of *dia-legein*, διά-λέγειν, the problem of dialectically searching for the inner structure of being and non-being taken in and for themselves. Certainly this was the way that the problem of becoming came into philosophy. To be convinced of this, it is enough to go back to the phrases of Parmenides himself.[1] In fragment 6 he tells us, "It is necessary to say and think that the entity is" (χρὴ τὸ λέγειν τε νοεῖν τ'ἐὸν ἔμμεναι).[2] In fact, being "is" (ἔστι γὰρ εἶναι).[3] In no way does non-being have being (μηδὲν δ'οὐκ ἔστιν).[4] Here the problem of being and non-being comes in, but only to eliminate non-being. As if that were not enough, Parmenides elsewhere, at the start of fragment 7, tells us, "In no way is it possible for you to force non-being to be" (οὐ γὰρ μήποτε τοῦτο δαμῆι εἶναι μὴ ἐόντα).[5] "But keep your thought away from this route of inquiry and seeking" (ἀλλὰ σὺ τῆσδ' ἀφ' ὁδοῦ διζήσιος εἶργε νόημα).[6] Not only that; Parmenides is going to draw the unavoidable consequence of this posing of the problem. If in fact becoming is a problem of joining being and non-being, Parmenides will roundly affirm that non-being is not; hence, being as such has no becoming. It is ἀκίνητον, motionless. Motion does not exist in being. Becoming does not exist.[7] Being is completely motionless; great chains keep it completely motionless and virtually imprisoned within itself.

d   The first way, then, in which the problem of becoming qua becoming came into philosophy was a rather strange form, in that dialectic that came under the form of the dialectic of being and non-being.[8] Parmenides rejects non-being as something that is not, and consequently he rejects becoming. And this is essential to the problem.

Plato

e   Plato felt that this was not possible.[9] And in his great dialogue the *Sophist*,[10] he tells us very cautiously, Παρμενίδης ὁ μέγας, "Parmenides the Great"—Plato calls him the "Great"—while we were still children, *from beginning to end* (ἀρχόμενός τε καὶ διὰ τέλους), has attested to this in the form of prose (as we would say) and in verse from beginning to end, τοῦτο ἀπεμαρτύρατο, πεζῇ τε ὥδε ἑκάστοτε λέγων καὶ μετὰ μέτρων.

Plato quotes the fragment of Parmenides (a quote that preserves the fragment for us), "In no way will you be able to force non-being to be: resolutely keep your thought away from this route of inquiry (διζήμενος)."[11]

Plato adds that this is not as clear as Parmenides thinks. It has serious shortcomings, this statement of Parmenides. Plato mentions two. It would be possible to find more in Plato himself, but I limit myself to these two in the text of the *Sophist*. Plato says that what we, evidently, call "non-being" cannot be attributed to anything in particular, but to some things we say are and to others we say are not.[12] This means that "non-being" is not a kind of nothingness that floats out there in a vague sort of way.

Then, everyone who says, says something. Every logos is a λέγειν τι, it is a saying "something."[13] Now, saying something means that that something "stands" as meant. When I say non-being, that means something, μὴ εἶναι [not being], is a τι [something].[14] How is it therefore possible to say strictly that non-being is not?

Not only that: is it very easy to say that things are, and that becoming implies a moment of non-being? Yes; it is easy to say it, but let us think that the more a thing "is," the less it is identified with everything else. Precisely what strictly distinguishes one thing from the rest is just a moment of non-being: "It is this and it is *not* something else." It is the same, ταὐτόν. But, at the same time, it is θάτερον; it is other than all the rest of things.[15] We find, then, that in that case, the very structure of being and of logos necessarily implies this moment of otherness. We find not only that non-being is, but we also find that the multitude orients us about this thing that non-being is, "the other." To say of something that it is not is precisely to say that it is "other." Non-being is precisely θάτερον, the other.[16] Having arrived at this point, in an indirect way Plato says to his reader, "Do not come to think that by saying this I commit an act of parricide."[17] Surely he does commit it! That goes without saying! He states precisely the being of non-being. And not only does he say that, but when he finishes that fragment of the dialogue,[18] he again quotes the same couplet of Parmenides: "In no way will you manage to force non-being to be; / resolutely keep your thought away from this line of inquiry." And he says, "Now you see what has happened; we have not only shown that non-being somehow is, but we have moreover found the *eidos* of non-being, the figure of non-being. And that figure is just 'the other.'"[19] Being would be sameness, and non-being otherness. In fact, therefore—Plato says—motion participates in being and non-being.[20] But I am not going to enter here into the analysis that Plato makes of motion. It is certainly other than being, and in this case it participates in non-being; but also, to a certain extent, it is the same thing that is being and that is non-being, and therefore, strictly speaking, becoming "is." This is a difficult mental combination, so difficult that Aristotle cannot admit it.

Aristotle

For Aristotle the problem of becoming, as unity between being and non-being, ceases to be then a mere dialectical unity and changes into a physical unity: into the reality of things.[21] What then is becoming? Of what does that unity of being and non-being consist in the physical reality of things?

All motion, says Aristotle, is in fact a change in the broadest sense of the word.[22] Aristotle reserves the name ἀλλοίωσις for nothing else than accidental changes,[23] but let us include here within change its own substantial generation.[24] Motion, then, is a transformation, a change.

Now, Aristotle also says that motion always presupposes a mover.[25] This is clear for Aristotle: there is someone or something that moves. The dialectic of the unity of being and non-being is not enough; it is necessary to take into account the one doing the moving. And this is where perhaps we are going to discover what the peculiarity of being and non-being is, in the very character of the moving object.

Of this moving object Aristotle says that it is a subject of motion. It is the subject that is undergoing the motion. It is a ὑποκείμενον, a subject that undergoes it.[26] This is clear enough at first glance. Evidently there is someone who is moving. And that which is moving is something that in one form or another remains as subject of these variations; if not, there would not be motion, there would be a kind of evanescence of the thing in question.

Motion is not, strictly speaking, a passage from non-being to being and from being to non-being, but is rather a passing from one way of being to another.[27] To lose being and to get being: coming to be. In fact, Plato's own form of argument echoes in a physical dimension: non-being is, in one way or other, that which already was, but which is destined to lose being.[28] If one is not now in the Plaza del Rey, for instance, non-being with respect to being in the Plaza del Rey is being here, for me; for others it may be standing in Calle Alcalá. Every one of the ways of being, to the degree it is not one that is about to stop, serves precisely the function of non-being. Aristotle will then say that the true problem of becoming is just the inner joining of a thing within physical reality, within what it is, between that moment of being and non-being that Aristotle in no way will eliminate from becoming. Becoming is a change. And to change implies precisely a moment of non-being. To conceptualize becoming, Aristotle will say that things, besides being what they actually are, have potency, δύναμις, to be other things, and that motion is precisely a mode of actuation of that capacity (ἡ τοῦ δυνάμει ὄντος ἐντελέχεια, ᾗ τοιοῦτον).[29] I will come back to this point below.

It is precisely the imperfect act—Aristotle will say—the act of a potency to be something that is still in progress; it begins to be in act but still has not come to be it definitively. For that reason, Aristotle says that it is an act, though ἀτελές, an imperfect act.[30]

Yet however physical it is, the problem of becoming implies for Aristotle a moment of being and a moment of non-being. Aristotle's genius lies in having coined concepts like that of δύναμις, of potency, to illustrate with them immense metaphysical dimensions of reality. Now, has he exhausted the problem of becoming in doing this? For up to now (I omit referring to other Greek philosophers such as Heraclitus, Democritus, etc.) the problem of becoming is always the problem of being. In it the edge of non-being perforates being in one form or another.

2. Three Basic Assumptions

It is easy, then, to discover that throughout these various ways of focusing on the problem of being as a dialectic between being and non-being—whether in Parmenides' sense of denying motion, in Plato's sense of admitting it, and so admitting the reality of non-being, or in Aristotle's sense of a physics of being; whatever form it takes, we find that this conceptualization of the problem has three basic assumptions, easy to observe after what has already been said.

In the first place, the problem of becoming is a problem of *being.*

Second, in becoming, what is and is not is precisely a *subject that becomes.* This is a second hypothesis.

Third, in this subject, becoming consists of *changing,* of changing continually.

Here are the three radical assumptions on which all Greek philosophy of becoming is built: the idea that it is an ontological structure; the idea that it is an ontological structure proper to a subject; and the idea that what happens to this subject in becoming is precisely the act of changing.

Now, are these three assumptions totally obvious? We have the right—naturally—to grow seriously uneasy and to center our philosophical reflection on these three assumptions, each one taken by itself.

Becoming Is a Change

To begin with the third of the assumptions, that becoming is a change, it seems more or less clear that in becoming there are changes. I will enter later into the problem, but for now the question arises, Does something become because it changes, or does it change because it becomes? For if the latter were true, appealing to the example of change would leave the problem of becoming untouched. At least it would leave it in midstream. Nowhere is it written that becoming is *primo et per se* [first and for itself], in formal terms, a change. This naturally may seem shocking. I recall that some years ago, when I was speaking not in regard to this theme but about whether God's existence hinges on the definition of motion, I pointed out to one of my addressees that all this might be so, but that this was a philosophical conception of motion that there is no duty to accept. I remember the astonishment with which he said to me, "Well, the fact is that I can't conceive any other." Yes, clearly, this is the question: we are used to not conceiving anything except what comes rolling down to us through twenty-five centuries of history.

At least the question—and it is not true that I feel capable of answering it—evidently remains unanswered: Does one become because one changes, or does one change because one becomes? For if one changes because one becomes, the problem of change neither leads directly to becoming nor formally exhausts it. The problem of what there is in becoming of the dynamic, of dynamism, is not formally identified with the changing character of things. That is another story.

The Subject of Becoming

Here is the second of the assumptions. We are told that in becoming there is something that becomes. This is evident; how can it be denied? But the problem lies in the function which that something serves. Is it understood that this something is a subject that endlessly remains at the base of the motion, a subject upon which takes place that changing vicissitude that is becoming? Or is it that purely and simply becoming in some measure formally relates to reality itself in one of its dimensions, without this reality formally and compulsorily needing to display the character of a subject, of a ὑποκείμενον? To be becoming is not the same as to be the subject of becoming. In this case the problem of the nature of what becomes stands unresolved.

2
Reality and Being

A As I have already pointed out, traditionally the problem of dynamism had always been taken to be a problem of becoming, which was a unity—however totally unique one may want—but still a unity between being and non-being. Hence it was a problem of ontology, a problem of being that relates to reality, considered as a subject, as a substance to which precisely something that is becoming happens, something which, strictly speaking, would be a change, a mutation.

B Now, these three assumptions are more than debatable.

C Is it true that the problem of becoming is a problem of being and non-being?

D Second, is it true that something that is becoming is formally a substance?

E Third and last, is it true that, formally, becoming and dynamism are a change?

F By answering these questions I might not be clear, but at least I might indicate what I meant by the title *Dynamic Structure of Reality*.

Being

A I shall consider the classical idea of being from the perspective of a great distance; I am not going to review the history of this problem, which is extremely well known; I limit myself to recalling at this point the basic concepts so I can refer to them as to a system of intellectual coordinates. Obviously it is not here a question of copulative being, that is, of "to be" serving as the copula, a logical connecting link between subject and predicate; it is a question of being that relates to things that are, something a classical text would call "substantive being."[1]

B This substantive being can be said to have many possibilities. For example, a mathematician can speak of a non-Archimedean space . . . although, at least to date, it is not known whether such non-Archimedean space has physical reality. (I dispense with what a mathematician would say: that the same thing also applies to Euclidean space; perhaps. This is not the issue I go into.) Therefore I take non-Archimedean space.[2] Naturally, non-Archimedean space is not that to which substantive being is primarily referred. Instead, by substantive being is meant, and is precisely said to be, *real* being, that which has existence—the *esse reale* [real being] itself. Still and all, it turns out to be clear enough that in the classical conception, *realitas* [reality], "real" being, is an adjective whose substantive or noun is *esse*. Reality is a moment and mode of being; what dominates is precisely *esse*, being. Reality is just a mode of being, the most important, the most decisive, if you will, the most basic, but a *mode of being*.[3]

C   Now, you may think this is not as obvious as it appears at first sight. You can say that the first mode of reality is just substantive being. For example, iron has being, which is being-iron. Yes; and what if you are then asked, What do you understand by being-iron?

D   In the first place, depending upon the addressee and the intention of the question, there will be different answers. One answer can be to give the atomic structure of the atom of an iron molecule, etc. Other answers can be given, no doubt; but none of them is *being*-iron, but only *iron* itself. Of what does that moment of being consist? Let us not confuse ferric *reality* with *being* iron, which is precisely at issue. If we respond to the question What is iron? by setting down the characteristics of iron, we have the *reality* called "iron," but we have not yet begun to have its *being*; iron is one thing, but quite another what iron *is*.[4] And yet, somehow iron has a substantive being.

E   In the second place, iron and any other reality of the universe—at least of the universe that we all handle and know—are realities, though intrinsically "respective" [referred to other forms of reality]. No reality is mounted upon itself in such a way that *afterward* it enters into relationships with others, even though this entrance could be construed as essential to them. It is not a question of "relationships," no, but of the fact that intrinsically and formally each reality is in itself, *in re*, "respective."[5] Now, if by reality is understood something that is actually real—that goes without saying—then it will have to be considered that the reality can be actual in two different dimensions: (1) taking the properties it has, that thing by virtue of which the reality iron is ferric reality; (2) what the actuality of iron is in that respectivity [referentiality] vis-à-vis all other things. I have thematically given the name "world" to that respectivity.[6] Hence it would turn out that that actuality would be the actuality of iron in the world. This actuality is "being." I have never said (even though that statement has been gleefully attributed to me) that being is respectivity: I have never ever said that! What I have said is that being is the actuality of reality in that respectivity, which is something different. Iron would be—and as we shall see, this is less anthropomorphic than it may seem—something like that act, that actuality by virtue of which iron affirms itself as iron vis-à-vis the other realities in the world: what this reality is, is iron. Precisely, that is certainly substantive being.[7] But who does not see in that case that substantive being is mounted precisely upon reality and is a second act of reality? And in fact, two completely different descriptions of any phenomenon can be given, based on this double actuality. For instance, in the case of the beginning, the birth of a child or of an animal, one can say that it was born, that it had some parents, that there was a phenomenon of generation, a phenomenon of gestation, of birth. Indeed so, that can be said perfectly well. This is an explanation in terms of reality. Now, I can give another explanation. I can say, "That child has come to light. He was born to the light of day. He has come into the world." But this is not alluding to the real phenomenon of the production of the reality of the new child: this is giving notice precisely of his new actuality, his actuality in that thing we call a world. This second event could not occur in any way without the first. Being, from wherever place it is taken, is more or less mounted upon reality.

In the third place, being is a further act, naturally. If one wishes to hold fast to the metaphor of light, φῶς, with respect to the character of being, as that which surrounds and illumines everything, one must say that there is no light without a light-source. Precisely there is where a sophism could emerge. It is thought that the brightness of a light-source consists of something like this, that its own brightness appears in the light that that light-source is shedding all around itself. But this is a complete illusion. The brightness begins by being something in itself. And it sheds light all around. And only to the degree that that light that illuminates everything round about can flow back over its own bright light-source, only as brightness as such has a physical property and not merely one grounded in the property of light, to that degree alone can we speak of the being of the substantive thing. We can say that it is the brightness seen in its own light that emanates from it in some form, evidently, though in a secondary way. That is, first we have the light-source, reality, afterward we have the light, being, and we have the light insofar as it is flowing back over the very light-source from which it emerges, as being flowing back over reality. This back-flow is precisely what constitutes the being of the substantive thing.

In the fourth place, the being of the substantive thing, as I have been saying, is a kind of affirmation of reality, of each of the realities in the world. Therefore, to my way of thinking, it is a complete error to speak of *esse reale*, real being. What we need to speak of is *realitas in essendo*, reality in the midst of being. What comes first is the *realitas*, and the *esse* is just its second act. It is *realitas in essendo*, but it is not the *esse reale*. Hence this reality, far from being a moment of being—the most important, if you will, but it makes no difference—begins by not being a moment of being but by being something previous to being.

H   Now, this is not splitting hairs. In the first place, it is clear that since being is the actuality of things in the world, it concerns them; it concerns them as a second act, but even so it concerns *them*. It is not true that being primarily has to be something that is achieved, won, accomplished. No. The mere fact of being reality, and to the degree that something is so, already implies precisely that actuality. Even if there were no human beings, reality would still have being precisely as a second act.

I   As I have been saying, this is not splitting hairs, although it may seem so, because there is a case, that of the human being, in whom these structures appear, I will not say not dissociated, because they are not that, but rather distinguished with greater clarity. In fact, let us consider what humans are when they speak of themselves. They say, "I." This "I" is not the reality of humans. How could it be? Human beings have that reality even though they may not be performing whatever act is needed to be me. Humans are realities with bodies and psyches, with social dimensions, etc., whichever ones they may have; it is not a question of giving here a definition of the human. But humans are realities. And what we call "I" is precisely the second act. That is the act in which my own reality affirms itself in a reduplicative and formal way in a second act, in the action that it is performing. For instance: *I* eat, *I* walk, *I* talk, *I* buy, *I* quarrel, *I* take a stroll.

J   There is always this second act. This second act is not juxtaposed to reality. No. The second act consists of reabsorbing the whole reality into the first act and of declaring it, during the second act, identical to the reality in the first act: this is what we call "intimacy." The "I" reverts precisely to reality itself. It is reality in the second act. Consequently, what must be said is that the "I," which is not the reality of humans, is nonetheless their substantive being, the reality *in essendo,* in the midst of being. Now, this being of the substantive thing is not completely finished and done. For there is a first respectivity: the respectivity and the actuality of my own reality in the world of my actions, which is not my doing; but it should be said in the case of humans that that being is such that it is precisely an actuality in order to be something else that it is not yet. Hence human beings—and that is exactly the meaning and course of their lives—have to go on giving shape to their substantive beings, and go on giving shape to them in each of the instants of their lives. Reality will surely keep changing, but in a different way. From birth to death with all possible human vicissitudes in mind and body, the changes of that reality do not formally coincide with the forms assumed by being except to the extent that the "I" itself reabsorbs those variations into its own life.

Reality

Reality is prior to being. Now it may be asked, If it is prior to being, what does it mean to call something "real"?

Naturally, it is possible to start with the concept of existence and contrast what is real with what is unreal. What exists is real, what does not exist is unreal. Now, is this the primary point of departure? I have always thought that it is not. I have thought that to understand what reality is, it is necessary to contrast it to a certain mode of presence of things in which these do not present themselves to us formally as realities but as stimuli. A stimulus is not unreal in the sense of non-existent. Neither is it reality in a formal sense. A stimulus is precisely infra-real. Reality, on the contrary, presents itself to us as something more than a stimulus. The stimulus itself presents itself to us as stimulating reality, that is, as something emerging from what is stimulating us and which belongs in itself to that which stimulates us. Precisely the moment of reality is this "in-its-own-self [en propio], [this] 'in-its-own-right' [de suyo]."

Things present themselves to us human beings in great measure as something that is related to us, but related to us "in their own right," for what they, the things, are in themselves. Just for that reason it is necessary to dissociate, to my way of thinking, the concept of reality from the concept of existence. Naturally, it is not true that what does not exist is real, certainly not; but it is not enough that it exist for it to be real. Let us take, for instance, the case, frequent in the world of ancient Greece, of Mercury, who appears with an umbrella in Athens or in Epidaurus, where the works of Aristophanes were performed; or Jupiter, who appears as a charioteer. One would think that they are subjective visions. No. Clearly neither Mercury nor Jupiter appeared in any way, and yet for the Greeks for whom those visions appeared, it was not a question of subjective visions. A Greek understood that although there was nobody who saw Jupiter as a charioteer, Jupiter would go walking as a charioteer through the streets of Athens or would come down from Olympus as a charioteer, or that Mercury had an umbrella. For a Greek this was not a subjective illusion. Nevertheless, we very correctly say that this is not real. Why? Is it true that it does not exist? No. Jupiter apparently exists as a charioteer; there is no room for doubt. In this sense he has existence. But he is not real. Why? Because that existence does not pertain to Jupiter in his own right. In his own right Jupiter has another form that is not that of a charioteer. Exactly. The moment of the in his own right [de suyo] unitarily absorbs the essence and the existence, and

19

in this previous absorption the real is constituted insofar as it is real. It does not exclude essence and existence, but includes them *radically;* essence and existence are bonded into something previous, unitary, undivided, which is precisely being something *in its own right.*

Reality is not a mode of being. Reality is precisely something prior to being. And being is something that is grounded in reality as a thing *in its own right.* Hence the problem of becoming primarily and radically relates to reality. It does not relate to being. It relates to being in a derivative fashion, to the extent that being is the second actuality, the re-actualization of a reality in its respectivity. But becoming is precisely earlier than every joining of being and non-being, because it is something that falls into reality qua reality, and qua reality is prior to being in a reduplicative fashion.

To be precise, therefore, the first assumption of the three with which the world of the ancient Greeks confronted this problem is revealed to be incorrect. The problem of becoming is not a problem of being, to my way of thinking. Then the question arises: this reality that is moving, is it the moving object as a subject of motion? That is the second question.

Reality and Structure

Introduction

A Aristotle has defined the mover as a subject that stays intact, in some form or other, through the vicissitudes of its movement, of change and of dynamism; it is a ὑποκείμενον, *subjectum* [subject].[1] And this is precisely what is the problem. Is it true that the primary and radical character of reality is being ὑποκείμενον, being *subjectum*, being sub-stance? Aristotle has tended ever more rigorously to identify reality and the quality of being a subject. Against this idea I have written many pages and will not repeat them here.[2] Yet I will put in writing not precisely my critiques of Aristotle but positive ideas that I would have to add.

B Aristotle defends and formulates his idea of reality as the quality of being a subject [*subjetualidad*] by contrasting substance to accident. Substance is something that can exist in itself: a lion, a rock.[3] A rock for Aristotle was not an artificial thing, but a natural thing with a certain unity . . . just as a lion is. On the other hand, a color, reason, logos, these are things that do not have existence by themselves but are inherent to others. Reason, for instance, is something accidental, not in the sense that a human being may lack it, but in the sense that reason, logos, in itself cannot have existence by itself but is the logos of something, that is, of a definite human being. Consequently, all the accidents belonging to this someone are inherent. At the same time, this substance plays a role as subject of these accidents. As a consequence, who can doubt that the radical form of reality, as Aristotle would say, is being ὑποκείμενον [subject], is being a *subjectum*?

C This is clear at first glance. But let us give a concrete reality to that idea. Let us take a man. Let us consider one of his essential notes [*notas*]; for example, he has a beard. This gentleman shaves, and then he removes his beard. Let us continue to perform the same operation with all his essential notes. This gentleman is of such and such an age; his years are removed from him. He has such and such a complexion . . . He can change skin color since he sunbathes and grows darker . . . If everything is taken away from him, then, clearly, it is as if we defoliated an artichoke: what is left of this man if all notes are removed from him? Where is the subject? This is a question of some importance. The fact is that the opposite operation can be attempted. Let us consider that what we call "things" are not precisely substances to which some accidents and properties are inherent, but substantive systems of notes and properties. Then the thing changes its appearance.

It changes its appearance because in fact among the many notes that reality can have there are some that I have called "adventitious," arising from connection with others. For example, it is possible to have a skin color determined by the sun and get very brown, tanned. But there are other properties, other notes that somehow—I will not enter into how this is—belong to him by themselves. For example, having eyes, having a gaze, having two arms, having a definite organic and psychic structure, etc. These notes are those that reality possesses *in its own right* in a certain way. Now, what must be asked here therefore is, In what way do these notes form a system?

I have said that I was not going to do more than state some aspects, because otherwise I would have to explain my book [*On Essence*] in detail, and it is not proper to do that in this study.[4]

The Constitutional System of Notes: Substantivity

These notes, insofar as they form systems, are found to be characterized by some characteristic moments.

In the first place, the notes are co-determining one another mutually among themselves. The notes that comprise an organism, let us say, keep determining one another. I know someone will tell me—because someone has already done so—that for some Scholastic philosophers also, evidently, matter and form mutually determine each other—for example, for Suárez. This is evident. When he speaks of the substantial form of an organism, Suárez presumes that the organism is somehow organized, and that therefore the form determines it *quodammodo* [somehow], he says. And in that *quodammodo* is precisely the form. Yes, but let us be perfectly clear: Suárez's form and organism are found to be in the relationship of act and power between themselves. They co-determine one another but in the way an act determines a power.[5] Yet I am speaking here of a co-determination as of *two perfect acts:* one actual note and another actual note. This is the composition of the first characteristic of the system: there is a co-determination. By virtue of this co-determination, each note is not fully what it is except in connection with others. I will stress this point more precisely further on.

C   In the second place, a substantive reality is a somehow finite, closed system of notes. Clearly. A reality that was open to all its notes would be something like Fichte's "I," open to the infinite degree to its predicates and, naturally, that "I" never came to rest in any, and in fact never acquired any.[6]

D   The thing is clear. The system necessarily has a certain moment of closure.

E   Yet that is not enough. For the closure could be brought about in many ways. For instance, take a linear closure. If a piece of paper is taken in which points are being marked on a line, I can say that each point is conditioned by the preceding and conditions the following point. The first conditions the rest but will not be conditioned by any of the rest. And the last will be conditioned by all but will condition none. Now, this is not what happens in a system. A system has a cyclical structure, that is, the initial point converges with the final point, and consequently the system is the set of a series of notes which mutually codetermine one another in a closed, though also a cyclical, form. Hence it cannot then be said in any way that these notes lead to an open reality that would be indefinite. Now, in this sense the system of notes is *constitutional*, understanding by such that it belongs to the reality *in its own right*.

F   Thus the sufficiency of a system of notes as a system with the characters here stated is precisely what we have called a "substantivity" [*substantividad*].[7] It is a sufficient unit in the order of constitution. These systems have substantivity. Those lacking such sufficiency have no substantivity.

G   Naturally the character of substantiality is in no sense the same as the character of substantivity. Even without entering into the problem of whatever substances may be in the Aristotelian sense, there is no room for doubt that those substances, whatever they may be, are grounded precisely in substantivity. If there are substances it is because there is substantivity, not the reverse.[8]

The Basic, Constitutive System: The Essence

A   This system not only has these characteristics but, in the second place, this substantive, constitutive system possesses many notes that do not immediately display the characteristics I have just described. For instance, I can say that albinism is evidently a constitutional note, since albinism is genetically controlled. Now, it would really be absurd to propose, at least at our current level of knowledge, that albinism is a character that rests on itself, for, as we know, it rests on a chromosome and a gene through a given union of nucleic acids, etc. That is, the albino character merely expresses in a determined form what genotypically (and phenotypically in the case of race) may be something more radical and deeper. That is, all substantivity is mounted on a basic primary system, which is the one that would no longer be simply *constitutional*, but would be *constitutive*.

B   Then the basic, constitutive system of all notes necessary and sufficient for a substantive reality to be what it is, is precisely what I have called "essence."[9] It is the cohesive [*coherencial*] primary unit.

C   In this constitutive system, I was saying, the notes of the system determine one another, codetermine one another mutually between themselves in an actual way. This means that if I take any note *in* the system in question (not outside it—that would be something else), while I am taking it *in actu* [in the act], such as it is in a determined system, that note does not start out by being a note that later is in a relationship with other notes. Rather, its entire reason for being a note is to be a "note-of," precisely "of the remaining notes"; it is conditioning the others. Intrinsically in its character as a note is that moment of the "of," that moment of genitiveness, by virtue of which it is by itself and in itself in reference to the remaining notes that comprise the essence that are constitutive of it. In different languages this character has been able to be expressed in many different forms. In Indo-European languages and in many Semitic languages, the character of genitiveness is expressed, for example, with the flexion *domus Petri*, in Latin, the house "of Peter." In other languages, for example in Spanish, lacking declensions, it is expressed with prepositions: the house *of Peter* [*la casa de Pedro*]. But Semitic languages can express this relationship in a different form, which is not by saying the house "of-Peter" but the "house-of" Peter; in other words, "of" affects "house" and not Peter. This is what is therefore called the "construct" state. In fact, being a note-of confers precisely upon the system a character that I would formally call "construct." I say it is construct whereby "construct" means not that one note keeps having others added to it, but that each note is only what it is when primarily and formally belonging to the others and referring to them.[10]

Reality as Structure

A Now, if this is so, in the third place, there is no distinct subject hidden behind the system itself. There is nothing but the system itself. This evidently means not insofar as it has many notes but insofar as it is a construct, and only insofar as a moment of primary, radical unity manifests itself within it.

B   This unity is primary and radical, that is to say, it is not synthetic. One might think that that unity is the synthesis precisely of the notes. No, it is the reverse.

The unity is what is primary. And what we call the "multiple notes" is what is actualized and expressed more or less like analyzers in the multiple notes, something which is primarily the radical, incoercible unity of the system in question. Hence, naturally, the notes are not inherent to a subject but, I repeat, are coherent among themselves. They are coherent among themselves, and in them the construct system is actualized.

C   Now, insofar as that unity confers construct character upon the system of notes, these notes present precisely what the radical unity is in itself: it is exactly an *extruct* [*extructo*], it is *structure* [*estructura*]. This is the formal definition of structure.[11]

D   Reality is radically and primarily the quality of being not a subject [*subjetualidad*], but a structure. It is structure.

ξ   Structure is the actuality of the primary unity in a construct system of notes. In it, in this actuality, the formal effect of the system consists of determining the position of each of the notes within the system. It does not consist of having each note emerge from a subject, but of having each note occupy a perfectly determined place within other notes. These notes, taken by themselves, may not be exclusively peculiar to the system in question. Let us take the case of a living organism. How can it be claimed that a living organism is a substance endowed with life? What is meant by substance? There are many substances in great quantity in an organism. In the human being, besides all the organic ones, there is psychic substance—if you want to call it that. It is not a question that the living being is a substance; the living being is a structure. It is a structural unit. Each one of those moments can keep on renewing itself and does renew itself through time without doubt. But nonetheless, the structure is staying the same. It is a unity. And within this unity that is the living being, each one of the notes has a perfectly determined position although they may not belong formally, exclusively, to the living being in question.

F   Many years ago, with different terminology, when I was lecturing on questions similar to these and had a little time for conversation at the end of the lessons, I formulated this question: Is weight a biological note? A great biologist answered me, "No, in no way." How is that not so? If someone weighs 198 or 220 pounds and falls down, it is easier to break an arm or a leg than if a person weighs 88 or 66 pounds. How can it be said that weight has no biological function? It is one thing that the weight be shared by things that are not organisms, and quite another that it have no biological function: it has a perfectly determined place within the organism. The organism is not a substance, it is precisely a structure.

Reality as Constitution

Now, what I call "constitution" is the manner that each of the essential systems has for being one. That is exactly the constitution: the modes or manners of being precisely one. The constitution is not characterized by the notes taken in themselves, nor by a kind of more or less capricious and obscure substance that holds some properties in itself and within its bosom. No, constitution is the way that something is one. All substantive systems have essential unity, with each having its own, but each is "one" in its own way, determined by its notes. And the mode in which the constitutive notes modulate the primary and radical unit is precisely what I have called a "constitution."

In short, reality, as I said at the start of these pages, is precisely something *in its own right*. And this *in its own right* is something radically structural. Reality is constitutively structure, not constitutively substance. Hence one must insert the problem of becoming precisely in reality. This is needed not only in a more or less vague way, that is, only insofar as becoming pertains in its own right to things (precisely "in their own right" is something whereby we say that they are real), but insofar as it pertains to reality, through what reality is at its root, namely, a structure.

Becoming is not something that happens to the subject, but something inserted in the essential structures themselves of substantivity, of real substantivity. These structures, I repeat, are each highly different from the others. Each one is a unit in its own way. And becoming is something to be found inserted precisely in that structural unit, in that structural and construct system of notes, that constitute the substantivity of something.

Is the moment of becoming that is inserted in those structures the moment of change?

In its greatest generality, it cannot be said that becoming is change.

I said that Greek philosophy has bequeathed us three assumptions, or better said, it has bequeathed us a philosophy of becoming, mounted on three assumptions: first, on the assumption that becoming is a problem of ontology; in second place, on the assumption that reality is precisely the quality of being a subject; and in third place, that becoming is just a change, an alteration.

Of these three assumptions, the first two, in my opinion, are not exact. First, because the problem of dynamism, the problem of becoming, is a problem of reality and not of being; second, because it is a problem of structure, not of a subject. There now remains floating before our eyes the problem of what dynamism may be if, to be precise, it is not formally change.

26

4
Dynamism and Change

Introduction

In the two preceding chapters I have pointed out why and in what sense, in my view, the problem of becoming is not a problem of being and non-being, but is primarily a problem of reality. I noted that, in my view, all realities are respective [referential], and being is the actuality of a reality precisely in respectivity as such. Consequently, the problem of becoming relates *primo et per se* [first and by itself] to reality and not being.

In the second place, I said that reality is not formally a subject, but something different: it is precisely a substantivity endowed with a structure and with a construct system of notes. A construct system of notes means that each note is intrinsically a note-of something. It is not synthetically coupled with others, but from itself, insofar as it is a note physically realized within a definite substantivity; it intrinsically has the character of being a note-of something with the remaining notes that compose the system in question. In such a sense it is a construct of this system. Now, this system has a primary unity that is not a subject hidden behind the system, but the radical unity of the system, a unity that is shaped into a construct system of notes. Only insofar as this construct system of notes expresses in its constructivity what that primary unity is, those notes are, with respect to this unity, an *extructum,* that is, a structure.

Realities are structural substantivities, not primarily subjects. Precisely for this reason, reality has that dimension, that character of being *in its own right,* by virtue of which it is contrasted to any stimulus, which is not *in its own right* itself but which simply stimulates to an action.

This is what gives rise to the following problem: if something engaged in becoming is not the subject but a structure, then we would need to be told of what the dynamism of that structure consists. In other words, what is a be-coming in precise terms? Is it a change?

ε   I have already said that the substantivity is what becomes by and in the structure that it possesses. Only by keeping this constantly in mind is it possible to find an orientation, to my way of thinking, about what dynamism of the reality is, the dynamism of those structures. To that end I start by mentioning two very different conceptions, naturally with different ancestry and different scope in the history of philosophy. Both are important: the first, clearly, because it comes from Aristotle, and the second because it is the assumption of all nineteenth-century science. I will examine these two conceptions and will try not to invalidate them—that would be intolerably pedantic—but I will simply raise issues about them difficult to resolve, to show how in fact they leave room or at least some space for further reflection on the theme.

Aristotle and the Substantial View of the Universe

Λ   The first conception is the one represented by Aristotle. I will take it as a synthetic exposition of the whole world of ancient Greece. For Aristotle, becoming is the result of the nature of each thing by itself and of the interaction of some things with others.

ß   Aristotle naturally takes for his point of departure each thing by itself. Each thing, he tells us, is an οὐσία [substance], in the sense of ὑποκείμενον [subject]. It is a substance. He adds a preposition to what Parmenides said about being. Parmenides said that it is κείμενον, something standing there. Aristotle prefixes a preposition: it is a ὑπο-κείμενον [sub-ject], a sub-stance. The operation is one of considerable scope. A κείμενον is not the same as a ὑποκείμενον. I do not claim that Parmenides has said this, but I want to say that it is just the line of thought within which Aristotle is inserted.

c   This substance is a φύσις, a certain nature with material and formal dimensions, which it is neither necessary nor important to examine here for my purposes. Here is what each thing is: each thing is a substance in the strict sense of a ὑποκείμενον, endowed with matter and form, and in virtue of them endowed with material and formal properties, in the order of accidents. Accidents are inherent to substance.[1]

D   In the second place, and in virtue of its nature, this substance is a source and root of what Aristotle calls δυνάμεις [potencies], precisely its faculties, its capacities: this is the problem of the δύναμις [potency]. These δυνάμεις or potencies spring from the very reality of substance for Aristotle[2] and to some degree or other differ from it.

ι   Certainly Aristotle always maintains a double concept of what δυνάμεις is.

The first is the clearer and is important here. He expounds it in many passages of his books, as for instance in the *Metaphysics:* "ὅτι . . . λέγομεν δυνατὸν ὅ πέφυκε κινεῖν ἄλλο ἢ κινεῖσθαι ὑπ' ἄλλου . . ."[3]: "We say simply that the capable, the potential, is that which can move another, or be moved by another" or move "something insofar as it is other."

F   This is a first meaning that Aristotle gives to the word δύναμις: the capacity to move the other or to be moved by the other; or rather, he says, "[to move] something insofar as it is other." It can move itself, but only insofar as it is other, naturally. This dualism is constant in Aristotle. It has repercussions constantly on his conception of οὐσία [substance] and of the motion that will emerge from substance. One thing certainly can move itself, but insofar as it is the other. There is always this moment of otherness: it is precisely the moment of non-being, which always permeates this Aristotelian conception.[4]

G   The word δύναμις, Aristotle says, also has another meaning: λέγομεν δὲ δυνάμει οἷον ἐν τῷ ξύλῳ Ἑρμῆν. "We say that something is in potency—potentially—as for example Hermes—the statue of Hermes—in the block of wood." And he offers several other examples immediately afterward. Everything else is act, ἐνέργεια.[5]

H   Aristotle does not define ἐνέργεια. Naturally, it is not because it is a simple thing to give a rigorous definition of what act is, but Aristotle in short would say, clearly, that it is the statue of Hermes, and that the way the statue "is" with respect to the block of wood, within which it does not yet exist, is δυνάμει [in a potency]. Hence δύναμις simply means a *possibilitas* [possibility]. But certainly it is not a *possibilitas* in Leibniz's sense, that is, a compatibility of notes.[6] It is not a question of that. Rather, it is a question of there just being in reality factors capable of producing another reality, a reality that is potentially a being, or δυνάμει ὄν, as long as it is not produced. If one wishes, for example, the oak is patently δυνάμει ὄν [potentially a being] with respect to the acorn as long as the acorn has not yet produced the whole oak. But, in sum, the first meaning is what really matters to us. It is not a question here of what is possible, but of the first meaning [capacity to move]. In other words, there are some δυνάμεις, some capacities or faculties, that spring out of the substance of each thing, one or another distinct form of this substance, and are the means by which this substance acts upon other things.

I   This activity, that is, reality in act and consequently the activity itself while it is acting, is what Aristotle calls ἐνέργεια. The word ἐνέργεια has many meanings in Greek (as do almost all these words). The one under study here especially (we are at work in philosophy) is the sense of "act"; but, as I say, it is not the only sense that the word holds in Greek. For example, one can say, μεγάλη ἐνέργεια τῷ φαρμάκῳ πρόσεστι, "Much energy, great energy belongs to the medicine." In other words, it is very energetic, very active. We also employ the word in that sense in English. In that context, ἐνέργεια has the meaning of activity. Aristotle pays no heed to the sense that activity has in terms of activity, but to what it has in terms of act, to what is acting insofar as it is act.

J   Now with these two notions in hand, Aristotle hopes to understand what becoming is. Becoming in a general sense is change, and within it Aristotle says that there is a composite of potency and act.

K   Although Aristotle emphasizes the generation and corruption of substances, he thinks that that generation and corruption is always from one substance to another.[7] Consequently, what is decisive is what relates to the structure of each substance, by virtue of which there is generation, and also motion, and also becoming in each of those substances.

L   Now, how then does Aristotle conceive becoming, whether in the sense of change in general or in the sense of motion? (The difference matters little in the present case.) Aristotle naturally understands that motion, becoming, is not simple δύναμις [capacity]. Quite the contrary: that a person is capable of building a house, an ἀρχιτέκτον [architect], does not mean that he is actually building it. As a consequence, it cannot be said that there is motion while there is nothing more than δύναμις [capacity].[8] Now, if there were an ἐνέργεια [act], if there were a house in fact put up, neither would there be the operation of building, that is, motion.[9] What is motion, then?

M   Aristotle employs two formulas to tell us what motion and becoming are. One is a bit simple, but it considerably affects his thought: he says that it is ἐνέργεια ἀτελής, that motion is an imperfect act.[10] Imperfect does not mean to say that it has defects but that it has not yet reached its end, that it has not yet reached being a "finished thing," as we say in English, a thing perfect in the sense of ended. Motion is an unfinished act.

N   Now Aristotle finds it extremely important to say where the positive character of this unfinished act lies and where its unfinished state as such is to be found. Aristotle tells us in a formula that has caused much laughter throughout the history of philosophy, yet which is very simple and forms the only definition of motion that has come down in all the history of philosophy, as must be admitted. Motion is not pure potency, except when it is acting as such potency without having finished producing its entire effect.[11] That is, when substance is the mover.

O   For Aristotle the description of the motion is not the important part of motion, but rather the condition of the mover matters more to him. Of what does κινητόν consist, that is, substance insofar as it is the mover when it is moving? Aristotle says that it consists of the fact that its potencies are acting as such potencies without having produced their complete act. If they were dozing off, let us say, in the state of pure potency, there would not be motion; neither would there be if they had produced their entire act. Motion occurs precisely when they are acting as potencies. To say this in plain language, motion consists neither of being able nor of being, but of being actively able. When it is in fact being actively able, it is then that there is motion; that is the motion, the condition of the mover. To be in fact actively being able is κίνησις [motion] as such.

That is the famous definition of Aristotle: the actuality of the potential being insofar as it is such potential: ἡ τοῦ δυνάμει ὄντος ἐντελέχεια, ᾗ τοιοῦτον.[12]

This is becoming. For Aristotle it is always a change from potency to act, which emerges precisely from the δυνάμεις [potencies] of a substance, those δυνάμεις that in turn emerge and spring from the οὐσία [substance] considered to be a substance endowed with matter and form.

Finally—and here I will not make a full exposition of Aristotelianism, as it would be too long—for Aristotle the act is always prior to the potency.[13] Therefore the problem arises as to what puts a mover into motion. Aristotle says it is the interaction with other movers, with other substances.[14] The universe, in fact—here Aristotle works completely within a serious conception of the Greek world—is a system, a τάξις [order], as a Greek would say, of substances. Each thing begins by being what it is. Furthermore, all that things are, and the way they can act, are fitted into a certain order, into a τάξις. By virtue of this, each substance, in some form or another, receives determined actions from other substances, or acts on other substances, as a consequence of which each one of them begins by being by itself.[15] In fact this is what happens in motion.[16]

By virtue of the τάξις [order], that is, through the interaction of some substances with others, the δυνάμεις [potencies] of each substance are really different or at least are somehow different from the substance itself. One substance exerts actions upon another or receives passions from another, and this produces that phenomenon which is precisely κίνησις, motion.

There is no doubt: the concept of δύναμις [potency] is one of the most grandiose and brilliant concepts produced in the history of philosophy. All who love to laugh at metaphysics can laugh all they want: I invite them to put another concept in its place. This is indeed a genial and brilliant concept. Now, that does not mean that this conception of Aristotle does not have some points that could give rise to some very important issues.

In the first place, is δύναμις in fact distinguished from substance? How does it differ?

Aristotle always takes for granted that that distinction exists. But the example that he gives is equivocal. It is the example of architecture, which is an acquired potency. If being an architect were a δύναμις [capacity] that sprang from the substance of the architect himself,[17] it could be asked to what extent it is justified to say that being an architect differs from having a capacity for building. This is more than problematic. The problems increase in number if we are told, as do all partisans of real distinctions, as, for instance, the Thomists (who carry real distinctions to the level of frenzy in the history of philosophy), that substances are really different from their δυνάμεις [capacities].[18] This does not go beyond being a mere statement.

Being able to build is not to be actively building. Certainly, but does this mean that the power of building—if it were not an acquired potency—is something different from the structure itself, from the object to be built, from the builder as such?[19] If in place of building something more natural is considered as, for example, walking, or digesting, hearing . . . Yes, they are faculties, clearly. I can close my eyes and not see. Yes, to a certain extent, yes; but only to a certain extent. But does that mean that those faculties are different from what I am as a human being?

In the second place, another consideration can enter with regard to becoming, itself.

Aristotle takes becoming as a change, as change itself. Now, change is inserted within an *activity*. This is a dimension on which Aristotle never insists. He never does because for him becoming is a change from non-being to being. Indeed; but if at the base of this change an activity is perceived that is being active in the midst of that change, then the appeal to change as such does not help to illustrate the problem of becoming. For then something changes because it becomes and does not become because it changes. The fact is that, to be sure, there exists this double dimension in motion: the dimension of change and, in some form or other, the dimension of activity. Not all motion is change in the same form. Scholastic philosophy already recognized as much: the motion of exertion [activity] or progress-toward [change] is not the same, nor is motion in the sense of a transitive change, or a change of place, a growth spurt, etc. Even Aristotle has to admit this when he speaks, for example, of the contemplation of truth or the act of love.

On the contrary, there is activity.

Surely it will be thought that Aristotle has already said that the condition of the moving being is the δύναμις [potency] that "is acting." Indeed; but just here is where the difficulty lies. For then, in this conception, there are two transitions in motion, not only one. One, the most apparent in fact, by virtue of which my δύναμις, which was dormant, is now in act, producing the thing, signals a change. There is no doubt. But there is a deeper change, whereby substance leaves its dormant state to begin to activate its potency. *One* case is, therefore, the transition from inactive potency to active potency; the *other*, the transition from active potency to its own act. To what is this due? Are there then two motions? A complication appears here not easy to resolve in Aristotelian philosophy.

β   In the third place, Aristotle appeals to the concept of τάξις [order], to the "taxonomic" [táxico] or orderly structure of the universe. Now, this concept of τάξις is enormously problematic.

γ   First, where is it said or proved that the universe is composed of substances, each of which begins by being what it is, independently of the rest? Considering all that has been ascertainable in the research of reality since Aristotle's times, it turns out that the contrary happens. Each of what we call "things" is a fragment (in the strictest sense of the word) of the universe. The fragments do not have the character of substances in the Aristotelian sense. Not even Aristotle himself would admit this.

δ   It is nowhere said that in fact what we call "substances" are fully that in Aristotle's sense. Rather they are fragments of the cosmos. At most there would be therefore only one substance in Aristotle's sense, and that would be the whole cosmos. Now, to the whole cosmos the concept of τάξις [order] is not applied. It applies only to things that form part of the cosmos but not to the cosmos itself.

ε   In the second place, Aristotle understands that this *taxis* has a unique moment: it is the ordering of some substances by others. Hence, patently, the ordering would be a corollary of the character of the substances. Now, is this so? Is it evident that the world is composed of substances, each of which is as it is, and what we call the universe is a result of a "taxonomic" [orderly] joining of these substances? What if the reverse were true? It is precisely the other conception of becoming that deserves to be considered.

The Nineteenth Century and the Systematic Vision of the Universe

A   The other conception of becoming, more or less hammered out in the second half of the nineteenth century, and clearly coming down to our own time, consists of starting from a point of view opposite to Aristotle's point of departure.

B   The universe, *primo et per se*—to say it in a pedantic and Scholastic way (though Latin also has its expressive force)—is a system of connections. This is the world in the usual sense of the word. I am not going to enter here into clarifying the degree of inexactness I find in the concept this word affirms; it is unimportant in this case.

C   The world, the universe, at least the physical universe, is constituted before all and over all by a system of connections. This system of connections has in itself a certain substantivity. Science does not use the word, but it applies here.

This is for example what is called a "field" in physics—for instance, an electromagnetic field.

D   An electromagnetic field is something completely different from what Coulomb thought.[20] For him, one electrical charge attracts or repels another. An electromagnetic field, Maxwell would say,[21] is just the reverse. It is a system of lines of force, of undulating structure, not relevant for the present. Let us imagine a kind of elastic thread tied at the ends. If one of the ends is untied, it goes toward the other, undoubtedly. Yet it is not because one end attracts the other, but because the elasticity of the thread intervenes. Naturally, the attraction or repulsion of electric charges is owing to the structure of the field, not the reverse, as if the field were produced by a "taxonomy" of one charge acting on another.

Ɛ   *Primo et per se* [first and by itself], it is a question of something that constitutes a field, the field of the universe. Therefore, what we call "things" are simply points of application of this field. These connections clearly have some points of application, and these points are what we call "things." Things would be like the knots of a net; but primary reality would be the threads of that net and its meshlike structure. It is a derivative of the net that they cross one another in the form of knots, constituting at each knot that something which we call a "thing"; but this thing is not what is primary. It is just the opposite conception to Aristotle's. Aristotle starts with the knots and understands that they are not knots, but rather that the threads come out of each of the knots. Here the reverse is understood. Concrete things, real material things, are the points of application of the field.

F   What is first and fundamental is the system of connections, that is, the field, and in second place, the things are the points of application of the field. In the third place, this field is endowed with certain laws in its structure. For instance, in the case of the electromagnetic field it is clear. There is an electromagnetic field constituted at each point by three vectors, two at right angles, which are the electrical and the magnetic, and a vector of propagation at right angles to the plane of the other two vectors, etc. They are linked by some differential equations, by virtue of which the solutions to these equations are a distortion of this vector all along the line of propagation in undulating form, etc.[22]

G   Therefore the field has certain laws. These laws, we are told, are *dynamic* in themselves. What counts is not things, but just the system of laws that there is in the universe. This is what is primary and fundamental. Things have no more permanence, no more consistency, than the working of those laws confers on them; by virtue of such laws the points of intersection are constituted in that net.

H   Hence these laws—dynamic in themselves—make becoming not precisely a change, but instead make the world intrinsically and formally a mode of process [*procesual*]. This means a dynamic process, with certain laws, within which are things as points of application. If things become, it is because they are points of application in this field, not because this field would be the filamentous, "philic," or phyletic result of each of the things that there is in it.[23] Change would be a consequence of "being a mode of process" [*procesualidad*], something completely different from a change. The dynamism would be a mode of process, something completely different from a change. In this sense, the universe would be absolutely dynamic in itself.

I   It would not be excessive to raise a few searching questions here. For this conception of becoming points toward them, as does everything in this world.

J   In the first place, here the concept of field and the concept of mass are handled in a very carefree fashion. Now, Einstein proved in his famous equation that the difference between mass and field is merely quantitative. He discovered the energy of mass, and the mass of energy, not only in some particular cases—this much was known before Einstein—but in all its generality.[24] How can it be said that things are the points of application of a field?

K   In the second place, here we have a description of the field as something that is precisely a kind of continuous medium, endowed with certain structures, certain laws, a gravitational field, an electromagnetic field . . . within which there are certain things that would be their points of application. In theory there is no doubt, but this is just the most problematic aspect. Where is it precisely said in contemporary physics (not in Maxwell's) that this is the structure of the field?[25] In fact, electromagnetic forces are not, as Coulomb claimed, attractions and repulsions at a distance of electric charges. What if they were streams of particles that came out of one point to go to another? What if light were a stream of photons, not an undulating alteration? These are things very much within today's physics. How, then, could it be maintained that things are the points of application of a field? The whole idea of being a mode of process just disappears.

L   Third, we are told that that universe is ruled by certain already existing laws, and that things in it evolve. But current physics and cosmology are not just limited to describing more or less hypothetically (as everything in science— it would seem that human beings can call "science" only mathematical wisdom), though with ever greater probability, that the universe began at a certain initial state, at least the present-day universe. (I do not refer to the universe as a creation from nothing; science has nothing to say there.) In other words, science not only affirms that the present state of the universe derives from an initial state by virtue of certain laws but also has had to observe that that evolution does not consist simply of changing the configurations of the universe (for example, the production of galaxies; within galaxies of interstellar dust, the formation of stars in fragmentation, collision, etc.). There is something more, and it is precisely that in its evolution the laws of the universe change. It is not said anywhere, not even in today's cosmology, that, for instance, the laws of the gravitational field might have begun by being actually existent laws with all their predominance in the initial state of the universe.

M Then it would have to be asked, What explains that change of the laws, other higher laws? Without doubt this is not dialectically impossible. Yet with it, where would we ever stop? The laws of the universe can vary, to be sure; but then their variation cannot be described in the terms that I have just set out.

N Finally, and especially, we are told that becoming is being a mode of process [procesualidad]. Yes, but the issue is, What is understood by this being a mode of process? It is evident that process consists of procedere, in Latin, "proceeding"; in this case the Greek word is not so clear: ἐκπόρευσις, to come out of, to depart from. Now, we are not told what comprises that pro- of procedere. Nor are we told what composes the very mode of process of the world, but only that the becoming of every thing hinges on certain laws of the field within which the things are immersed. Yet what is being a mode of process itself?

O I once again repeat that I am not trying to invalidate these conceptions; that would be absurd. Yet I am attempting, at least, to observe in a precise manner the unclear, deficient sides that, in my view, those two conceptions display.

P The two conceptions start with the dualism between things that are and the becoming, call it what you will. Whether it is understood that things are the subjects serving as points of departure for actions or, on the contrary, that actions result from the connections of the world as points of application of becoming, one thing remains unassailable: there is always this dualism. In that dualism things always perform the function of subjects. This is inexorable. In the Aristotelian conception, this happens because they are the subjects from which emerge the δυνάμεις [potencies], and to them precisely becoming happens. In the other conception, that does not occur, but the contrary takes place. Yet the contrary consists of every thing being subject to becoming.

Q Subject "of" or subject "to," this does not change the essence of the question. It is always the character of reality as being a subject [subjetual]. In the first case it is much clearer than in the second that what is real has the character of being a subject [subjetualidad], yet in the second it is no less real.

R Now, I have tried to call to mind that at least to my way of thinking, reality does not formally have the attribute of being a subject but is instead structural. Therefore it is necessary, without invalidating the notions that I have just set down, to focus the problem of dynamism from the viewpoint of structure.

The Structural Dynamism of Reality

I am going to present my focus on the problem of the structural dynamism of reality in five steps. I will not label them, but simply number them.

First Step

In previous pages I pointed out that reality is a substantivity that essentially and structurally is found in the condition of respectivity [referentiality].

Respectivity, in the first place, relates to the constitution of each thing. It is that character whereby no thing begins by being what it is and later is placed in relation to others, but just the contrary: what each thing is, is constitutively a function of the rest. In this primary sense, all reality is constitutively respective.[26] In its own constitution it is a function of the rest.

In the second place, this respectivity, as I pointed out in the previous sentence, is not formally a relationship. This is especially true because every relationship presupposes *relata* [related things]. Here we do not have *relata*, since each thing is a function of the rest. It is something that constitutes the related object itself; it is not based on the character of the related object, but rather constitutes it. By virtue of this respectivity *in re* [referentiality in the thing] it is nothing different from the thing itself. It is precisely its inner, its intrinsic, constitution.

In the order of reality as such this respectivity is what I have called a "world." It is the respectivity that all things have among themselves only because they are real. I will not go into this matter, since it holds no importance for present purposes.

In the order of particulars [*talidad*], this respectivity is precisely what constitutes the cosmos. This respectivity by virtue of which each thing is what it is—not simply being real, but what the real is—the *talitas* (Latin, "particularity") of each of these things is what each constitutively is as a function of the particularity of the rest.

In the third place, this respectivity has different dimensions. It has a character of outer respectivity. Evidently, I repeat, a thing has being as a function of what the remaining things are. Yet there is also an inner respectivity, which I have already noted at the beginning of this chapter: the construct character of a system. Each note is precisely a note-of the rest. It is only what it is respectively [referentially] to the other notes.

There is the inner law of the substantivity of things by virtue of which they are constructs. This construct character is precisely the character of inner respectivity that all substantive realities have. The notes of the substantivity are in this sense the construct of a structure. This structure is only what it is by being shaped into some notes, each of which is what it is only as a function of the rest. Therefore—as I have repeatedly said—the formal, proper effect of a structure upon the notes is not that of originating them, but that of assigning them a definite position within the system. The respectivity of the real is precisely that whereby reality is just something *in its own right* [*de suyo*], as I have mentioned previously. This in-its-own-right is the primary character that I would not say defines, but that surely comprises the primary consistency of reality, to my way of thinking.[27] It does not consist of being existence. There are existing things to which we can deny the name of real. Take, for instance, the figure of the charioteer that Jupiter can take on for a Greek in the streets of Athens, as already mentioned before. Why is this so? Because that is not the figure that Jupiter has *in his own right.* There is this character of the *in-one's-own-right* in and within which both the essence and the existence of things must be inserted so that they can be called realities. To say the same from a different angle, things are *in their own right* respective. Each one is intrinsically and formally turned *in its own right* toward the others. In other words, there is no τάξις [order], but each thing is previously constituted in outer respectivity toward the others and is constituted in inner respectivity with itself, because no thing is a coupling or an outer connection of notes, but precisely a *structure.* It is not something extrinsic, but something intrinsic.

I   In itself and by virtue of the mere fact of being real, every thing or moment of a thing is physically respective [referential]. In the first place, intrinsically, and not because of the interaction of other notes or other substances. Further, formally, because nothing is a reality except in its constitutively respective character to all realities, to the reality of the notes, and to the realities that there are in the universe.

J   In an intrinsically and formally respective way, reality is precisely something *in-its-own-right.* To say this another way, reality *in its own right* is intrinsically and formally respective.

Second Step

K   These real things are above all systems of notes. What are these notes? Merely pointing it out will clarify what the structural unity of substantivity is. Respectivity is not a conceptual moment, so to speak. It is patently not a question of my seeing a thing, contemplating it, possessing it exhaustively in my intelligence, and, after something else appears, of seeing what one is with respect to the other. No, this would be an extrinsic connection, and I started off by saying that it is an intrinsic and formal connection.

L   Respectivity is a physical dimension of things. It is absolutely physical. A respectivity is not merely mental or relational, with a more or less abstract character, nor even as a concrete one. For it is not a concept. It is a strictly physical moment in the traditional and philosophical sense of the word. It is real with the physical reality of something. Respectivity has a formally physical character. The notes imply in themselves formally a physical turning toward the rest of the notes. Precisely because this respectivity is a physical character, and no one note is what it is except in reference to the rest, no thing produces effects unless it is turned toward the rest. In other words, every note in its own, intrinsic respectivity, and hence a fortiori every substantive system with respect to another substantive system has in its physical respectivity a character of "action" in its physical sense.

M   Before everything else, no substantivity nor any note lacks this character of action in its own reality. It is certain that there are notes in which this moment apparently is not being active [accional]. This is easy to see. It can be said, for instance, of a color that it is not active in itself. Yet after passing from that example to others, how could it be denied that a substance has the character of an action? Take a stomach: what would a stomach be as a note of a living being, of an animal, if it did not keep on producing certain effects, which are not added to its gastric reality, but constitute it formally as such?

N   The example of color is an equivocal example. That means that we do not perceive, so to speak, the character of being active [accional] belonging to color. One needs to study very little physics to know that what we call "color" is a more or less quiescent system of action. It is a question of a thing strictly being active: an incidence of light upon determined forms, upon a body, etc. It is true that not on account of this can one say that notes are active forces, as Leibniz said.[28] Absolutely not. For all those active forces have a *quale,* some perceptible quality.[29] Precisely to the degree that I do not perceive in that *quale* a dynamic moment is when the notes appear to me in that state of quiescence. Such is the case of color. But if I take the note in its integral reality, each note, certainly in its own *quale,* is an absolutely determined action, by virtue of which the notes are active in the first place in *themselves.* There is no doubt: they are active in themselves. Second, they are active *by* themselves. They are not stimulated, stirred up, by other substances or by other notes. In the third place, they are active *formally.* In other words, respectivity is intrinsically and formally being active [accional]. Since this respectivity is what formally constitutes the reality *simpliciter* [without qualification] of the notes and of the substantive systems, that means that integrally this substantive reality and the notes comprising it formally have the character of being active [accional].

Third Step

This reality, I said, has a substantive structure. That substantive structure consists of being what it is "in its own right" [*de suyo*].

Everything is real to the extent that it is *in its own right*. Everything ceases to be real to the extent that it is not *in its own right*.

Now, this patently means that every reality is precisely an *in itself* in some way or other. Its own character of substantivity confers upon it this character of being something *in itself*. It is *in its own right*, to be sure, and by being in its own right, it is something *in itself*. Now, the notes, I said, are in themselves and by themselves formally active. This means purely and simply that reality *in itself* is formally active. This means that a substantivity is what it is not simply by virtue of the quiescent aspect of some notes that in an abstract way may comprise that system, but it is what it is precisely in being the active unity [*unidad accional*] that comprises the very system of notes.

In other words, a thing, a substantive reality, is not simply what it is by virtue of the notes it qualitatively possesses, but in the physical reality of all that those notes are by way of being active [*accionalmente*]. It has being, let us say, by being what it is and all that it can give of itself. All that it gives of itself— giving of oneself is an intrinsic and formal moment of the structure of things.

Things, precisely because they are *in their own right*, have an active moment that consists of *giving of themselves*. This *giving of themselves* is the very expression of their activity.[30]

Potency, δύναμις, is not something that springs out of reality, but "is" the very constitution of reality qua reality. Every reality is active in and by itself precisely and formally by being real. This is what I would call "dynamism." It is reality in its constitutive *giving of itself*.

This dynamism, this *giving of oneself* [*dar de sí*], is not a subject, whether as subject to anything or as subject of anything, but is dynamism in itself: it is dynamic structure formally as such.

In the second place, this dynamism, as I have already pointed out, is not a *vis*, a force in the sense of dynamic mechanics, nor in that other sense for which this dynamic mechanics has served its brilliant discoverer Leibniz in metaphysics.[31] It is not a question of a *vis*, a force. There are moments in reality that are not dynamic. What I mean is that those moments are only the aspect or the *quale* of an integral reality that is formally active in and by itself.

The δύναμις [potency] is not anything different from reality. It is reality itself as real, purely and simply. The effects that this reality may produce form another issue. A thing has no reason for producing all the effects that it can give of itself. What I mean is that when it produces them, it is giving of itself. That

40

giving of itself is nothing different from the very reality in which things are constitutively what they are.

Fourth Step

ẋ Now, the fourth step consists of recognizing that dynamism and becoming, understood as a giving of themselves, are not necessarily a change in the first place. Quite the contrary, that will be all the less so the richer the reality that gives of itself. It could happen in some exceptional case that there would be a giving of oneself without any change. The supreme case is precisely God, Who because He is infinite, gives of Himself all that He is without losing or changing anything. How would it be possible to deny the dynamism of God in Creation?

ɣ   In the second place, it is certain that in things every dynamism intrinsically implies a moment of change. Yet that moment of change is not what constitutes the dynamism, but is rather the concrete structure whereby that dynamism gives of itself.

ż   Change is not something that constitutes dynamism, but just the opposite: change is that according to which and in the form in which occurs precisely the reality that is giving of itself and the giving of itself of that very reality (which are one and the same thing).

ɑ   Not only does that occur. Not only does it happen that in fact the giving of itself, the dynamism, is not *formally* a change, but that precisely something can become, in the most radical sense of the word, not in *itself* but precisely in *another*. In this case it does not change into itself. Let us consider, for instance, the case of love. It is a dynamism. But the one who becomes is not one *in the self*, but one *in the other*. The "in the other"—that is where the becoming is, not in the one itself. So much the less does that hold true if we apply this becoming, this notion of giving of oneself, to divine love. Precisely it has been said, and rightfully so, in medieval metaphysics, that love is aimed not at the qualities of the beloved but at the physical reality of the beloved. It is precisely for this reason that love consists of a becoming, of a giving of oneself, really, into the effective reality of the other. It is something that could not happen if becoming were formally a change.

β   Becoming is not formally a change. Certainly change enters as a component in all dynamisms of the universe; yet it is a component that does not constitute dynamism, but is the result of it or gives it its inner structure. Dynamism is nothing but reality in its giving of itself.

Fifth Step

ɣ To take the fifth or last step, dynamism, thus understood as a giving of itself, is neither becoming in generation or in corruption, as Aristotle said, nor is it a process either. Reality is in itself, by being real, constitutively and constitutionally dynamism. Only to the extent that dynamism implies a change, only to that extent can we speak of a process. Yet the process is the expression of the dynamism; it is not the dynamism itself. This conception of dynamism as being a process [*procesual*] is an extremely external conception. It is a mere description. It may well serve the ends of science, which takes things in a merely functional, external way. This I do not debate. I began by saying that I was not trying to invalidate any of these concepts, but that I was striving at least to incorporate them into something that I regard as more radical.

For what is false, to my way of thinking, is to say that the world *has* dynamism. The world has no dynamism. It is equally false to say that the world is in dynamism. The world is not in dynamism, but is dynamism. Being dynamism does not consist of having the character of being process [*procesual*], but is, in its constitutive reality, a giving of itself, which is nothing but precisely actively being what one in fact already is.

Dynamism is not something that one has, nor something in which one is—this is precisely the error of the whole conception of being process[*procesual*]—but one is dynamic. Dynamism is something formally constitutive of the world. The world is formally in its own reality something that consists of giving of itself. This giving of itself what it already is, is precisely dynamism.

There are degrees in dynamism so understood, and in giving of oneself: from the mere action and reaction of matter, the principle of action and reaction that weighs heavily in the first pages of Newton's *Principia*,[32] to giving in love. But this indicates that dynamism has its own, precise structures, by virtue of which the moment of change lying precisely in dynamism and becoming is more or less patent and effective.

Now, it would be an enormous error to think that the transcendental structures of being hinge only on the structure of electrons or inanimate matter. We are always inclined to believe that when we allude to love or to persons, we are speaking of some anthropomorphic and metaphorical things, but that what counts are the electromagnetic fields and the electrons. Yet, why? Are not those other things realities? Does not dynamism in fact have a structure that relates to the different structures of dynamism in a different way, and that applies in an analogous fashion to all those structures? The dynamic structure of local motion, the dynamic structure of physical phenomena, are not the same as the dynamic structure of a living being, of a human person, much less of the whole of history and human society. This shows us, clearly, that dynamism has precise structures, that it is impossible to speak of dynamism without qualifying it. I will deal with those structures throughout this study.

In the preceding chapters, I have set out my reasons for thinking, first, that in contrast with the merely ontological conception of becoming, it is reality that becomes. Therefore I have insisted on the need to incorporate this problem into reality as reality and not as being.

ι   In the second place, reality is not substance, "subject," but is constituted by structures; reality is not composed of substances, but of structures; it is integrated by structures.

κ   In the third place, those structures have a dynamism. By dynamism I understand what that structure has that is precisely being active [accional]. Also I have pointed out the two most important existing conceptions about this dynamism: Aristotle's that the δυνάμεις [potencies] derive and spring from a substance, and the nineteenth-century and modern conception that things are something like points of application of a field constituted by laws of physical or some other order. I have pointed out, moreover, that the difficulties that, in my view, both concepts present require adopting a different standpoint. I do not claim to invalidate those two concepts—that would be intolerably pedantic on my part and naturally very false—but certainly at least my thinking will just serve the purpose of integrating and radicalizing the problem of this dynamism.

λ   I said that dynamism consists basically of the active character of each reality, precisely in itself and by itself, with the consequence that structures are structures of activity. By virtue of them, what we call "reality" is not constituted simply by notes that are somehow static. Reality is dynamic and active by itself and not by virtue of some potencies emerging from it. I will stress this point further on.

μ   In short, reality is precisely what it is in an instantaneous and momentary fashion, and it is everything that can give of itself. Dynamism, furthermore, consists precisely of that giving of itself, by virtue of which dynamism does not mean change: change is a moment of dynamism and becoming. Becoming does not take place because of change, but change because of becoming.

ν   With this I have brought into focus the problem, What comprises the idea of the dynamic structure of reality?

ξ   What are in fact those dynamic structures of reality? That will be the theme of the second part of this study.

ο   What are those structures?

π   The first thing it is necessary to stress is that it is not a question of making a kind of balance of all the dynamic structures that the universe in fact offers when considered from various angles. This would be a kind of scientific balance-sheet of reality, which, though very important and naturally not wholly foreign to these considerations, does not constitute their formal, proper point of view. My point of view is purely and formally philosophical. Hence I must state, first of all, what comprises this philosophical standpoint, I repeat, from which I shall deal with the dynamic structures of reality.

Traditionally (I will later try to justify this way of proceeding into my theme), what constitutes the problem of the concrete character of dynamism in reality is what has generally been called "causality." In its dynamism, reality is causal.

Consequently, the philosophical viewpoint is in fact for this problem the viewpoint of causality. This is very different or at least sensibly different from the study of the different modes of causation in reality. It is not the same thing to study causality as to make a scientific balance-sheet of the different ways that things are produced in the universe. Therefore I adopt the point of view of causality by interpreting dynamism as a causal dynamism.

Part 2

The Dynamic Structures of Reality

5
Causal Dynamism

Introduction

A First of all, to learn precisely what causality is, it is best to focus some pertinent historical considerations on two points.

1. Aristotle

B In the first place, the classical viewpoint governing this whole question is Aristotle's.

C Aristotle carefully distinguishes *cause* and *principle* in his words and in his brief definitions, but in practice he does not distinguish them: πασῶν μὲν οὖν κοινὸν τῶν ἀρχῶν τὸ πρῶτον εἶναι ὅθεν, he says—and it is the only thing that Aristotle defines—"*a principle consists of something arising from something else.*" That from which there arises ὅθεν, "whence" something (arises), that is precisely principle. "The cause"—αἴτια—is a mode of principle."[1] And he says nothing more.

D It would have been desirable for Aristotle to tell us what he meant by cause. But he does not. In fact he says that causes are principles, but there he ends the issue. Naturally the issue ends in a way that will be very decisive in the history of modern philosophy. For it will then seem that the problem of causality is a special case of the principle of reason. All this culminates in Leibniz, forming the antithesis, to my way of thinking, of what should be said about causality. Causality is not a mode of sufficient reason; it is something else.[2] In any case, Aristotle tells us that αἴτια, cause, is a mode of being of a principle.

E Aristotle, in his typical mode of being intellectual, immediately mentions as many kinds of causation as there are in the universe, in reality. I cite a brief passage from Aristotle to make direct contact with his thought and to determine exactly what he tells us about cause. Of the thousand places in which he speaks of it I choose the second chapter of Book V: Αἴτιον λέγεται ἕνα μὲν τρόπον ἐξ οὗ γίγνεταί τι ἐνυπάρχοντος.[3] "In a first sense it is said—in a first manner it is said—that cause [αἴτιον] is that out of which [ἐξ οὗ] something becomes, that which is intrinsic, which is in the depths of the being that becomes; as bronze with respect to the statue, or silver with respect to the jewel, and the genera of all these."

This is the first sense of causation for Aristotle. It consists of being an inner principle for that which becomes and is caused, and an inner principle from which in fact something becomes, namely its ὕλη, its matter. But in another way, ἄλλον δε, we say that cause, αἴτιον, is precisely the εἶδος [form],[4] the παράδειγμα [pattern], Aristotle will say, the configuration of something qua entity, and the paradigm—let us leave the paradigm aside; this is the reason that something is what it is, ὁ λόγος τοῦ τί ἦν εἶναι,[5] and all the genera in which this notion is divided, καὶ τὰ τούτου γένη.[6] Thus, for instance, as an example of genera—he says—the parts of which a definition is composed, etc.

This is the second sense, the second mode of causation: it consists of conferring a certain configuration upon reality such as it is: it is the formal cause: ἔτι ὅθεν ἡ ἀρχὴ τῆς μεταβολῆς ἡ πρώτη ἢ τῆς ἠρεμήσεως.[7]

In a third sense, cause is also the first principle of change—of motion—or of rest. "As whoever wants something is a cause, as is also the father with respect to the child, and in general all that does something with respect to what is done, and all that transforms something with respect to what is transformed."[8] This is the third meaning of causality for Aristotle: the source of change, something traditionally called afterward the "efficient cause," in Latin, *causa efficiens*. Finally, he says, ἔτι ὡς τὸ τέλος[9]—Something is also a cause if it acts as an end. This end ἐστὶ τὸ οὗ ἕνεκα[10] . . .—the end is that with a view to which we do something, or is something, as, for instance, walking with respect to health. Why in fact do we walk? He says, διὰ τί γὰρ περιπατεῖ;[11] And we answer: to be healthy, to maintain our health. By saying this, we think that we have indicated what a cause is: εἰπόντες οὕτως οἰόμεθα ἀποδεδωκέναι τὸ αἴτιον.[12]

Aristotle gives us summarily in this paragraph the four modes of causation in nature, which are the material cause, the formal cause, the efficient cause, and the final cause.

Naturally it cannot be denied that we are a bit disappointed that Aristotle apparently should have said, but does not say, what it is that unites these four modes of causation among themselves. He does say that all causes are principles, but he does not say what it means to be a cause.

In fact the sense of the word "cause" has undergone a major restriction in the course of history, in which the concept of material and formal cause, qua causes, is more than questionable and has practically disappeared. Finality is thought to be something proper to and exclusive of human actions. As a consequence, the problem of causality has ended up being reduced to the problem of the efficient cause. This is a lamentable reduction, but be that as it may, the bias for it is already in Aristotle's own exposition of the problem of causality. We also understand that Aristotle says that the efficient cause is the first principle of change . . . the first principle of motion or of the rest of something. To be sure, this metaphysical concept is more than debatable. Can it be said that the only thing that makes a cause efficient, and the only thing to which efficient causes apply, is motion alone? This is supremely problematic. It could be thought that action or activity is a more general thing than motion. This is patent.

However it may be, Aristotle does not define of what causality consists. He subsumes it under the category, the idea, of ἀρχή [principle], and he paves the way for the limitation of the problem of causality—efficient causality—by means of a conception that is far from being evident but which has had a decisive influence in the history of thought.

2. Modern Philosophy

The modern world imposes serious revisions, fundamental revisions, on this Aristotelian notion. Such revisions do not consist precisely of modifying the idea of causality, but of carrying it to a different plane. Galileo begins by doing this.

Galileo, in a babbling way—like every creator who is going to initiate a new period in history, even without knowing it—in his *Dialogues on New Science,* debates with himself about striving to eliminate this viewpoint of efficient causality. He says that he wants to make a *new science,* in which—I will not quote his text because it is well known—he is going to tell us *how* things happen. He measures some dimensions, some lengths of times.[13] . . . I would not say that he measured force, because Galileo did not assume a dynamic viewpoint—that was proper to Leibniz or to Newton—but he does measure a series of things. He sees how in fact, given certain numbers, there are certain results expressed in other numbers, a function of the first numbers. In short, what Galileo does *seems* to be a special way of studying causes, the very causes of Aristotle. Yet that is not so. For the law that Galileo is about to formulate is not a causal law.[14] In the first place, there are many things that, from the standpoint of cause, would remain outside Galileo's physics. Galileo, in fact, was not the creator of the concept, though certainly of the reality, of inertial motion. A body left to itself without external influences, collisions, or contacts, would indefinitely follow the motion of a straight, uniform line.[15] Now, one might wonder, by virtue of what cause? The cause of an inertial motion remains outside the purview of physics. Physics starts with bodies that overcome inertia, yet has in no way posed the problem of the cause of inertial motions. This omission is serious for the notion of causality. Yet it is real without any doubt.

In the second place, even if we reduce the breadth of efficient cause to what Galileo inquires of the world and to what the world responds to him, the problem and Galileo's response are not precisely a problem of causality, although he might have thought otherwise. It is a problem of law. Galileo wishes to tell us how motions happen in the universe. He would leave the debate of causes to Albert of Saxony and all who shortly before his time argued about the "extremely difficult issue" that they called "the fall of heavy bodies." They argued about whether, in fact, when a body moves in space under the influence of gravity, the motion of the fall is mixed with the motions of translation which that body may undergo.[16] It seems that the thing was easy to solve. From a boat it is possible to drop a stone, watch how that body falls, and do the same experiment when a boat passes under the arch of a bridge, and jump from the railing to the height of the mast itself. Nobody ever did that experiment. They said that the idea of motion sufficed. It is curious that no one ever attempted the experiment. It is so curious that it has always shocked me. In sum, however it may be, the law of inertia, the principle of inertia, is not a causal law in the Aristotelian sense. It is a law that links the different factors that come into play within it; it links them into a concept that is not directly a concept of causality. So far from this concept does it lie that they could reverse the terms of the law. Instead of saying—as later was indeed said in dynamics, for instance, by Newton[17]—that force is what produces the acceleration in mass, it could be said that mass is the subject of the law, and that it is the quotient of force divided by acceleration, etc.

These are not causal laws. The problem of causality reduced to the plane of efficient causality has passed from the plane of efficient causality to the plane of law, in Latin, *lex*. Now, confronting this law that necessarily links some terms to others, Hume's philosophical critique arises that says, "This matter of laws, what is it all about?"

Hume severely criticizes the idea of causality. I could never have the experience that pulling a cord produces the sound of a bell. What I can say is that regularly, with a perfect normalcy, each time that there is a tug on the cord in determined conditions a sound is produced in the bell. But it completely escapes the senses that the tug produces the sound. What we call "laws" are pure and simple habits of stating the succession or coexistence of determined phenomena offered to sensible perception. Naturally there does not exist a perception of causality. This causality, if it existed, would have to be a question

50

of pure concepts, as, clearly, on the contrary, Hume will make the empiricist critique of concepts. This means that the idea of causality stays reduced to a habit or a custom, as he himself says.[18]

R   This thing seems irresistible to Kant. Yet it is appropriate to quote his text to see in what form this critique of Hume seems irresistible to Kant. Let us not build any unfounded illusions.

S   In the introduction to the second edition of the *Critique of Pure Reason,* Kant says, "Let us take the proposition, 'Everything that happens has its cause.' In the concept of something happening, I certainly think of something that exists, prior to which there was a certain time and naturally another time after, another after that, etc. From this concept I can deduce as many analytical judgments as I wish."[19] In other words, I can have the concept of a thing that begins, see that that beginning is included within a previous time and a consecutive time, and make all kinds of direct physical and metaphysical analyses of that thing. But the concept of a cause is this: the concept that something exists that is different from that which is happening, this can never be obtained from analysis of the concept of that which is happening.[20] In what is happening, I can certainly make all the analyses that I wish, as Leibniz said.[21] Never will I find in this the appellation to another thing different from what happens, within which would be, precisely, the cause of the happening of the first thing. This is not an issue to be resolved with analytical judgments, Kant says.[22] In other words, the appellation to a second thing is a synthesis with respect to the analysis of the first thing. Clearly the thing would be simple if, in fact, the basis of this synthesis were to be found in experience. Now, there is where Hume has taken it upon himself to demonstrate that this is impossible.[23]

T   Consequently, the principle of causality is not a principle of reality. It is a pure principle of cognition,[24] a theme which need not concern us here.

U   Let us make it clear that what Kant means to say is that the value of causality is not based on an analysis of concepts or on a perception of realities, but that causality itself is a condition of intelligibility proper to human intellect.

V   In the second place, Kant not only makes this exposition of the problem of causality, but also I believe, for the first time (at least following Leibniz, perhaps as explicit as Kant),[25] speaks of a *"principle" of causality.* The problem of causality from Aristotle to this moment had been the problem of analysis or of a perception—call it as we wish—of some things that in fact happen in the world and that are causal factors. As of Kant, though, the "principle of causality" is mentioned.

W   The principle of causality is said to have necessarily an absolute value vis-à-vis doubters of that value.[26] The *principle* of causality is no longer debated, but its *character* as a principle is. It does not relate to this problem that the attempt be made to join Kant in saying that the form of efficient causality—and this is the only causality of which it is a question—is precisely temporal. Kant will insist a great deal on this point. The temporal form of causality is for Kant the condition for the application of the principle of causality to real things.[27] Yet the principle by itself is a principle. As a principle, it expresses only the conditions of intelligibility for the human intellect itself.

X   In the nineteenth century, this idea of the temporal form of causality associated with what I previously said with respect to Galileo will acquire a somewhat different character. It will come to be said that in fact science has nothing to do with causality, and this is absolutely true. Science only tries to explain how things happen.[28]

Y   Perhaps a certain presumption of modesty has led it to be said that science studies only how things happen. And the "hows" particularly sought are those presented with regularity.

Z   Those "hows" of science are laws, but in no sense are they causes. In these "hows," in the second place, it is a question of studying, given a determined phenomenon, what are all the conditions and phenomena that have contributed to the appearance in reality of this second phenomenon. The great postulate for this, without which there would not be science, is that the phenomenon in question is rigorously determined by all its antecedents. This is absolutely the case for all imaginable things. It is a rigorous determinism. There is nothing in the effect that is not rigorously determined by the antecedent, by its antecedents, or by the whole system of antecedents that it may have. That is what has been called "determinism." This is absolutely right as the exposition of scientific labor. This determinism has had to go on slowly and laboriously broadening its scope: from the realm of mechanics to the rest of physics and all the remaining sciences of nature. (It was already more problematic to apply it to biology, but this also took place.) Yet what is the concept of law applied to society, to sociology? What is the concept of law applied to history? This is more problematic. Be that as it may, some laws and regularities have been found little by little which, if not laws and regularities in the sense of an absolute mathematical deduction, at least are regularities taken as a whole: certain statistical regularities. In the conquest of determined laws of reality, although many realities escape determinism one by one in an elementary way, nonetheless taken together, there is a statistical determinism upon which the sciences of reality are grounded.

α   This is absolutely undeniable, but it never ceases to present serious disadvantages from the philosophical viewpoint, which is the only one that matters to me here.

β   It is important to stress that science does not only behave this way, but must behave thus. The contrary would be for it to fail to fulfill its own scientific principles. It is quite another thing to determine whether or not this touches on the problem of causality. Nowhere is it said that determinism is causality: if there were a causation that were merely unique in nature, would it for that reason cease to be causality? Not only would it be a causality, though excluded from deterministic laws in the rigorous sense, but where it is said that everything happening in nature is obedient precisely to some determinism? In short, everyone is aware of what has happened in contemporary physics, the physics of elementary particles. Although it is difficult to admit, scientists assent to it with serenity. Yet the creators of the mechanics of the atom have never believed it: neither Einstein, Dirac, Schrödinger, nor Planck.[29] I recall the impression Planck personally caused on me when he told me he would go to his grave with the sadness of not being able to accept the physics made on the basis of his discovery. That is what I heard Planck say.

γ Yet, be that as it may, nowadays, despite all failed attempts to the contrary—and all the attempts to the contrary have failed—the indeterminism of elementary particles is absolutely undeniable.[30]

δ But there is a third, more serious, disadvantage, related to philosophy.

ε Slowly, in a brief exposition of these themes like the one I have just made, if what Aristotle said about causes is compared to what I say here about determinism, there is a μετάβασις [shift].[31] Philosophically there has been a slip, a serious one.

ζ Aristotle has not defined what causes are but has described what each of them is. Therefore I have transcribed the paragraph where he says what the cause contributes to its effect. For instance, matter is something that stays intrinsic to the developing being (not immanent as bad translations say, since ἐνυπάρχον means "intrinsic"), and enables this being to be engendered from its matter. The form gives it a determination;[32] the efficient cause gives it a principle of change;[33] the final cause, a τέλος, or end.[34] Although there is no doubt about all this, let it now be compared to what happens to a physicist who states a law, by virtue of which he finds that a phenomenon in question seems very strange, very rare, to him. He researches some conditions, formulates some laws, even creates and hammers out some brilliant hypotheses, and uses them to explain this phenomenon, the one in question. Let us put ourselves in this situation, in the most optimistic of cases. There is a deep difference from Aristotle, who has taken cause as his point of departure, while the scientist has taken the effect as his. This is an essential difference.

η This deterministic vision of the world is a vision starting from the follow-up, from the effect. Nonetheless, the problem remains of how that vision of the world would be if one started from the cause. To avoid speaking of cause,

53

it would at least be possible to refer to starting from the antecedent. Given an event, without a doubt it is a gigantic task to find the determination of the world in such and such a form. Now, to find out how in fact, in a primary and radical way—not a secondary and derivative one—an antecedent is going to determine the course of phenomena, is already another issue. Science does not pose this second problem, which, however, is a radical and basic one. All this means that despite this exposition, we remain in a certain way faced with the same problem: What is meant by causality? What is the inner structure that links causality to real and effective dynamism, whose characteristics were rapidly sketched in the foregoing pages? This is the problem.

The Functionality of What Is Real

A First, beginning with Hume's and Kant's critique, to avoid getting lost in a void, it is necessary to ask how the human being arrives at this vision of causality, of things as a cause.

B Kant says that Hume awoke him from his dogmatic slumber.[35] I have already said that Kant accepts in integral fashion Hume's critique so as to reveal that there is nothing in sensible perceptions that gives us the vision of causality. There would be no room for any other measure than that of going to the concepts, as Leibniz did in his aim of reducing the principle of causality to the principle of reason, and the principle of reason to that of identity or contradiction.[36] For Kant this is impossible for the above-stated reasons. Hence the problem of causality is converted into a problem of pure human understanding. Now, about the point of departure, which is Hume's critique, I will call to mind what I have often said on various occasions. It is that in fact all empiricism has the idea that sensible perception, or perception in the usual sense of the word, is constituted by what we all know: we see tables, lights, colors, we hear sounds of a ringing bell, etc. All these are perceptions. As I said in previous pages, we have the perception of the tug on a cord, and the perception of a sound in the bell. Two successive perceptions, one ends and the other begins. This succession is not a law and still less a cause. However absolutely true this may be, as here stated, there still remains the question of whether the human content of a perception is reduced to the specific, particular content it has by virtue of pure sensing. This is something different.

C I have written many pages to convince myself at least, if I do not manage to convince others, that in fact human sensing is an intellective sensing.[37] The human being does not sense only green, blue, red, pungent, hot, but he senses *really* the hot, *really* the pungent, *really* the red. This moment of reality is what I have called the "impression" of reality. This is not because of a second impression added to the first, but because it is the very formality with which sensible impressions are presented to the human being in contrast to the animal, for which these particular contents are mere stimuli.[38]

D The human being is essentially in this respect a sentient intelligence. In other words, the human being senses in an intellective way not only things described as real, but the very reality of them. The impression of reality forms part of the perception.

E Hence we arrive at a situation which for Hume and Kant must be a bit embarrassing. In a succession of perceptions—between the tug on the cord and the sound of the bell here mentioned—that succession has two elements: one, certainly, the fact that the sound of the bell is not presented to us only as a sound described purely as sound but as something that happens. Where does it happen? In reality, without a doubt. Before, there was *really* no sound before and there *really* is sound now. This moment of reality belongs to sensing. In the second place, not only does this moment of reality belong to things, but undeniably the one perceiving that in reality there begins to be a sound perceives that at least the appearance of the sound *in reality*, its attainment of reality is something that depends on certain conditions. Although they may not be causes, and even were they pure mental or psychological habits, as Hume would say, it would all be the same to me. For this would be enough to say, in that case, that the production of a sound—in the example that I have given—the appearance of the sound would be something that is at least functionally conditioned by other phenomena.

F Now, since this function does not concern the particular content of the sound, but the character of reality the sound has, of reality as such, we find that in sensible perception there is a perception of the functionality of the real qua real. This is precisely causality. Causality, to my way of thinking, is purely and simply the functionality of the real qua real.[39]

G This leaves unresolved the serious problem of what a cause is. This is another issue. Hume could be perfectly right when he says that the tug on the cord is not the cause of the bell's sound. Everyone might say that this trivial example implies splitting hairs. However true this may be, let us consult science: how many masses of examples there are in which it has been believed that the cause of a determined phenomenon was this or the other, when in reality it was neither: there was a different cause that produced two simultaneous or successive effects, etc. Ascertaining what is the cause is a problem different from the one of ascertaining what is the condition of causality.[40]

H The same can then be objected to Kant, who fully accepts the critique of Hume. It is certain that the idea of causality cannot be obtained through an analysis of concepts. Yet it is not certain that it is impossible to obtain it, and it is in fact obtained in a sensible perception once we take the precaution of defining human perception, sensible perception. In other words, in a perception not only what *is* real, but that it is *real* is perceived.[41]

I   This should be the point of departure: the idea that the functionality of the real—which I call "causality"—can be understood precisely from two angles.

J   1. It can be understood from the angle of something that is acquiring reality, as, for instance, the sound of the bell that previously was not and now is; but it can also be understood from the viewpoint of what I call its "functionality." Whatever the thing may be with respect to which the sound of the bell is a function in its real appearance—whether the tug on the cord, or whatever you want, or the free will of God—it is all to the same effect for what I am saying. Where is it said that occasionalism is an impossible metaphysics?[42] It is not. It may be an error of fact, but that is irrelevant here. It is not an impossible metaphysics.

K   2. Yet it can be understood from the vantage point of the cause. If there is real and effective causation, whatever that cause may be, something is its effect, because it depends on what is called a "cause." What is called a "cause" has some influence on the reality of the effect. It is the influence of the real qua real. These two notions purely and simply comprise the functionality of which causality consists: the dependence of the effect and the influence of the cause as moments of the formality of the real qua real. Modern science, as I pointed out before, has taken functionality and causality purely and simply from the viewpoint of the effect.[43] This is a limitation, independent of the fact that what science wishes to seek in these effects is not their coming into play but the law. Now, causality, I said, is not the same as cause. Functionality of the real qua real can be perceived and is directly perceived, yet in the immense majority of cases what is the cause is unperceived. This is a different issue. The problem of causality is not the same as the problem of cause. Never, of course, is causality missing in a sensible perception, but never is the cause given in an immediate way. What is in fact the cause? There is a functionality that is causality, which refers to a cause, and precisely in this referral it is necessary to place the strict problem of causality as a moment of dynamism: the functionality of the real qua real, that is, causality is a moment of dynamism. Let us recall how I understand dynamism: as indicated at the beginning of this chapter, it is a giving of itself. Then the problem of causality thus focused can be summed up in three points:

L   In the first place, dynamism and causality.

M   In the second place, what is causality from the viewpoint of the causal determination of the cause.

N Finally, what is causality from the viewpoint of the effect.

O This viewpoint, it can be seen, differs from the merely scientific one.

Dynamism and Causality

A I must monotonously repeat the starting points of the ideas that I have been expounding so as not to remain in a vacuum.

B In earlier pages, I stressed that reality is intrinsically and formally respective [referential].[44] Nothing is real if it is not real with respect to another reality. By virtue of this, reality, both the reality of every substantive thing and the reality of the connection of some things with others, is construct. In other words, every thing is a *thing-of* all the others. The *of* is not a later or posthumous addendum to the reality of something, but forms a formal, strict part of the very reality of something. It is possible that, by abstraction, I might not speak of that *of* and of that construct state and might limit myself to seeing the *quale* [perceptible property] of a note or of a determined reality.[45] Yet in its physical wholeness, that *of* belongs intrinsically and formally to reality. The construct is essentially respective. Now, as I said, this construct is the expression of a primary, real unity of which substantivity consists: a unity that does not spring from any subject, but which is the unity of the system itself, of the construct. This unity is expressed precisely in the construct character of the notes that a reality has or that a system of substantive realities possesses. This expression of unity in and by the construct is precisely what I call "structure." Reality is structural precisely because it is actualized in a system of notes in a construct state.

C In the second place, everything real is active by itself. The word "active" is an improper word here. (Languages have not been made to waste time in philosophy, the way I do, and it is always difficult to find words that mean exactly what is meant to be expressed.)[46]

D Leibniz, for instance, said that reality is *vis,* force. He had something concrete in mind: the dynamics that he had just created.[47] Here it is not a question of reality being a force in this sense. Clearly it could be thought that at least it is activity. Yet neither is this so. For activity, as I will show with precision, derives from what I am about to say and from what I am saying now but is not that of which reality consists. For then it would be necessary to appeal instead to a notion, to something like a reality that is active by itself.

E Concerning a problem that has nothing to do with this, some hairsplitting Scholastic philosophers once said that, for example, fire is an active principle by itself. It needs nothing to activate it. It is enough to throw in the firewood, and it burns. Fire is active by itself.[48] Leibniz's viewpoint would be this: the fact of its actively burning or inchoately igniting.[49] Now, this is not what I intend to say. I mean to say that reality is active by itself, and that its connection with another reality is enough for it to enter into activity. It is a kind of activeness [*actuosidad*]. But this is not a good expression either.[50] Still, it remains clear, in the first place, that respectivity grounds this kind of activeness: reality is active by itself. In the second place, this activeness is the one that in its respectivity [referentiality] produces activity. Activity is grounded in activeness, and activeness in respectivity. Each term presupposes the one before. Therefore what I am saying has nothing directly to do with the dynamism of Leibniz.

F   Finally, in respectivity there is not only the system of notes that comprises a substantivity, but there is the respectivity of one substantivity to another. To that respectivity completely applies what I have just said. Consequently, that giving of itself that, as indicated, constitutes the dynamism of the world is a giving of itself precisely into activity. Then that activity determines each of the things that comprise the world and, finally, performs not only the function of causality but also the function of a cause. Functionality is the expression of causal activity. Therefore the dynamism of the world is an intrinsically and formally causal dynamism. I thereby mean that the problem of activity is not inserted within causality, but precisely the reverse: to my way of thinking, the problem of causality is inserted within activity.[51]

G   Since the time of Aristotle it has been usual to say that substance has δυνάμεις [potencies] that enter into action owing to the influence of other substances that are in action and that precisely put the οὐσία [substance] into activity. Yet I think that it is strictly the contrary: the first predicate of reality is precisely its being activity in the sense that I have just explained (grounded naturally in "activeness" and the latter in respectivity). Only to the extent that it is activity can it be described as causal for some of its dimensions. Causality is a moment of activity, and not activity a moment of causality. This is so because the functionality of the real is based on the inner and outer respectivity of substantive realities, active by themselves, an intrinsic, formal respectivity, in other words, an actual respectivity in *activity*.

H   To be exact, causality is a functionality that is not proper either to the cause or the effect, but is a unitary function of both. It is simultaneously and together in the function that performs as the cause and the effect. In this functionality the cause is precisely *determined* as a cause, and the effect as an effect. Therefore the functionality has a name that is easy to evoke: causality in its concrete structure is precisely *determination*. For the moment this matter has nothing to do with determinism.[52]

Causality and Cause

A   Causality, I said, is a character, the radical character of structure in its dynamism.

B   The problem of who is the cause is a problem that *quoad nos* [relative to us] (at least *quoad nos* human beings) is inserted within the problem of causality. I use the expression *quoad nos* so as not to complicate things, for even in the case of God this is true. Divine causality is inserted within its own active potency, and not the reverse. But let us leave this aside for now because I am not writing an exposition of theology.

C   The problem of who is the cause, of what is the cause, is inserted within the problem of causality,[53] and not the reverse.

D   Certainly, to be concrete, if one takes a particular causation, a function of the real qua real, something particular, one discovers that the cause is always essentially problematic. Who can ever be sure of having discovered a real cause of a phenomenon, much less of claiming that this cause is adequate? This is absolutely capricious.

E   It could be thought (and out of this, for instance, came the names of electrical phenomena) that negative electrical charges produce repulsion if some are in front of other negative charges, and attraction if they are in front of some positive charges. The cause would be the charges, and the effect the attractions or repulsions. And what if the contrary were true, as Maxwell maintains—that the charges are the points of application of an electromagnetic field? What is the true cause? The cause would be the field.[54]

F   This is always problematic.

G   The idea of a natural law cannot be overturned by the scheme of causality. Causality has a rigorous, precise order: a cause precedes an effect, and this does not happen in any law. Every law, at least in its formulation, is essentially reversible. Any of its terms can be taken as the subject of a law.[55] Hence, I repeat, ascertaining what is the cause within causality, in a particular case, is always essentially problematic.

H   Further, no substantivity—and this is more serious—is fully the locus of causality because there is no substantive reality (outside the human one, though this holds true only in limited dimensions), there is no substantivity that is fully substantive. Consequently, none is a cause in a plenary mode.[56]

I   If substantivities (including living beings, but excluding human beings), if all substantivities formed only part (in one or another form as fragments of one or another character) of a unique reality, patently causality could not be predicated in a plenary fashion of any of those elements.[57]

J   In the third place, not only is the cause problematic (and there is no particular substantivity that is the locus of a causality), but the locus of the causality is to be found in the respectivity. I have already shown that in fact causal dynamism is something essentially grounded in intrinsic respectivity, because of which one thing is really respective to another.[58] It follows that causation and determination are applied in a strict, formal way to this respective system, which constitutes the world and the cosmos. This system is the one that is substantive, the only system endowed precisely with causality. It could be called *natura naturans* [nature producing out of itself], or the All, but always after making serious corrections to the traditional meaning.[59]

K   In the first place, it is not a question of a subject of cosmic phenomena. Nor is it one of a root from which these phenomena emerge. It is a question purely and simply of a structure, of something purely structural, active in and by itself. In that activity it embraces precisely all the partial structures it contains.

L   All this is something completely different from the idea of a *natura naturans* in the classical sense of the expression.

M   With respect to each of these structures, the activity of the All, by virtue of respectivity, is precisely the functional determination of each of the substantive realities comprising the world. Causality is determination of the real in the activity of the whole. In this fashion causality, which shows up precisely in every thing, in the becoming of each one of them, is only the shaping of a causation that is incumbent *primo et per se* [first and by itself], purely and simply on the whole insofar as this whole is precisely active.

N   Now, this applies, I said, independently of every idea of scientific law. Where is it said that reality is nothing more than a system of regularities? All objections that have been raised to the idea of freedom always stem from saying the following: here is an act, for instance, a person who has chosen a thing . . .

O   "Wait a minute," we are told, "I am going to use Leibniz's fiction of an infinite analysis,[60] and if I were capable of determining to an infinite degree all the precedent and concomitant conditions of this free act, of this free decision, I would see that in fact this free decision is rigorously determined by its antecedents and concomitants." This is absolutely true.

P   Yet that is not the problem of freedom. The problem of freedom is who sets the antecedents, and how. This is the issue. If we suppose that the decision exists, I could make an analysis and determine all its conditions, and set them in a differential equation. Now, it is a completely different thing to know who has set precisely these antecedents. Do they exist simply there as realities that derive from the cosmos? Or is it an ego that, properly speaking, sets those motives, an ego by virtue of which these motives can never be called antecedents? Where is it said that the motives of a free act are antecedents? They are determinants, but they are not antecedents.

Q   The free act is determined rigorously and deterministically by all its anteced-ents. What happens is that this factor does not stop the act from being free, since those antecedents are to some extent set by the subject itself. It is a self-setting. Consequently, the antecedents do not fit the scheme, "consequent-antecedent."

R   From wherever it is taken, however, whatever the angle from which we ad-dress the problem of causality and the causation of the realities of the world, we find that causality is a moment of activity and not a consequence of activ-ity. Now, this seems like a metaphysical restriction of the problem of causality in an enormous way. For where then is the so-called absolute value of the prin-ciple of causality?

S   It is all well and good that the world is after all an activity. This may be a fact. But if causality is inserted within *that* fact, where is the necessary meta-physical value of the *principle* of causality? The question is quite justified. Nonetheless, it would be turned against its formulator if it were argued to him, Do you wish to state what comprises the principle of causality? Now, no one hesitates to formulate the principle of contradiction, except as to whether or not time enters into the formulation of this principle. Things cannot be and not-be at the same time, said Aristotle.[61] Kant would feel that time is superflu-ous in that statement, but the structure of the principle is definitely the same.[62] Would someone give me an equally univocal formulation of the so-called prin-ciple of causality? Where is it and of what does it consist?

T   I know that there are very aggressive polemicists on the issue. Every finite entity is composed of essence and existence. Here would enter the principle of causality. Yet the distinction between essence and existence seems to me, for instance, inadmissible, and it seems equally so to many, many others who are not me but greater than me.[63] Within Scholasticism itself, what is the formu-lation of the principle of causality to which one would like to assign the qual-ification of absolute?

U   The principle of causality still awaits a univocal formulation. That is the first point. To my way of thinking, it is not that I refuse to answer what the idea of causality is in that principle; what I do is leave the form of "principle" apart from the statement. I have in fact said that all reality presented as a function of another is real in and for a causal dynamism. For causality consists purely and simply of the functionality of the real qua real. Now, the All to which I have alluded has peculiar characters. It certainly has some particular charac-ters—the All was instituted, for example, by some sort of bucket where the energy was located, where there are some electrons, a few photons, and that bucket explodes, space expands, galaxies are formed, etc. All this is absolutely true, and in this sense the All has a particular character.[64] Nonetheless, it could in fact have happened otherwise, without a doubt. It is not stated, further, that the All has never come *before* the initial state. Yet the fact is that reality not only has a particular character, but it has in addition the character of being real. Respectivity does not only relate to the particular content of reality—a thing that I have called a "cosmos"—but it relates to reality as such, which is respective as such—a thing I have called a "world."[65]

From the particular standpoint, what I have called the "All" is a condition purely of fact: in fact, the cosmos is thus but could perhaps have been otherwise. We do not know. And if it could not be otherwise, it would have to be proved that it could not have been otherwise—it is all the same.

Yet there is a respectivity in a different sense. It is the respectivity of the real qua real. For in fact that cosmos, that system that never goes beyond being a structural system, is a structural system that, as a system, may be the primary unity that is molded into the construct.[66] Reciprocally, that unity has no other reality except in the system into which it is molded. Consequently, in its own way, it is a function of the structural system itself. Hence reality as such is not exempt from these considerations on causality. Consequently, as pressed as we may, and would, find ourselves to define the so-called principle of causality, nevertheless it seems obvious to me that causality is inserted within activity, and it responds as a result to a condition of the real qua real. Nothing more or less can be asked of a metaphysical consideration.

Everything else, the absolute character of a kind of principle hung from the sky, is perfectly capricious. This is how causality appears in cause.

Naturally it can at once be asked, How does it appear in the so-called effect?

That is the third point.

Causality and Effect

I said that the effect is rigorously determined, without this being determinism in the full sense of the word. For determinism is always determination according to a law, a *lex*. The law is a regularity in the "how" things happen.[67]

Now, it is obvious that cause is not a law. There can be causes that do not obey laws in this sense. It is evident, in turn, that the law is not a cause. How could it be claimed that law is a cause? A law states precisely the intrinsic necessity for the way something happens but stays silent about the necessary character of this functionality. This is not the problem of science.[68]

Science does not concern itself about causes in the metaphysical sense, but in the usual, everyday sense. For instance, it neither does nor need distinguish what a metaphysician means when he solemnly says, as has been said many times in history, "These are not *causes,* they are *conditions.*" This is an issue debatable in itself, but obviously lacking in meaning for a scientist.

Science takes the word "cause," understood as determination, in a very broad sense. It does not take it in a rigorous, strictly metaphysical sense. Science seeks how things happen.

In the second place, moreover, that "how" is strictly particular. Science starts from reality being there, from its becoming, from human beings doing things with reality. It does not pose the problem as to what "beginning" means and what "ceasing to be" signifies in reality. A scientist would be left completely cold if told that the consequence of a law is the final point of a new creation in every case, or that it is a kind of emanation or prolongation of the starting point. This matters nothing to the scientist for the purposes of his science. He states a law: the law links A and B between themselves with an equation or with a more or less necessary consideration of a functional type, but there is no room in it for thinking that it is something that relates to the real qua real. The "how" that science seeks is a merely particular "how." Never is it a "how" that relates to reality as such.

Finally, in the third place, "how" is always relative. On certain levels there are regularities, and there are laws on a certain level. But that same law may cease to be a law on a different level. For instance, if what I do is take a not too fine and rigorous system of lenses and examine the passage of light through them, evidently I have a law of the propagation of light in a straight line. The idea of light rays is as commonplace and old as mankind. Yet it applies on the condition that the presumed light ray is not made to pass through an orifice with dimensions of the order of magnitude of the wavelength, because in that case the light does not pass like a ray, but diffuses like a fan. In other words, the law of the propagation of light in a straight line ceases to be a truth on that level, and the truth is something different: that light is of the nature of a wave, and not just a ray propagated in a straight line.[69]

Essentially, there are levels in the order of particulars. But the "how" that is *not* causality is, however, what *manifests* the causality. In other words, the functionality of law is the particular expression of causal dynamism. It manifests causality not because it manifests that the antecedent of a law is precisely the cause of the consequent—something we will never know, nor have any reason to ascertain. It manifests causality, however, because it evidently manifests that something becomes transparent or manifest, and that something is precisely the causality that the whole universe is exerting, of which this determined phenomenon is a manifestation and a participation.

Therefore the door always stays constitutively open to other kinds of determinism, of determination, which are not formally according to laws.

In causality so understood, it is necessary, to my way of thinking, to pose philosophically the problem of what the dynamic structures of reality are.

J   Causality, to be concrete, is precisely the form of processive [*procesual*] dynamism. The process, I said, is not dynamism, but expresses dynamism.[70] Now I say that the lawfulness of this process is not causality, but expresses causality.

K   Reality, in its radical unity, is therefore causal dynamism.

L   Consequently, it is necessary to consider what the structures of this causal dynamism are.

M   I have considered the structures that reality possesses, beginning with the character of those dynamic structures that, as I have first pointed out, in one or another form, express and manifest themselves in what we call "causality."

N   By causality, I have said, is understood in the first place the functionality of the real qua real. In the second place, *in* this functionality, as the real, which is real insofar as it is formally an "in-its-own-right" [*de suyo*], this reality, in fact, *gives of itself* really. This giving of itself in the functionality of the real qua real is precisely causality.

O   Immediately afterward, I set out three points: first, the relationship between dynamism and causality; second, dynamism and cause; and, third, dynamism and effect.

P   With respect to dynamism and causality I have tried to show how necessary it is to distinguish with care between *causality* and the determination of a *cause*.

Q   Causality is the functionality of the real qua real. Now, at times it is possible to ascertain what the cause is that produces that thing, and at other times no. In the last analysis, every solution will always be problematic and also hypothetical. It is not a question of identifying causality with ascertaining a particular cause.

R   Entering directly into the theme, I called to mind once more that reality is constitutively respective. Now, the moments of that respectivity are active by themselves. This character is completely different from that of Leibniz's *vis* [force], a kind of activeness [*actuosidad*]. By virtue of the character that reality has of being active by itself, placed in the respectivity of activeness, by reason of its action, it precisely determines an activity. *Activity* is grounded in *activeness*, and this activeness is, in turn, grounded in *respectivity*. Activity, insofar as it is the determinant of all that happens in it, is precisely *causality*. Hence the first formal moment of causality is the distinction of determination with respect to cause.

S   The second point here treated has been the problem of causality seen from the viewpoint of cause. Again I repeat that all content of causality that is immediately given in the apprehension of sentient intelligence also has something problematic, the concrete determination of the cause. This is not only a practical difficulty, but a difficulty rooted in the point of departure of the problem. The fact is that we use the plural for many substantivities, when the truth is that in reality (without taking into account the human being in some aspect of human reality) no thing has the fullness of substantivity: all are moments more or less abstracted and extracted from a single substantivity that is proper to the whole. Hence the determination of a cause always hinges on the variation of the point of view, as the substantivity of a thing is considered in its fullness—a thing that would be false—or in the respectivity of the whole. This whole is not a subject nor is it a root; it comprises the pure structure of respectivity insofar as it is active in and by itself. Hence, in short, true causality would be found only in the whole as such.

This poses the final problem, which is causality from the viewpoint of the effect, about which I have limited myself to saying that this causality cannot be confused in any way with what has been called determinism.

Determinism is a certain aspect of a thing, a very determined aspect, in turn, of the causality in the effect, which is the determination of the law. Not everything that occurs in the universe has the character of a law. Especially the fact that an effect has a reality by virtue of the cause does not mean that this effect or this cause is repeatable. In other words, determinism at most is a scheme of a special type of causality, but it is not causality in itself.

Considering causality as a moment of dynamism, that is, considering causal dynamism in its integrity, I will shortly set down what the concrete structures of this dynamism are.

In the first place, it is necessary to recall that dynamism consists of giving of itself. Reality is in and by itself active qua reality. By virtue of this, respectivity as a whole—both inner and outer respectivity—in its giving of itself is something that assumes the character of causality.

Dynamism, therefore, is formally causal.

In the second place, dynamism is grounded in respectivity. Therefore it will be necessary to make use of it to conceive what the different types of causal dynamism are.

Clearly respectivity is not univocal. The respectivity that there is between provisionally substantive realities—substantivities, I have said, are fragments of a totality—has a patently different character in accordance with the essence involved.

On the one hand, every essence consists of a primary, actively coherent unity of notes that are formally constitutive. These notes comprise a unitary system, actively coherent and primary, a system necessary and sufficient for a thing to have all its constitutional notes and to be able to have all the adventitious notes. It is the "extruct" [*extructo*], or construct system of notes, but also an "extruct" in-its-own-right [*de suyo*]. Therefore, it constitutes the "itself" of the "giving of itself." Then it is necessary to say that essences, from the viewpoint of their actively coherent unity, and from the viewpoint of their constitution, can belong to two completely different types.

β   In the first place, we have the type of those essences that certainly in themselves are constitutive systems of necessary and sufficient notes. They enable the reality whose essence they form to have at least all the characteristics proper to its substantivity, as well as the possibility of receiving characteristics or notes by interaction with a source external to the substantivity. They are, consequently, in this sense, realities *in themselves*. Yet these essences have a particular quality: they are realities in themselves, *nothing* else. Hence their respectivity is much easier to apprehend than in the other type of essence, since each one of the substantivities is something in itself, but it is intrinsically respective [referred] to something that is extrinsic with respect to the substantivity in question.

γ   There is a second type of essence in which this does not happen. Those essences are structured in such a way that in their moment of activity and dynamism they behave not merely with the particularity of the thing that those essences are and the particularity of the thing that the remaining things are with which they are in respectivity. Instead, they formally behave with the character of reality possessed by their own essence. This is what is exclusive to essences that are intelligent and volitional. Intelligence and will are not primarily open *because* they are referred to things that they are not. They are primarily referred to their own character of reality, a character formally defining their openness. The first thing that intelligence does, whether it knows it or not, whether it realizes it or not, is dealing with problems that intelligence primarily has to resolve by taking them precisely as problems of reality, in other words, by behaving with the reality proper to that intelligence and to that will. This does not happen in the case of closed essences. For an electron to exercise its active or passive electrical actions, it would not help at all to add the behavior of the electron with respect to its character of reality. There is no parameter, no factor in the structure of the equations of electromagnetic fields that allows introducing the moment of reality. On the contrary, where a human being is concerned, it is not enough to say that it digests, thinks, feels, etc., but it is necessary to say that it has an intelligence by virtue of which that human faces up to itself as a reality. That is the basic difference between open essences and closed essences. Hence from the viewpoint of dynamism, these two essences behave in a structurally and essentially different way.[71]

δ   They behave in a different way because, while closed essences do nothing more than be what they are in themselves and exist in respectivity with other essences that are in themselves, something completely different happens in open essences. Yet this something, however, does not completely distinguish the open essence from the closed essence. It would be an enormous error to think that in the open essence its openness consists of an "addendum" of a relational type to the notes that make up the essence—in this case of a human being—a closed essence, something in itself. This would be absolutely false. In the final analysis, this has been the root of all nineteenth-century subjectivisms, which have thought that the human being begins by being a reality closed over itself and afterward naively attempts to believe that it does or does not place itself in connection with something lying outside itself. This is completely capricious in its point of departure. The openness of the open essence is not added to the structures by virtue of which this essence is something in itself.

Yet neither can it be said that the openness of the open essence rests on itself. The great mistake from Heidegger's philosophy onward is the claim to view the openness as something mounted on itself, as if all that the open essence were to be afterward in its actions were the precipitate decanted by the pure existential openness of the essence.[72] It is not one thing or the other. The openness of the essence is an intrinsic and formal modification of something that is "in itself," a modification that emerges from the fact that this essence, which is in itself, has certain notes called intelligence and will. By virtue of these notes, this essence behaves with respect to itself in its own character as reality.

If these human essences did not have those notes by virtue of which each one of the essences is something in itself, there would be no place to speak of openness. On this difference between open and closed essences it is necessary to rely on seeing the different types of causal dynamism existing in the universe.

These dynamic structures, I say and repeat to satiety, are the ways of giving of themselves that substantivities have by reason of their essential structure. Yet open essences always basically presuppose that this essence is something in itself. This means that, some way or another, dynamisms of open essence differ from those of closed essence. Nonetheless, the dynamism proper and peculiar to that open essence, insofar as open, is mounted upon and is a modification of the dynamism that this very essence has, insofar as it is a closed essence, insofar as it is something in itself.

In other words, in the first place, dynamisms are different and diverse, but further, they are organized in a certain form. Some are grounded precisely upon others. In the second place, the dynamism of an open essence qua open is grounded on the dynamism of the essence as a reality in itself. The form of this grounding will have to be ascertained.

In the third place, this idea of the organization of the dynamisms should not be confused with what books have traditionally called the "order of causes." It is not a question of taking the four causes—material, formal, efficient, and final—multiplied in very many types of realities, that all converge upon a wondrous order, the order of the universe.

κ   Quite the contrary, here the point of departure is an initial, radical respectivity by virtue of which each substantivity is in re [in the thing] essentially
and constitutively respective. Here it is not a question of an order of causes
but of something different: of a *grounding of causality*. I adhere to the *pure type
of causality*—at least at the beginning—as opposed to the cause, and I say that
the different dynamisms are diverse. They are found to be organized, because
dynamisms, in their various types, are *grounded* upon one another. The most
elementary dynamisms are basic dynamisms for this reason. Reciprocally, the
other dynamisms are not reduced in any way to the basic ones—this cannot
happen. Yet they could not be what they are unless grounded in the elementary, basic dynamisms. This is clearly seen in the problem of a certain type of
dynamism: variation and change. There is a tendency to think that change and
variation is precisely the prototype of becoming.

λ   From Plato dates the idea that the sensible world with its variations is a pure
becoming, and that on the contrary the world of ideas rests on itself and is the
ὄντως ὄν, the really true entity.[73]

μ   Now, from the viewpoint of what I have here expressed in a clumsy and
babbling way, the situation is completely reversed. In variation there is a maximum of change and a minimum of becoming. To the extent that something
rises in the scale of realities, there is more becoming and less variation.

ν   The richer the substantivity, the more it gives of itself and the less it changes.
But this does not mean that the change is not precisely the basic dynamism of
all the other dynamisms.

ξ   I begin the study of these different causal dynamisms by starting with the
basic dynamism.

$$\sim 6$$

The Dynamism of Variation

Introduction

A This basic dynamism is mounted on the difference that exists in all substantivity, and in every substantive reality, between notes that are constitutive and constitutional to it and notes that are adventitious.[1] These notes are adventitious because they arise from the intrinsic respectivity [referentiality] in which in fact all the substantivities in question are to be found.

B These inessential or adventitious notes—call them what you will—have not gone unnoticed in classical philosophy. Yet that classical philosophy has viewed those notes as *in-herent* notes whose formal reason for being is precisely the inherence in a subject. Now, this is more than problematic. I will not repeat once more what I said rightly or wrongly concerning the mode of being a subject [*subjetualidad*] attributed to the real: being a subject is not the formal characteristic of substantivity, but being a substantivity means being a system of sufficient notes in the order of constitution. Hence these notes are not strictly *in-herent*. The *res* [thing] to which they would be inherent is not a *subjectum* [subject]. To use some word, I called them "adherent" in *On Essence*.[2] Here the word "adherence" does not have the physical sense of an adhesion of a paper to a table because it is humid, for instance. That is not relevant. It is a question of the etymological sense of *ad-haerere* [cohering to, from Latin *ad-* to; *haerēre* to stick, cling], just as *in-haerere* [cohering within, from Latin *inhaerēre* to exist permanently in] should also be taken in its etymological sense.

C Hence, to my way of thinking, the formal constituent of these notes is not *in-haerere*, but an *ad-haerere*. It lies in the *ad* and not in the *in*. It is a question of *ad-esse* [to be present] and not of an *in-esse* [being possessed]. As is known to those who know far more than I, it is not a question here of taking the *ad* in the sense of *esse-ad* [being toward], which is the character of an accident determined within Aristotelianism, i. e., that of the relation.[3] Here I deal with *ad-haerere* in the purely elementary sense, that is, of being attached to the system in some form or another.

D   Now, these notes are not simply superimposed upon the substantive system. On the contrary, the thing is always only one thing. This means that although these notes by themselves may not be *res* [things], nonetheless that which is the *res* (which is the essence to which these notes are adherents) exercises a transcendental function with respect to these notes. Hence we say that these notes belong to the *res* and acquire the character of the *res* as adhering to it [*adherencialmente*]. The essence not only is the *res* but also reifies [*reifica*], produces the *res*. This does not mean that it makes the notes the *res*, but it makes them *one thing in the essence*. These notes determine the *res* reifying it [*reificantemente*], and this is precisely the essence or substantive reality.

Ɛ   Hence these adherent notes are to some extent or other the expression of an irreducible aspect of respectivity itself in which substantive realities are instituted into reality.

F   Now, there is a giving of itself in substantivity that concerns the capacity of having different adherent notes. This capacity, this dynamism with which they are obtained, is what we call "variation." To vary in the most trivial sense of the word means precisely that the more or less adherent notes vary, notes which one reality has in its respectivity with others. Yet it is best to be a bit more precise about the concept of variation.

G   In the first place, recall that it is a question here of a giving of oneself. This may seem paradoxical. For if, in the last analysis, notes come to the thing through its relationship with other realities, how can it be said that the thing gives of itself? Doubtlessly this is true to a point. And not only is it true to a certain point, but it is a rigorous truth. Yet it is not the full truth.

H   Let us take the adherent note most extrinsic to a body, in the final analysis—and most tangible in reality: its place. It is not essential that a body be in this place. It could be in another. Clearly place is not essential to it. Yet it is essential for it to be *some*place. That is another issue.

I   Hence, giving of oneself is neither alien to, nor absent from, these adherent determinations. Certainly it can be a matter of indifference, or not essential, for a body to be here or there. Yet it is essential for it to be somewhere. An essence, although it may not be constituted by notes adherent to it, nonetheless prearranges in its essential, formal constitution the possible type of adherent notes that that essence is capable of having. Therefore the very structure of giving of oneself means in this case "to prearrange."

J   Giving of oneself, in this basic, elementary sense—which could not be more elementary, but neither could it be more basic—consists of prearranging that which can be a substantive reality by adhering to it. To give of itself means to prearrange.

K   I say that place is a very trivial but radical example. With good reason, to say in Greek that something is absurd (an expression seeming to contain a contradiction in concepts) is to say that it is ἄτοπον [placeless]: something that refers precisely to this adherent note that is place. Something existing nowhere is absurd.

L   In turn, the dynamism of this prearrangement is the one that most includes the moment of change. As a consequence, against all appearances, change and variation is the least giving of oneself and the least dynamism to be found in the universe. Changing is precisely a giving of oneself, but it is the minimum one. Hence it is the least of all dynamisms, and consequently the least of all causalities. Nonetheless, the moment of giving of itself (of becoming) is not absent here. Why? For the reason I have pointed out. For substantivity prearranges the field of adherent notes that a thing can have. Also, precisely the moment of variation is, if not what makes it possible, at least what is inserted in something positive, which is the giving of itself. In the following pages I will clarify what this means in concrete terms.

M   In the third place and finally, I repeat once more than it is not a question that in variation there is a *subject of* the variation. But it is a question of some adherent notes that consequently conform inessentially to the entire reality and therefore make this entire substantive reality not a subject of a variation but a substantivity that is *in variation*. The variation relates to the whole reality, not to the reality qua subject.

N   To some extent or other, all becoming is based on a variation in the sense here explained, not because becoming is formally a variation, but because variation is the basic form of dynamism of all dynamisms of reality.

O   Hence it is necessary to say concretely what the *dynamism of variation* is; and it is necessary to consider that the dynamism of variation hinges on the types of variation that can be examined in reality.

P   I therefore consider here the different types of variation that there are in reality.

Q   Aristotle called all these variations I will mention ἀλλοίωσις. He referred the concept of ἀλλοίωσις to the order of quality.[4] That is irrelevant now. I take the word ἀλλοίωσις in the most generic sense of variation, hence, as a synonym of motion, or κίνησις. Now, Aristotle says that there are no more than three types of variation; to determine these types it is enough to review the categories. There are no motions or variations with respect to relation, etc. There are no more than three possible types of accidental motions: motions relating to quantity—the motion of increasing or decreasing quantity. There is also the variation of quality. There can, moreover, exist a variation of place. There are therefore local motion, quantitative motion, and qualitative motion.[5] This threefold division of κινήσεις [motions], of variations, has rather stubbornly blanketed the entire history of philosophy. It is not because it is untrue, because doubtless it is true; yet that truth is handled with a bit of imprecision in Aristotle's threefold conception.

R In the first place, let us take local motions, as Aristotle puts it. There is a tendency to identify local motion with mechanical motion, as Aristotle himself does.[6] Now this is absolutely false. In Aristotle's times this was clear. But since the second half of the nineteenth century this was seen to be completely false. There are changes of place that are local motions and which, nonetheless, are not of mechanical character. In fact, variations of place within a field—variations of place produced by the propagation of an electromagnetic field—how could they not be changes of place? The proof is that with the appropriate apparatus, radio waves are received at a distance while they are still propagating. These motions and variations are not of mechanical character. Every attempt to reduce the electromagnetic field to mechanical forces has absolutely failed. It is necessary to take the electromagnetic field as a field irreducible to mechanical motion. A mechanical motion is something that is a function solely of masses and distances and whose force follows the direction of a line that unites the centers of gravity of the two masses in question. That is mechanical motion. Now, this does not happen in the electromagnetic field. Here the variation of a horizontal electrical vector causes a magnetic vector to appear at right angles to it. The attempt to reduce this to forces of elasticity in a possible hypothetical medium, like ether, has always failed in the history of physics.[7] In no way is it possible to identify a change of place with a change of mechanical character.

S In the second place, in this enumeration it seems that it is a question simply of diversity. Strictly speaking, this is also incorrect. Doubtless in the final analysis, change of place, local variation—apparently completely elementary and derived from a coarse metaphysics—is the basic dynamic structure of all that happens in reality. When I say basic, I mean nothing more. It is not a question of saying that it is formally the only type of activity. This would be a grotesque mechanistic doctrine. Yet I say that without local motion, all other dynamisms that there are in reality would not exist or be possible. Think about growth: growth is not simply a change of volume. It has some source. In plants auxins or growth factors will be discovered, etc. All these biochemical reactions include in great measure a local motion, a displacement by virtue of which growth is produced. Growth is not displacement by itself. Yet there would not be growth without that local displacement. In qualitative differences the same thing happens. Yet to take, for instance, the kinetic theory of gases, thermo-dynamic theory, the kinetic theory of temperature,[8] there, without doubt, displacement is a basic structure for every qualitative change, etc. Now, Aristotle limits himself to distinguishing these kinds of motion and says that at any rate local motion is the most apparent of all motions.[9]

T   In the third place, in his conception of motion and of this classification of motions, Aristotle starts from the substances comprising the universe. He cannot help but begin here, as this is quite an obvious point of departure. He reasons as if motion were something that, for whatever reason, emerges actively or passively from the moving subject.[10]

U   Now, in what I have set out here, I have tried to point out that all dynamism—in the present case, the dynamism of variation—has no meaning except from the standpoint of a respectivity. Aristotle completely leaves out this viewpoint in his philosophical conception of variation and dynamism.

V   Consequently, it is a question of starting from a basic, primary structure of respectivity in the universe in which substantivities are obviously in respectivity and are active by themselves. Taking this character together as respective and active by itself, actualized precisely in the totality of respectivity, we have exactly the structure of the dynamism of variation.

W   Now it is necessary to ask the following questions with respect to this dynamism: In the first place, where is, what comprises, this radical, elementary dynamism? And, in the second place, briefly, why and in what sense is this dynamism of variation a radical dynamism, relating not only to the physical world, but to all reality?

First Point: Basic Respectivity

A   In the first place, it is necessary to consider the most elementary respectivity, which is that of material realities. Still, I insist that there is nothing exempt from a reference to a place. Precisely, as I said, to indicate that something is absurd, Greek uses the expression that it is ἄτοπον [placeless].

B   Everything that is real is somewhere. It may be debated in what form it is there, but that is another issue, to which I shall return. However it may be, without that reference to place, there is no possibility at all of speaking of reality. Hence, in this sense, all dynamism of variation is grounded primarily on the fact that things are in a place, in some form or other, and that the respectivity grounded in the place is consequently the basic respectivity of all dynamism or variation. What is more, ceasing to be always in one place and going to another is something that has no meaning except in respectivity. It would be a serious mistake (though one which it is possible to commit in different ways—Aristotle's is one, Newton's another—to absolutize, in a certain way, the place that things occupy. It is absurd to begin somewhere and then to refer to whether in fact there are in the world other things with respect to which the place that the first thing occupies is in a relation to them. The place of a thing is always constitutive and essential and formally respective to all other things.

C   Aristotle aimed to find an absolute place in the universe. This is capricious. But Newton, taking a turn in the opposite direction, claimed to say that bodies are in space and, consequently, place is defined with respect to space and not with respect to all other things.[11] Now, this is naturally capricious too.

D   Place is essentially, constitutively and formally respective. If I use the word "respective," it is, in this sense, respective to the places of all other things.

E   Things are, therefore, in respectivity by reason of the place they occupy, and this, I maintain, is basic respectivity, which should be situated at the root of every consideration about the dynamism of variation.

F   Therefore, it is necessary to inquire, in the first place, of what this basic structure consists.

G   In the second place, what is the dynamic character of local motion, since it is the most elementary form?

H   In the third place, the question must address local dynamism as basic respectivity of all variation.

1. The Structure of Space

I It is necessary to begin with place, understanding by such, I again repeat, a place that a body occupies respectively [referentially], relative to the others. Here we begin—and I at once assume a humbler tone, needed to make this a problem of general metaphysics, not of cosmology. I begin with the fact that the place held by a body is held by *occupying* it. By *occupation* is meant a kind of one to one, biunique [*biunivocal*] correspondence, as a mathematician would say, between the points of the body and its parts and that kind of outer periphery we call "place," precisely its τόπος. This biunique correspondence, by virtue of which this place corresponds to this part of the body, and so on in succession, is what we call "occupying the place"—filling it. A way, therefore, of being in the place, the most elementary way, is to be occupying it.

J Now, the respectivity grounded precisely on this occupation of a place is what we call "space." Space is the respectivity of real things by reason of the place occupied by them. I insist on the words "occupation," "reality," and "respectivity." Hence what we call "space"—an idea naturally completely alien to Aristotle's metaphysics and falsified as I indicated in Newton's physics—the idea of space is much more complex in its very structure than appears at first glance.

K   I will not try to say new things that no one has said of space before. What I intend to do is to say them in such a way that they appear from the standpoint in which I place myself. All mathematical texts say that space has three structures; now it is a question of perceiving why. I say that the respectivity in which some bodies are with respect to others by reason of the place they occupy, in the first place, gives rise to a structure, which is precisely what I have called being "next to." In that case, respectivity has no other character than that some things are next to others. It is space as a set of points; it is what, from the standpoint of the structure of space, constitutes the object of a [mathematical] science: topology. It can be said that space is continuous or discontinuous, is or not connected, has lacunae or not, whether the order of multiple connection is compact or not, and so on. This is the *topological structure* of space, of being "next to."[12]

L   Yet in respectivity there is not only being next to but also being in the direction toward. In other words, there is a determined parallel direction with respect to which all the other directions may be defined. Now, this is what a mathematician would call "affinity."[13] Parallel displacement is precisely what determines the direction of points in space. For instance, suppose Galileo's claim were true that bodies move by inertia in Euclidean space. Obviously, parallel change of place, affinity, would be defined precisely by the property we were taught since childhood: they gave us two definitions of the straight line—the shortest distance between two points—we can leave this aside for the moment—and that other definition, the line whose points all lie in the same direction. The problem comes with defining the directions. This structure is precisely affinity. "Next to" makes way for topology. In the "direction toward" lies affinity, parallelism.

M   Yet, in the third place, there is a respectivity that is putting one place, and hence the body occupying it, at a distance from another. This is precisely *metrics*.

N   "Next to," "in the direction toward," and "at a distance from" are the three basic, essential structures that space has: continuity, parallelism, and distance. Now, what is curious about these structures is that one structure in no way determines the following structure. Given a determined topological structure, a parallel change of place and a direction are definable in infinite ways. Topology does not determine a special affinity. Following this consideration, neither topology nor affinity univocally defines a metric. The possibility would be absurd. On the contrary, the only thing that mathematics can do, and did do only a few years ago, is to find the necessary and sufficient conditions for a topological space to be converted into a metrizable one, in other words, susceptible to being defined as a distance in it. It is a question of certain conditions whose determination constitutes the theorem of Nagata and Smirnoff.[14]

Yet the necessity and sufficiency of these conditions does not mean the necessary satisfaction of them. There are topological spaces that do not lend themselves to be converted into distances, metrizable spaces, etc. On the contrary, the reverse is absolutely true: a definite metric implies a definite affinity and also leads to an absolutely definite topology.[15]

Since reality has a definite metric, in this structure of space is where is inserted precisely the moment, the dynamic character of local variation—which is the second point I am interested in examining.

2. The Structure of Space as Respectivity

The structure of space is a respectivity in re [referentiality in the thing]. I am referring to the space of physics, not to the consideration of geometry, which is another issue.

In re [in the thing] is a respectivity in local variation, without a doubt. In the last analysis, what we call "space" is the space that leaves things in order to . . . The first extension of that "in order to" would be in order for things "to be there" [estar] among other things and especially to be able to "move" among others. Precisely there, the moment of local variation, is essential for this consideration of space—space as free play of mechanical motions, local motions.

Not only is this so, but precisely what we would call "geometrical" and "spatial" structures of physical space are nothing but the precipitate, in a word, that things occupying space decant into it. What is, for instance, a straight line in the example that I set down earlier of inertia in Galileo's sense? It is an inertial motion that we consider in a Euclidean space of three dimensions, etc., and that is a straight line. While this is true, it could be conceived as something else. It would be possible to conceive this space not as Euclidean, not as rectilinear, but even so, inertial motion would continue to exist as a geodesic line.[16] Space by itself has no structures, or rather has no structures but those imposed on it by the bodies occupying it, each in its place, and further by the system of displacements: this is purely of a physical character. The displacements considered in their pure respectivity is what constitutes the structure of physical space. Now, of those physical factors that determine its structures there are essentially three: light, gravity, and action: light, which determines precisely the limit of maximum speed in reality;[17] gravity, which determines its curvature;[18] and action, which in fact we do not know what it determines nor what it will determine in the future. It is quantum mechanics. Whether it will abandon its indeterminacy and its undular character, and what will become of it, who can say? Its great creators have never found it possible to eliminate the determination of some trajectories, etc. In sum, pure activists, like Heisenberg, for example, say it is possible.[19]

S   Be that as it may, light, gravity, and action are the great determinants of what we call the "physical structure of space." Naturally it is understood that whenever a body moves in space it is not necessarily subjected to the action of forces. In other words, a motion, a body left to itself in physical conditions, that is, in light, gravity, and action, determines these structures of space.

T   Given this assumption, motion taken in itself is not a state of the mover. This realization is precisely what constituted, to my way of thinking, Galileo's surpassing concept of elementary motion with respect to Aristotle. In motion Aristotle is searching before all and above all for the *ens mobile* [moving being]. He took as his point of departure precisely that there was a being, a substantiality with a state of motion and variation. Then Aristotle said of this subject that it moves, that motion is ἡ τοῦ δυνάμει ὄντος ἐντελέχεια, ἦ τοιοῦτου,[20] that it is the actuality of the potency qua potency, that is, the imperfect act, ἀτελές, as he would say.[21] Now, this is nothing evident or obvious. For the first obvious thing that needs to be said is that motion is always a respectivity in which the mover is found with respect to other bodies. With respect to what subject is the body to move? With respect to space, absolute space? What if absolute space does not exist? Space is a respectivity of some bodies with others. Motion implies essentially and constitutively a relativity, a principle of relativity. Relativity is not the motion itself; on the contrary, motion has a very absolute character. What is relative is to know what is moving and what is at rest, for it makes no sense to say this in an absolute way. It depends upon what we want to consider in motion and what at rest. Motion is essentially and formally a variable respectivity, in other words, a structure or parameter that exists in reality. It would be capricious to follow the debate with Aristotle or with Leibniz, because what would have to be said would be that what is not true is that mechanical motion as such, local motion, is born out of the conditions of a subject. Instead, the whole universe is *in* motion. So-called motion is a parameter independent of the consideration of the universe.

U   The universe is not constituted by some substances from which follow local motion. If we assume the standpoint of creation, God has created some things but moreover has created them in motion. There is nothing more to say. It is an independent parameter. It is absolutely inefficacious, inadmissible, to try to explain motion by starting with the condition of the mover.

V   The example of the classical principle of relativity in rectilinear mechanical motions is quite a commonplace (the railroad station in which clearly one does not know which train is moving). It is no less true, as Einstein tried to demonstrate, in special relativity, etc.[22] This holds for the case of gravitational fields. It could be said—let us come back to the trains—that if the train suddenly puts on the brakes and stops and a suitcase falls on my feet, the one onto whom it has fallen is me, not onto someone in the other train that is opposite. But that is not the question. It is a question of knowing whether it has fallen onto me because my train has a positive gravitational field, or on the contrary, because the train opposite exerts a negative gravitational field by which it causes the suitcase to fall down. The structure of gravity is the curvature of space. This curvature embraces the bodies within it. Yet gravity for Einstein is not a force, as I will at once show. It is a structure of space as in the case of inertia.[23]

W   Motion is a state, a dynamic invariant in the universe, naturally in a definite system. Motion can in turn vary. Yet the fact is always that things move precisely because the universe is in motion. The universe does not move because things, through an interaction of some on others, put each other in motion. The structure of the universe is in and by itself constitutively dynamic. Clearly in this sense it should be said that the universe changes because it becomes, that is, because there is a previous giving of itself, which is precisely what constitutes the activity of the respectivity of the totality in question.

X   Naturally this is only an apparent avoidance of the issue. What happens here is the contrary: it centers the issue of causality on motion. Where is causality in motion, in local motion? Apparently one would appeal to mechanics proper, to force as the cause of motion. Yet this is an absolutely illegitimate answer for several reasons.

Y   In the first place, not every motion in physics is produced by a force; not by any means. In the case of an inertial motion, whatever its origin, or even though God might have created it in a pure state of inertia, this inertial motion does not carry a force in its bosom. All these medieval speculations about impetus, etc. never rise beyond being meaningless speculation. Clearly not all motion is produced by a force.

Z   A force is needed for a different purpose: to change the speed of motion, indeed, to produce an acceleration. This is the very definition of Newton: force is the product of mass times acceleration.[24] This is absolutely true, although it makes it quite impossible to identify the concept of the cause of motion with the concept of force.

α   Yet, in the second place, the fact is that the concept of force is in itself and in all its universality, even when limited to this case of accelerations, absolutely problematic within physics. In sum, until Einstein it was possible to talk about forces, for instance, the force of gravity. Now Einstein has completely relativized the concept of force. For Einstein there is no reality but fields: the electromagnetic and the gravitational ones; and what we call "force" is the way the human being feels the intensity of the field at a definite point. Yet it is not a force that produces the field. Force does not have causal character. Gravity is a structure: the curvature of the universe. The force of gravity does not exist for Einstein, not even in the remotest sense.

β Not only for these physical reasons, therefore, does cause differ from force, but now for philosophical reasons this identification is impossible. The fact is that the identification confuses causality and cause. These are two different things.

γ Despite every impossibility of defining the final root of local motions in the universe—I deal with local ones, not others—motion inexorably has the moment of being something happening in reality. Moreover, the human being, in his sentient intelligence, is precisely perceiving the motion of variation of place, for example, as a functionality within the real. Every variation is a variation *of* reality *in* reality. No motion is produced by chance in an arbitrary way, but all motion is a variation with respect to the place occupied for whatever reason one wants (I do not enter here into the problem of reasons). Clearly there is perception of the functionality of the real qua real and in this case of the real insofar as it has this adherent note we call "place." Precisely this is what I have called "causality." Here there is, naturally, an essential difference between philosophy and science. The scientist who reads what I am writing will say that this does not interest him. Naturally it does not, because I am not attempting to produce a mechanics nor to integrate differential equations of motion. What I do say is what are the conditions reality should fulfill for there to be those motions whose equations the scientist describes; and I say that that condition is that there be causality. Now, in no way does this mean that the cause of motion has been determined. For the truth is that *it is questionable whether the cause of motion really exists* in the sense that something unleashes motions. This is a mere hypothesis, as obvious as one might wish, but completely arbitrary. Where is it written that the motion of the universe is unleashed by *any* things, much less *one* thing? The universe is in motion in and by itself. There is nobody or no thing that has unleashed universal motion. If it is desirable to speak of cause, it will have to be said that it is the totality of the universe. Integral respectivity, the totality in question, is what would be the cause of variations of place happening within the universe, but not because there is a special, definite thing that has unleashed the motion in a definite substance and is propagated to another, and so on. This does not go beyond a merely imaginary hypothesis. The cause of motion is purely and simply the active character of reality in its place, neither less nor more; and reality taken in its respectivity, that is, in the totality of the universe.

δ The universe is in motion. There is nothing that has unleashed a motion or motions of the universe (I speak of local motions, to be exact).

ε Now, this dynamism consists of a giving of itself, and, as I said, it reveals everything that a body can give of itself by reason of its structures and notes in order to occupy different places in space. What is less obvious is that not every body can occupy any place in space. Yet it is essential that it occupy some place. Probably it is essential that it be able to vary, but this does not mean that the range of possible places is accessible to all bodies. A bottle cannot be on the surface of the sun because it would disintegrate. A body can occupy many places, but not every one imaginable.

Precisely because it cannot occupy all imaginable places, we said that it is manifestly a giving of itself. It gives of itself, given its physical conditions and its notes, the enormous but not indefinite or infinite gamut of places that a body can occupy in space. Hence in this case, although the becoming is minimal and the change maximal, local motion is nonetheless not exempt from the condition of becoming. It changes, in short, because it becomes. For there comes into play the capability that it has of occupying different places in space. This capability comes into play not because it is a potency different from substantivity and energized by something outside it, but simply because it is the body, even in its spatial note, that is active by itself and necessarily has to be in spatial, topical activity with respect to the other substantivities of the universe.

3. Local Dynamism as Basic Respectivity of All Variation

Local motion is the basis for all other variations, quantitative or qualitative. This is the case for the same reason that, according to the Scholastic philosophers, quantity is the *accidens radicalis* [root accident].[25] Now, *root motion* is change of place.

Naturally with some justice the reader may ask why I have made this clumsy explanation about space when it seems obvious that the universe and the respectivity of things in it have not only spatial but also temporal structure. Why have I not spoken of time? Because, although it may seem like heresy to say so, time does not directly relate to reality as such. It definitely relates to the actuality things have in their respectivity. And the actuality of the variation of place, of this dynamic of variation in the spatial respectivity of the universe, is precisely what we call the "being" of that dynamism.

Now, the mode of being of dynamism insofar as it is "diachronic" or "transcurrent" [*transcurrente*] is what we call "time." Time is the subsequent act, a subsequent act with respect to motion; and this does not happen to space.

Time is a mode of being of motion, but it is not what formally constitutes motion. Thus considered, time also has a complex structure, very parallel to spatial structures. In the first place, it has a kind of spatial character—I say a character of continuity, a kind of topology of time, a *chrono-logy*. Clearly Indian thinking, or at least a great part of it, would have much to address concerning the atomic structure of time as not being continuous, etc.[26] That is a topological problem.

λ   In the second place, time has a completely determined structure of affinity: it elapses unilaterally in a single direction, unidirectionally from the past toward the future. The possible reversal of time does not happen except a little artificially in determined equations of quantum physics, in the collisions of high-energy particles.[27] Yet let us leave this matter in the air, because as often as I have wished this to be explained to me, it never was. I even asked Heisenberg himself, who always unleashed great speeches at me, without giving me a clear exposition.

M   In the third place, time has a measurable structure, which is chronometry.
v   Chronology, the unidirectional structure of time, and chronometry are the structures of time, understood as the subsequent act, or the actuality of the real, physical, spatial dynamism of bodies, from the standpoint of actuality in respectivity.

Second Point: Basic Character of This Respectivity

A   This structure of local variation, as indicated, is immersed in one form or another in the radical basis of all quantitative and qualitative variations. Even in its maximum generality as material order, it must be taken with much greater scope to see or even guess how very radical and basic is this appeal to respectivity that I call "spatial."

B   The truth is that in fact until now I have started with material reality, characterized by a special mode of being in a place that is occupying it. Yet this is not the only way of being in a place. For example, the human spirit is in the body of each individual. Nonetheless, it does not occupy it in the sense that we have defined. It cannot be said to what point of the body a point of the spirit corresponds. As many attempts as have been made to ascertain it—for instance, in psychophysical parallelism with the brain—it has immediately been seen that this is a problem generating more mental heat than light. Something does not make sense. Yet, the spirit of every human being, within the more or less defined limits of a particular body, naturally is in it, not in someone else's body.

C   Occupying space is a way of being in a place: it means being in it as *circum-scriptively*, as the Scholastic philosophers would say, since they too say good things.

D   But there is another way, as I have just mentioned, which is to be situated as *diffinitively*.[28] In other words, the actuation and presence of a reality is defined in space without suggesting that this definition applies to occupying space. Then the enormous transcendence of space, of place, becomes immediately visible in all beings of the universe. There is nothing exempt from some reference to space, however that may be, taken to this maximum extent. Even in history, it makes no sense to try to take a great literary work, let us say, a Greek tragedy or comedy, and attribute it to just any people on earth. This is senseless. It is indeed sensible to attribute it to a people occupying a definite place and no other. The culture of China is not comparable, it is different for 40,000,000 reasons from Greek culture, in the first place, because the one is in China and the other in Greece. This is clear. There is always in some form an intrinsic, constitutive reference to space according to the different ways of being situated in it. Of all them, however, the one I have mentioned is basic. It is the fact that material realities in their quantitative and qualitative variation are actively assuming a motion of τόπος, a motion of place, which is not mechanical motion and does not necessarily have to be, and that variation is inserted precisely in the formal structure of respectivity as such.

ε The world is really and constitutively in motion. Precisely for this reason it moves in each thing, and that moving of things consists of their giving of themselves, that is, of occurring within the ambiance of notes variationally prearranged by the structure of an essence constitutive of substantivity.

F When I began the study of the dynamic structures of reality, I wrote in chapter 5 what I have repeated in this one, because it is necessary to keep it in mind. It is necessary to start, to my way of thinking, with the essential and constitutive respectivity in which all universal realities are situated. This respectivity is not consequent upon its mode of reality, but is formally constitutive of it.

G These structures and the structural notes composing them are active by themselves. Hence I have wished to convey very expressly that it is not a question of reality being activity—that would be Leibniz's thesis[29]—but of something simpler: reality is active by itself. I call to mind in part what that Scholastic philosopher said about fire as an active principle for itself, which does not always burn because it lacks fuel, but which only needs to be fed fuel for it to burn in its own right. Now, the fuel of the universe is given precisely in respectivity itself. As a result, in fact, the world is in activity because each of its structural moments is formally active by itself. Activity rests on this character of being active by itself.

H Now, the various realities that compose the universe, I was saying, are not precisely substances, but structural systems. Reality is composed not so much of underlying things, but of structural things: of structures. These structures are structures that rest on themselves as they have a sufficiency of notes in the order of what we call "constitutional sufficiency." This system of constitutional notes rests within the substantivity itself in a certain more radical and deeper basic system of notes that are not only constitutional but also constitutive.[30] Precisely through their primary unity of coherence they constitute what we call the "essence" of a thing: that which is the reality *simpliciter* [without qualification] of things in the world.

I   This system of substantivities can have and in fact does have a system of notes that do not belong to the essence, nor spring from the constitutive notes, but rather have traditionally been called accidental. This expression seems quite ambiguous to me. I have preferred to call them "ad-herent," as opposed to what traditionally has been said of the accident, that its essence consists of being inherent. This difference is based precisely on the fact that the thing to which the constitutional notes are ad-hering is different from the thing to which the accidents are in-hering: accidents are inherent in a subject, a substance.[31] On the contrary, here it is a question of some notes which, because they are adherent, determine in an ultimately concrete way the substantive system to which they adhere.

J   Therefore it is necessary to start by studying what the structures of universal dynamism are.

K   I have begun precisely with dynamic moments relating to the adherent notes, and this dynamism is what I have called "variation." I have tried to show that all the variations are grounded in the last analysis, radically, on the most elementary variation: the case where variation takes place in something comprising, at least at first glance, that peculiar property of the reality of a thing that is being situated somewhere. In fact, things can be situated, are all situated, somewhere. Something not situated anywhere, at least within the world, would be an ἄτοπον, something therefore absurd, without reality. What I have called "dynamism of local variation," I said, consists, however, of having this note of being situated from the viewpoint of a giving of oneself. For it is in fact true that it is not essential for a thing, for instance, a glass, to be situated where it is, as it could well be elsewhere. Nonetheless, in the first place, it could not be just anywhere at all, and in the second place, it is essential for it to be somewhere. Hence the possible changes of place are so many other moments, however elementary one wants, of a giving of themselves on the part of things.

L   Now, in this basic dynamism of displacement are grounded in one form or another all the other variations. But to enter into the study of different types of variation is not relevant here.

M   Variation is a giving of oneself. And giving of oneself consists, in this sense, of prearranging from oneself the scope of adherent notes, even those of places, in which a reality can be.

N   This causal dynamism is not the only one. It is not the only causal dynamism, because realities do not just have adherent notes but are structural systems in themselves. Here appears another point on which it is necessary to bring to bear reflection about the dynamic structure of reality.

7

The Dynamism of Alteration

Introduction

A Above all, I repeat, all other variations, and the remaining variations that are not local, the whole range of variations, whether local or not, form the basic dynamism upon which all other dynamisms are supported and mounted. By this I do not mean that the others are in any way reducible to this one. In banker's language, this would be tantamount to speculating on declining stock prices. It is not a question of this. Nor is it a question of the fact that other dynamisms are simply a complication of these elementary dynamisms. What I mean is that the other dynamisms, in some form or another, are supported or *based* on realities that enjoy or suffer this basic, elementary dynamism, which is variation. Afterward I will clarify what it means to be *based*.

B Now, these dynamisms, which are not pure variation, concern the very constitutive structures of reality, of substantive realities.

C I call to mind and insist again that all realities of the world are intrinsically and formally respective [referential]. Also, their own essential systems, and those first of all, are essentially constituted in inner, intrinsic respectivity to one another. Consequently, the problem of dynamism relates not only to the adherent notes but to the structures themselves. This is a more complicated stratum of dynamism, because it relates to these structures not only in the entire set of their constitutional notes—this goes without saying—but also in their own constitutive notes, in the basic, radical system, in that which is their very essence.

D Such essences, which for this reason I call "constitutive essences," in fact constitute what each thing is. They constitute the terminus of a new dynamism in a dynamic respectivity.

E   The dynamic respectivity by itself, I repeat, means the fact that these essences comprising the world are essences active not only in themselves but by themselves, too, as a result of their own intrinsic and formal condition. This does not mean in any way that it is necessary to define the structures by saying that they are unstable. That is another issue. They may or may not be stable as a consequence of what they may be in themselves. Yet instability is not the primary character of this dynamism of essences; so it does not mean that an essence, because it has some constitutive characteristics, is metaphysically stable and also immutable. In no way. I mean purely and simply that these essences, in their constitutive character, and insofar as they are constitutive essences, are active by themselves. In other words, they cannot be what they are unless they give of themselves what they express in their actions.

F   Now it is necessary to focus on some characteristics of this respectivity, which, as we shall see, is dynamic.

G   In the first place, with little reflection it can be understood that all substantivities of the universe, at least those accessible through experience, in their broadest, remotest trajectory, are constitutively *emergent*. None rests on itself. In some form or other, they emerge; but from what? At least they emerge in the world, in that respectivity of which they form part, and of which they are inner moments. Here the word "emergence" does not mean "emergency."[1] Emerge, *e-mergere*, means "to come out of." Such is the sense of "emergence."

H   In the second place, these things, substantive realities, the substantivities, are not only emergent, but this emergence has an underlying stratified [*substratual*] character.

I   The whole emergence, whatever its meaning, is supported on a substrate. Here *substratum* does not mean a kind of prime matter from whose complication whatever emerges is a result.[2] It is not a question of that, but purely and simply of something purely descriptive in the final analysis. No substantivity, in its moment and in its character of emergence, comes directly out of nothingness, but each is supported on something previous. It is not reducible and generally not reduced to this, but it is a substratum without which that emergence would not have been able to take place.

J   From any given substance and any given point in the universe not just any substantivity can emerge. They always emerge upon a definite substratum, on the basis of a definite substratum.

K   This substratum, which is the one that counts here, is the *immediate substratum*. For mediate substrata can be found that are not, however, the substratum that matters to me here. The one of present importance is the immediate substratum upon which is supported a constitutive essence, so that the latter can emerge in the universe.

L   That substratum, precisely because it is one, is relatively indeterminate. It is not completely, but of course only *relatively,* indeterminate; if it were not, there would be no possibility of emergence. There would simply be a monotonous repetition of substantive realities in the universe. Thus, in the respectivity [referentiality] of substantivities, these substantivities are, in the first place, emergent. In the second place, they are mounted upon a substratum. In the third place, the substratum does not operate by itself in isolated fashion, but is immersed in a definite configuration. This is essential: with different configurations, the same substratum and the same dynamic characteristics would give rise to very different substantivities. The configuration is essential, absolutely essential to a substratum to explain precisely this dynamism of the production of substantivities and of constitutive essences.

M   There is an emergence, an underlying stratification [*substratualidad*], and that stratification is in a radical and primary state belonging to a configuration [*configuracionalidad*].

N   Now, this configuration, like everything happening in respectivity, is intrinsically and formally dynamic. Precisely the dynamism to which I am going to refer now is the dynamic configuration qua configuration, that is, a type of causal dynamism completely different from the dynamism I examined in variation.

O   In variation it was precisely a question of a dynamism in which a substantivity varies while essentially staying the same; here the dynamism comes upon the substantivity as such. Consequently, it is not variation but *alteration* in the strict sense. It produces an *alter* [other].

P   Alteration is a giving of oneself that is different from variation. While variation consists of prearranging the gamut of adherent notes that a reality can have, or at least in prearranging the field of those notes, alteration is something completely different: it is a giving of itself in which what gives itself is precisely an *alter,* an other. This is a dynamism of great wealth. However, its great richness is not simply juxtaposed to what came before but precisely supported by it.

Q   I insist once again that the dynamisms of the universe are not simply different but are organized. The organization does not mean a theory of competing causes, but, to take causality in its integral meaning, they are organized upon others in the sense that they are supported by the others in a dynamic and stratified fashion. Thus, for instance, it is necessary to say that upon the primary phenomenon of variation, precisely of place, are grounded all other dynamisms, as we shall see.

R   In fact, this dynamism of situating things in their place or in different places is a *distancing*. Distancing is the most elementary but unavoidable form of distinction. Every distinction, in the final analysis, in some form or another, is supported on a distancing by means of underlying strata. In this distancing is produced an alteration, an *alter,* as is natural. It is important to know what is the structure of this dynamism of alteration, of those "others" produced in the dynamism relating to the essence.

S   This dynamism has three possible types.

First Type: Change

A   In the first place, in this dynamism, which is incurred by and relates to the essential constitutive structures of a substantive reality, it is possible that, from their respective [referential] connection with other substantivities, from their respectivity, there is produced what we would commonly call, and what is strictly speaking, a *change of form.* In fact, one substantivity changes into other substantivities. The problem lies in defining what is meant by this change.

B   Here once more we need to confront Aristotle's conception, which at the beginning of his *Physics* deals precisely with the kinds of change. He cannot help but start with empirical changes confirmed in one's own experience.[3] Take, for example, moving from place to place. For the moment I disregard what I said before about the insufficiency of this conception.

C   Aristotle needs a subject, a moving subject that moves itself and goes from its place. An underlying subject is much more involved if we deal, for instance, with qualitative or quantitative variations—a plant that grows, an object that changes color, etc.[4] There is always a starting point or *terminus a quo* and an endpoint or *terminus ad quem,* and also a subject that passes from one *terminus* to the other.

D   Now, Aristotle transposes these descriptive considerations, which are in short rather poor but inexorable, undeniable, to the order he calls substances. Then he says that it is necessary to conceive *the idea of a change that he calls "substantial."*[5] For Aristotle there is a substantial change, something that is monotonously repeated in the Middle Ages and lasts throughout the sixteenth and seventeenth centuries even in theology books. According to this change, when I devour something I change it into my substance. This is, without a doubt, a manner of speaking. What is my substance for a piece of bread to be changed into my substance? This is a different issue. Be that as it may, Aristotle has the idea that a substantial change always implies two terms: one that which formally constitutes a substance—for instance, that it be meat, that it be an oak, that it be any particular vegetable, etc.—and the other into which the first is changed and which is a different reality.[6] For example, if I eat meat, it changes into my substance. There is another form of substantial change, for instance, in the case of generation, which consists of the appearing in reality of a substantial form different at least numerically from the first. Yet appearing in what reality? In the subject underlying it. Now, since it is a question of a substance, there is no substantially entire subject. Aristotle must hammer out that subtle, wondrous idea of prime matter, which has passed to current language. Prime matter is not matter, a definite thing, but is the indeterminate, potential principle by virtue of which that matter which loses a substantial form acquires a new substantial formality through the influence of the first form.[7] In this way the change would be for Aristotle a transmutation in the strict sense. In other words, a definite substance has a substantial form. Such a substance, through the action of another substance, loses this substantial form. The action of the substance that produces this loss is the one that *educes,* as a Scholastic philosopher would say, precisely from prime matter the new substantial form and gives it a new substantial character.[8] Now, this idea of substantial change, however much there is something changing [*transformante*], is not easy to admit without examination. For is that change a change in the strict sense? That would be the substitution of one substantial form with another. Another story is what is caused in any way by interaction with another substantivity. The fact remains that prime matter, endowed with form A, appears *afterward* endowed with form B. Can it be said that that substance has undergone change? No. Does the prime matter undergo change? No. Aristotle then resorts to an expedient: the "composite" is changed.[9] Yet how can one speak of this change? Is it in fact admitted that substantial forms exist perpetually in nature? So Aristotle believed without a doubt. I shall not enter here into the critique of this aspect of Aristotelianism, which would carry me too far afield for present purposes. Be that as it may, at first sight this would not be a change but a kind of substitution of forms. Yet let us disregard this and suppose there were a change.

ε   Aristotle's conception presents some difficulties.

ϝ   In the first place, the problem reappears evidently in all dynamisms. That which is the terminus of a change is not a subject but a substantivity. The idea of prime matter in Aristotle cannot have its own act. Yet Francisco Suárez started out by saying that it had its own act. Suárez understood, as a man of the Modern Age, that this idea of merely indeterminate prime matter was a bit difficult to abide.[10]

Ϟ   Be that as it may, it is not a question of a substance but of a substantivity. This is what is precisely in change: there is a substantivity. A substantivity is formally constituted by a structural character, not by a character of being a subject of some accidents. This cannot even be said of any substantial forms. Rather, it is a structure, formally speaking. Consequently, for the change to be a true one, what must change is the structure. It is not enough simply to substitute structures based on prime matter.

H   In fact, where is the change of substantiality in Aristotle's conception? It does not appear anywhere. Prime matter appears endowed with two different substantial forms, with the second caused by a substantivity that makes the first disappear and educes a second out of the prime matter. Yet, in the first place, that is really not a change.

I   In the second place—and I am arranging a series of difficulties, taking into account their historical appearance as well—thinkers of the Middle Ages, especially Scholastic philosophers, realized as much when they began to discern things in chemistry. There existed then what they called "the problem of the mixed," τὸ μικτόν, the problem of the mixture. Different substances are joined, and a chemical reaction is produced, as we would say in modern terms, and in this chemical reaction a certain new body is formed. Naturally, today we would set down a structural formula of atoms comprising the molecule. But setting this aside, I try to take this thing as they took it, very descriptively, as is natural, because in their time they did not know atoms or molecules. (Let us recall that even as late as 1908 Bergson wrote that the existence of an atom is more than problematic, so let us not accuse Scholastic philosophers for not speaking of atoms.)[11]

J   In that age they immediately asked themselves whether the component elements exist in the mix in an actual manner or not. There were two opinions. For some, in hydrochloric acid, for instance, there would actually be the chlorine as such and the hydrogen as such. Meanwhile, others would say no: a new, completely new substance is formed, with its prime matter and its form, and also naturally the elements, hydrogen and chlorine, that are obtained in an analysis but only by being produced over again. In this view the chlorine and hydrogen are not there *actually* but only *virtually*. These are two theses, one of *actual presence*, the other of *virtual presence*.[12]

K   Now, I have always thought that neither is true. For the two conceptions, the one of actual presence, the other of virtual presence, are constitutively mounted upon the idea of substantiality. But hydrochloric acid, the same as all realities of the world, is a structural system. If hydrochloric acid is a new body it is not because the substances that have led to it are maintained either actually or virtually, but because those substances have given way to *new systematic properties*, not capable of being distributed between the elements that gave way to the appearance of hydrochloric acid.

L   If hydrochloric acid had no further properties than the additive ones, that is, if it had no properties but the intermediate ones of the weight, volume, etc., of the substances composing it, it would not be a new body but a mixture. It would not be what the old chemistry regarded as a combination, which is something different. If we have a new body it is because it has certain systematic properties that cannot be distributed in an additive way among the parts comprising it. To offer a trivial example, let us take the case of potential energy. As is well known, the kinetic energy of a system of discrete points is the sum of the kinetic energy of each of the points comprising the system. This is a very elementary and trivial mechanical truth. Now, can this same thing be done with potential energy? It cannot. Potential energy is a function of the system and cannot be distributed among each of the points composing the system. This is a systemic property.[13]

Systemic properties are not reduced to an addition and a merely additive complication of elementary properties, but are new properties. To the extent that they are, the result deserves to be called "changing-into" in the rigorous sense. It is not a question of the substitution of one form for another for the purpose of arguing about the presence of previous forms within the so-called mix, but it is a *changing-into*, something completely different.

If the causality that Aristotle invokes for changes is precisely a *formal* causality,[14] it is necessary to admit with resignation that in changes the form may intervene if it exists, but in a form that *goes beyond form*. Precisely for this reason there is change. A causality going beyond form is completely foreign to Aristotelianism. With its idea of educing it is a question of a causal substitution of forms.[15] But it is not a true change of one structure into another, where something gives all its content to what we call "changes" in the universe.

In the third place, I shall consider by way of confirmation some of the more important changes that there are in reality. To what extent do they agree with the Aristotelian conception? I shall not consider more than two changes. One of them, for instance, is the change of matter into energy in the equation of Einstein.[16] There is a great tendency to imagine that what a physicist understands by energy is a kind of more or less evanescent fluid and that the mass is a solid thing. This is not what a physicist understands by energy. A physicist understands by energy a very concrete thing, even though it may seem abstract. It is the capacity to produce work, purely and simply.[17] What the equation of Einstein means is that mass, by itself, is the capacity to produce work, and that the work by itself in turn has qualities peculiar to mass. This is the equivalency. Now, the change of mass into energy is certainly obvious.[18] Unfortunately, there exist atomic bombs to prove as much. Yet what is the subject, and what prime matter is subject to that change?

Not only in this case in which the difference between matter and energy is merely quantitative, as I have just said, but in other cases, at least in reactions of very high energy, of the greatest energy accessible today in great research apparatuses, the collision of particles can produce every kind of particle. Among them it can produce the change of pure energy into matter, of matter into energy, and the appearance of particles endowed with all kinds of properties. I leave aside whether these particles are really independent in the radical sense of the word, or whether they represent, as Weisskopf argued, states of resonance of elementary particles:[19] these are all problems of physics in which I have no reason to enter because they are beside the point. The point is that there is a change of photons, which in a collision with electrons produce an electron by materialization or reciprocally.[20] Where is the subject? It is not easy to admit its absence. It is, on the contrary, a structural change.

Q   The change does not consist of the successive endowment of one substance, one piece of prime matter, with different substantial forms. It consists of one structure, from itself as structure, giving its place to a completely different structure.

R   There is to be found the moment beyond form: in the change of a structure and its giving of itself another structure. Hydrogen and chlorine by their electrical characteristics, by their atomic characteristics, by their positions in the periodic table, etc., make way, for this reason alone, for a new structure. That is precisely change. Everything that does not interpret structural dynamism as going beyond form is an avoidance of the problems of change.

S   Change is the dynamism of a structure that gives of itself other structures. As seen, it is constitutively mounted on a change of place. If elements making it up were not brought into close proximity, the reaction would not be produced. This does not only refer to happenings in chemistry. It could refer to the reproduction of human beings or of any animal. That is, without bringing about a local approach, there would be no possibility of producing this change. Now, this is not the only type of causal dynamism that relates to structures.

Second Type: Repetition

A   There is a second type of dynamism that, although it may seem paradoxical, to my way of thinking, is mounted upon what I have just described. It is the following: in the change of structures, through respective [referential] interaction, it may be that what the dynamism gives of itself is not a new structure in the sense that I have just considered—hydrogen and chlorine making way for hydrochloric acid. It is possible in that interaction that the change makes way simply for the production of a particle or an element precisely equal to those that have reacted. In that case we would have repetition.

B   *Now, without a doubt, repetition is a particular case of change.* If there were not a process like the one I have just described, there would be no possibility of replicating in reality B that which constituted reality A. Take, for instance, the electrons or neutrinos obtainable through a collision of elementary particles.

C   The dynamism of repetition is a moment of the dynamism of change. The result of this repetition is enormously important. For what the repetition produces is a *multiplicity* of elements that are equal. Since they are equal, at least in principle, this multiplicity does not exclude the singularity of each of the electrons, but it does no more than include this singularity. They are *singuli* [single things], not individuals. They are *singuli*, they are like numerical units. I can alter them, I can exchange one for another, one is not the other. Apart from the qualities that each has—their charge, their mass, their radius, etc.—their entire reality consists of not being the other electron.[21]

D   They are *singuli* and constitute a mere multiplicity.

E   Now, the change that effects the production of a multiplicity of *singuli* in this sense is precisely what gives all these *singuli* the character of what I have called a "natural class." They are *natural classes.*

F   The dynamism of the multiplicity is the dynamism of insertion into classes [*enclasamiento*]. In this dynamism there is less exchange than in the dynamism of change. Yet there is, however, a giving more of oneself. In fact, one electron produces another electron, but let it be clear what I mean: some particles produce others that are equal, etc., through mechanisms it is not relevant to set out in these pages, and through them there is more becoming in the sense of there being more giving of oneself. Yet there is less exchange than there was in change. It is the dynamism of insertion into classes. Now, insertion into classes is never making a new species.

G   The problem of species has always been presented as if it were an abstraction from something composed of *singuli* or individuals. Hence the species would come to be more than a kind of label, more or less justified in re [in the thing] for individuals or singularities that do not differ among themselves except in mere multiplicity. Now, this, to my way of thinking, is incorrect. For there to be a species, it is not enough for there to be a multiplicity of individuals. It is necessary that the mechanism leading to it be really and formally a mechanism of multiplication. Only when the multiplicity is the result of a multiplication will we have a different dynamic result: the production of a species.

H   When the second type of causal dynamism, which is that of repetition, has a character we shall call, *a potiori* [more aptly], evolutionary, then we have a third type of dynamism, by multiplication, which in a more general way I call "genesis." But I can also call it "evolution," describing the phenomenon *a potiori*. This is the third type of causal dynamism: genesis.

92

Third Type: Genesis

A Here it is a question of a genesis of structures, consequently, of an essential genesis.

B   Essences, realities *simpliciter* [without qualification] that constitute the basis of the universe, are in every instant submitted to grounding, to a genetic dynamism. I said that multiplication is essential for there to be genesis. For a process of dynamism to be one of multiplication, to my way of thinking, it must imply some conditions.

C   In the first place, it is clearly a question of a causal dynamism of each substantivity. Let us imagine that this were not so, but that *de potentia Dei absoluta* [by the absolute power of God] God produced substantivity B in the moment of a certain interaction between substantivity A and substantivity P. This would not be a multiplication in the strict sense. It would be the production of a different being. For there really to be multiplication, in the active sense of the word, it is necessary that the production be determined by the substantivities *themselves*.

D   In the second place, this action executed by itself must have the character of homonymy. In other words, in some form or another, what is produced in the multiplication must have a homonymous character with respect to the substantivities than have produced it. To put this idea another way, it is necessary that that action be *paradigmatic:* in some form or other, the producers, the substantivities productive of the genesis, must to some extent be paradigms kept and perpetuated by the substantivities brought about.

E   Now, precisely the unit of the various terms of a causal dynamism of this order, by multiplication, has a paradigmatic unity as a consequence. This unity is the one that strictly speaking at least I would call a "phylum." The words, naturally, are in biology, but I do not confer a biological meaning upon them.

F   I mean that it is a question of a phylum, precisely of a homonymous line with a paradigmatic character.[22]

G   Now, the phylum is a real reality in the universe. For a biologist, it is as real as an electromagnetic or gravitational field can be for a physicist.

H   It is not a question of a posthumous relationship between one substantivity and another. It is a question of something essentially constitutive. A substantivity, the daughter substantivity, would not be what it is except only insofar as it belongs to a definite phylum. Only then is when, strictly speaking, we have something more than a class; we have a species. This is the *dynamism of producing a species.*

I   Multiplication is not limited to producing an essence more or less homonymous with the first essence. This is not true. The truth is that all essences are constitutively individual, and that in their individuality they are essentially irreducible to one another. Causal essences in the genetic phylum, genetic essences, perform a concrete dynamic action by virtue of which the progenitors do not simply "transmit" a nature—these are abstractions—but formally are the "constitutive" and constituent action of the new essence in question, of the filial essence. It is a constituent action, not only a transmitting action. Only insofar as the new reality has a phyletic homonymy with the reality of its progenitors do we say that it belongs to a species. And because it belongs to a species, we say that the new reality belongs to the phylum, and reciprocally that the phylum is what has allowed the essence, which was nothing but constitutive, to change into what I have called a "quiddity," a specific essence.

J   I repeat that it is a *constituent* action, not simply a *transmission.* It is a true dynamism.

K   Now, this causal dynamism of genesis can concretely present two ways of functioning: one of them, the more immediate, is the genesis that I have called "generation." In fact, progenitors, for instance, produce some children in biological terms. Yet generation is not formally identical to multiplication. Multiplication will be generation if the moments characteristic of that multiplication imply some specific determinations. In the first place, the multiplication must be given from the formal and constitutive structure of the progenitors themselves. In the second place, the homonymy must not be simply an imitation of the parents, but a true transmission. Then the multiplication really has a character of generation.

L   The *constituent* action is a generating action to the extent that the substantivities are those that formally are *constituting* the reality of its effect.

M   It is not a question of educing a substantial form from prime matter, as Aristotle might think.[23] It is a question of precisely elaborating in a dynamic, absolutely real way the constituent action of the new substantivity. It is a "genetic determination."

N   Naturally this determination is not a determination that hinges exclusively on the character of the constituent essences of the progenitors. For in fact a son may look very much like his father but is never identical to him.

O   In one form or another, there are in progenitors what I have called a "constituent scheme."[24] Precisely that scheme is what serves for the constitution of the constituent essence of the generated being.

P   Dynamic causal action performed in accordance with a schematic plan, of a scheme already previously broken loose on the inside of the constituent essences, is what constitutes the possibility of a generation.

Q   Generation consists of giving of oneself in accordance with a scheme already broken loose within the constituent essence. It is a schematized giving of oneself. This does not always have to occur, as I shall explain at once. Nonetheless, provisionally, that is generation.

R   Giving of oneself consequently supposes that the realities that give of themselves do not have simply a prearrangement, as in the case of the variations of a greater or lesser range of adherent notes. Instead, they have precisely something different. It might be said that if there is *potency* it is to produce an effect. This is not necessary. I do not believe that it is a question simply of potencies; rather, it is a question of something more concrete, which are *potentialities*. They are precisely *genetic potentialities*. The substantivity of the parents, to return to the example from biology, is a giving of themselves of the inner constituent potentialities qua such potentialities that belong to the constitutive essences of the progenitors. They are potentialities for constitution.[25] Precisely the giving of oneself proper to generation consists of putting into play from oneself the inner potentialities for constitution belonging to the generating substantivities. Not every generating substantivity has potentialities for everything generated. Therefore, as I shall at once point out, potentialities have an extremely precise, definite structure.

S   Yet a second type of genetic dynamism can occur: it can happen that the scheme is not transmitted in complete form, because there are interferences in the causal dynamism and in the dynamic structures of this order in the progenitors. It is an intervention that would make something change, and these changes are called "mutations."

T   In that case the obtainable effect is plainly very different and very problematic. Generally what will happen is that the substantivity in question is destroyed. This is the most frequent and usual case. Yet something else may happen: the structure on which this mutation has fallen back can last only by integrating the mutation into its own structure. In that case we would not have a generation in the rigorous sense. We would have a mere *origination*, not a generation. Probably in this origination the term that has survived would not be of the same *phylum* as its progenitors, since it has a different scheme. Yet neither would it be completely foreign. It would be absurd to say that this is a generation. It would be absurd to think that the first bird has had reptiles as parents. What is true is that birds have their origin in reptiles, and this is quite different.

U   This is strictly speaking what constitutes an *evolution*. It is possible that the first term of the evolution is not viable. In that case, it is an individual that has been originated as such and disappears. But it is possible that the new individual is in turn really classifiable into a species [*especiable*]. Then a new phylum has begun with that individual.

V   The causal dynamism that is a giving of itself by virtue of change and mutations has made way for a new substantivity, a new constitutive essence.

W   Evolution is not mutation, but just the reverse: it is the capacity for integrating mutation. It is giving of oneself what one is precisely by integrating the mutation.

X   This is the contrary of change. It is a much deeper, more radical becoming. Precisely what it is doing is a giving of itself from the point of view of the substantivity. The mutation is the conditional moment—just like the variations—for a change of constitutive structure. But the evolutionary moment, properly speaking, is situated in the positive moment. The positive moment is the one according to which a structure, say, that of a determined reptile, has enough vitality to integrate the mutation and survives precisely in the form of a bird.

Y   Now, although the examples mentioned here come from biology, this is not merely a biological exposition of the problem, but it is a structural metaphysics—a metaphysical structure of the genesis of essences.

Z   All essences of this world emerge, as I have said. They have an emergent character in their substratum. The dynamism producing them is precisely the dynamism that I have just examined. Through some changes and through some repetitions, some generated terms or some originated terms genetically appear. What we call an evolution in the second case is precisely a genetic process in which specifically new forms are being produced from other previous ones as an intrinsic and determining function of the change of these earlier ones. But evolution is not situated at the moment of change. Quite the contrary, it is to be found at the moment of giving of oneself under the form of integration of the mutation.

α   Evolution is not the actualization of virtual powers, but the *potentiality for determining new virtual powers.*[26] Evolution is the actuality of potentialities, not of virtual powers. Potentiality is something superior to actuality and virtual power.

β   Certainly it may be said that it is a bit difficult to conceive that the genesis of essences, thus understood, is something more than a problem of concrete physical realities comprising the universe. In the last analysis, all generations, all evolutions, all changes, materialize through the *particularity* that the substantivities in question evidently have, because they are such-and-such. Birds are born from reptiles, which are reptiles because of certain structures, and are not born of amoebas, at least directly, but from another definite structure. Consequently, it is impossible to see precisely what that has to do with the structure of reality as such.

χ   To be sure, this would be true if we insisted on saying that what we call reality as such is like the concept of being in Scholastic philosophy: a kind of maximum abstract. It is not a question of that here.

δ   Every particularity, whatever it may be and in all its moments, has what I have called a "transcendental" function. It determines what is a particular in reality, only through the *particular* that it is. It is not a kind of contraction of all reality in the abstract into this definite *particular*. Rather, the particular, because it is definitely such, because it has that definiteness (rather than a definition), constitutes precisely that particularity in its character of reality. For it is precisely the transcendental function in which particular genesis, the birth of particular qualities, makes way for the modification of the very character of reality as such. Therefore this genesis is genesis of the *in-its-own-right* [*de suyo*].

ε   Every reality is *in its own right*. It must also be said (to take at least the ascending lines of evolution) that the superior termini are more in their own right than the inferior termini. Because they are more in their own right they are more themselves.

ϒ   If we think about the merely formal concept of the "in-one's-own-right" [*de suyo*], then this would be a mere trifle. Yet in re [in the thing] a primate is more of itself than an amoeba. Of this there can be no doubt at all.

η   It is a question, therefore, of a *genesis of reality as such*. Now, when it has been said that in reality as such there is no room for evolution (it is or it is not), what has been done is to return to Parmenides' argument. That is, being, reality, is or is not. To be sure, however, it can be in many ways.

θ   Here the degrees of reality are determined by the potentialities of reality that things have by virtue of their particularity.

ι   The potentialities in question are not simply potentialities in the biological sense of the word, but they are potentialities precisely for something to be real in a definite form. As I will soon point out, evolution relates to reality as such precisely in the form of determining the degrees of reality within it. The degrees of reality are not a series, a kind of scale of realities present in the universe, but they have a strictly dynamic character in which higher or lower forms of reality keep appearing. Both can happen. This is precisely becoming.

κ   It is a greater becoming in the sense of giving of itself. Production of a new substantivity requires much more giving of itself, for example, than the production of birds by reptiles, the change of hydrogen and chlorine into hydrochloric acid, or the repetition of elementary particles or change of place as in the case of simple variation. It is more becoming. Also it is less variation, say what one will. For although there may be some mutations, the evolutionary moment consists precisely of integrating them into the substantive reality, not of being passively dragged along by a change that would be merely extrinsic.

λ   It is a question of a becoming, a becoming in the strict sense of the word. To avoid getting lost in further considerations, it is necessary to delimit this becoming vis-à-vis two concepts easily confused with it.

μ   First of all, it might be thought that this becoming, such as I have described it in what I just said, somewhat resembles Bergson's élan vital. Now, this is not so in any way. Bergson supposes that reality is constituted, at least in its deepest and most important dimension, by an élan vital, by a vital impetus, by a kind of cosmic force. This impulse forces its way in different manners in the universe, and these different forms that it adopts in forcing its way through the universe would be each of the living beings and, a fortiori, each of the species.[27] Now, this seems absolutely capricious to me. For life is an élan vital, to be sure, if one wants to call élan vital something that we call "vitality" when we say, "Mr. So-and-so is a live wire." I leave aside the case of the human being in general, because it has other complications. Some primates are weaker than others, some are sicker than others, and all will end up dying one day. This is evident. Yet this is one sense of the word "élan" which is not the one coming into play here. For Bergson maintains that the élan vital is a process of discovery in which life continues to find new channels, discovering new ways and means.[28] Yet life does not discover anything in this order. For what happens to the living being in order to evolve is that certain generally extrinsic mutations occur to it. Which? They can be gamma rays, or cosmic rays, or whatever one wants; but evidently it is something that happens to the living being. What performs that wonderful gesture, splendidly described by Bergson in *L'Évolution créatrice* (*Creative Evolution*), is not the élan vital but precisely the collision of some structures with others. Now, becoming is not situated in this collision; becoming lies precisely in integrating that mutation.

ν   The concept that I have set out is not that of a vital impulse but of some *potentialities*. These potentialities of reality, evolutionary potentialities, are something completely different from an élan vital.

ξ   These potentialities, in the second place, it must be added, are not potentialities in the Aristotelian sense of the word, that is, some more or less indeterminate potentialities. Clearly they have some indetermination. But this indetermination is not absolute. It is not in a very precise sense. In the first place, at their point of departure all potentialities are embroiled [*incursos*] in a configuration. This is evident. If it were not for the configuration in which they are situated, those potentialities would not give of themselves what they give. This is absolutely essential. The configurations do not depend solely on the structure they are configuring.

ο   In the second place, these potentialities, within the structure, within the configuration, are in no way a kind of mere indeterminate δύναμις [capacity]. They have a very precise structure. The precision is such that the very potentiality qua potentiality varies continually in the course of the dynamism, from a germinal cell, that as such is more or less all-powerful (at least for the effects of the many forms derived from it), to the form it has at the moment of birth. At that point it is evidently no longer susceptible of taking on a new form; the system of potentialities—of biological potentialities—that a reality has is constantly restricting and modulating itself. Each essence consequently has a very precise and very definite system of potentialities that is being actualized only in a structural way, both throughout time and throughout the dynamism.

π   In the third place, those potentialities are giving forms, adopting forms, that are in no way like forms sown throughout the universe in an instant. Some configurations are born from earlier configurations and lead to further configurations. There is a whole cascade of configurations.

ρ   When making the critique of the constitution of molecules through this system of configurations, it has been said, how is it possible to maintain that the play of free electrons in the universe produces the most elementary molecule of proteins? Clearly this would be patent if things were this way, but they are not. The fact is that the elements of the universe in a first configuration have produced reality A. This reality in configuration, at the end of some time, has given reality B, etc. Even now, at a determined moment, the protein molecule appears. The fact is that the configurations are not sown at an instance in the universe but are connected in a rigorous cascade in which, in a very precise, formal way, the potentialities of evolving termini continue to be actualized.

ς   In this cascade, although all this may seem like speculation, no less than the most tangible realities in the universe are being constituted. They are so tangible that Aristotle did not hesitate to take them as his point of departure, as if they were something obvious and definite.

τ   In the first place, through this structure of potentialities (I repeat: I have used examples from biology for clearer illustration, but I refer to all essences in the universe), precisely a certain *hierarchical position* of some substantivities with respect to others is produced. It is precisely the Aristotelian τάξις [world order].[29]

υ   The Aristotelian τάξις is the first result of evolution and not a presupposition of it. The universe has, and has been acquiring, this more or less taxonomic form thanks precisely to an evolution. Let us think of the deep difference there would be between the primordium of a galaxy and what is now our galaxy—a spiral nebula, perfectly organized and endowed with a sun and some planets, and amidst the planets, the planet Earth that we know.

φ   The τάξις is precisely the achievement of evolution.

χ   In the second place, something very shocking intervenes, but it is a truth: I allude precisely to *individuation*. Elementary particles are *singuli* [single units] but are not individuals. The progressive constitution of individuality, of individuation, is precisely the achievement of evolution. The achievement of evolution is such that rigorously strict individualities do not exist except in the case of the human being, who is a product of evolution in the form I will make clear further on.

ψ   In the third place, precisely in this evolutionary course of potentialities and the making of potencies, speciation is produced. Certain genetic phyla are constituted by virtue of which the universe has a phylogenetic structure. That is, it has a speciation. It embraces not only some individuals, but all individuals constituted into species.

ω   In the fourth place, in this evolution different types of matter are being constituted. (It is not a question of a succession of points, but of mere enumeration.) We may think we speak of matter, even secondary matter,[30] in a very univocal way. This is incorrect. How can we imagine, for instance, what the matter of a white dwarf star, like the companion of Sirius, has in common with "normal" matter, when the matter of the dwarf, absolutely ionized, has such density, that each cubic centimeter would weigh more than 11,000 tonnes? What does the matter of earth, primarily molecular, have in common with the matter containable, for instance, within the sun, where there are some molecules, though very few, of hydroxyls? I could multiply the examples. The sun does not have a basically molecular structure but rather an atomic one, which is also almost always ionized. Different types of matter, therefore, are being produced. Life itself cannot appear in an indifferent way, in any manner at all. It only appears in those definite molecular types with a certain stability. That is an achievement of evolution.

a   There are also different *types* of space.

ʃ   This may seem to be a paradox with regard to what was said at the beginning of this chapter. It is not. Therefore I note that the distinction is supported on a distancing. This distancing is the one produced within the universe, space. The universe is not in space. It is spatious because it lodges space within itself. Its own inner evolution is producing space within the universe. This evolution is producing a distancing, I maintain, and space along with that. Further, it produces space with some definite structures. If we take a corner of the universe, we can consider it on a certain level as Euclidean. Once it was thought that this was the structure of universal space. However, it has been seen that this is not so, for the universe has a very different geometric structure. For instance, the structure determined by Ricci's tensor is non-Euclidean. If the tensor is zero, space is of a totally geodesic variety in the vacuum. If it is not zero, space is only locally geodesic.[31] If this tensor equals the inner tensor, we have the law of gravity. This is true, but Einstein was never sure throughout his life that this was a universal law. Given certain difficulties due to cosmic chronology, he felt that it was necessary to think that gravity was a more or less local phenomenon, limited to our galaxy or to the closest galaxies. Afterward, the difficulty encountered there was solved,[32] but this does not prevent the type of production of space from being perhaps even today an issue hotly contested among astronomers because of the expansion of the universe.

b The expansion of the universe is relatively clear. It appears, in the first place, in the explosion of a first configuration of matter contained in that configuration. In the second place, from the very expansion of space, by virtue of the intrinsic instability of this first constitution, the result is a new type of space with a very problematic curve.[33] If the expansion keeps speeding up in the form it is following, there at the limit, will the universe have a Euclidean structure, a closed structure, an elliptical structure, or rather a parabolic and hyperbolic structure? It is a question that stands sub judice, awaiting judgment. But in any case it is clear enough that the production of types of space is an achievement of evolution.

2 In this achievement of evolution, furthermore, are produced different types of laws.

γ We are in the habit of considering that there are no other laws in the universe than laws of action, those laws that link some antecedents and some consequences. But this is not true at all, strictly speaking.

e As long as the universe keeps evolving and forming configurations, there appear much subtler types of laws, more difficult to detect, which the human being has easily tended to believe are laws of action and which are simply laws of *structure*, structural laws. For instance, let us take gravity itself. Einstein put his finger on the sore spot: there is no force of gravity. Gravity is the structure of the curvature of the universe.[34]

ӟ Who can doubt that, in great measure, the laws of quantum mechanics are structural laws, though statistical ones, that determine a distribution but do not determine actions that can explain (something inadmissible nowadays) why an electron has one definite basic system instead of some other. Different possibilities can be offered, each with a different numerical coefficient. The numerical coefficient of a possibility is just what I have called a "probability." Then there appear laws of action, laws of structure, and other laws that offer a certain uniformity, which is statistical.

ӡc Finally, the most confusing part of all is that the universe is not comprised only of laws and initial configurations. It is composed of those four or six mysterious realities that are the *universal constants:* Planck's constant of action (h); the constant of the speed of light (c); the constant of the electrical charge of an element (e), etc.[35] What do these constants do within causal dynamism?

ӡ Some great astronomer, like Eddington, has thought that in evolution the system of universal constants changes too.[36] In sum, I am not technically informed enough about the material to be able to give an opinion. Yet however it may be, in its present-day form, there is no room for doubt that the universal constants are a product of evolution.

⟶

υ   I said that reality, taken in this way, is structurally emergent. The emergence consists of giving of itself an "otherness" [*alteridad*]. I repeat, this emergence and this otherness are not defined by a *particularity*, but by the transcendental function of this particularity, which is something completely different.

ῡ   It is usual to say that in the line of being there is no room for evolution. But this is false if "being" means "reality." If particularity is taken as a transcendental function, it can and should be said that there is room for speaking of evolution in what is real. The evolution of reality means an evolution precisely of the "in-its-own-right" [*de suyo*]. In this sense there are *degrees of reality*. Naturally, it is not that a human being is more real than an orangutan, if by reality is meant having physical existence; that is not question. It is a question of taking the matter in re [in the thing]. That which constitutes the "in-its-own-right" proper to the orangutan is much less in its own right than that which constitutes the "in-its-own-right" proper to a human. The "in-his-own-right" of an angel goes without saying; and naturally, a fortiori, that of God. This is something completely different.

κ   The causal dynamism of particularity as the transcendental function is the causal dynamism of reality qua reality, which implies not only a system of pure quiescent acts, nor only of potencies, but also of strict potentialities. These potentialities constitute precisely the active character that reality as such, in respectivity, has by itself. Therefore, potentiality is not the δυνάμει ὄν [a being in potency] of which Aristotle spoke, but something in a certain way the opposite.[37] It is precisely the ἐνέργεια or act of selfhood [*mismidad*] in structural variation. It lies in the capacity that the real has to be itself precisely by integrating the alterations. This is evolution. Evolution does not consist of changing but of giving of itself by integrating.

λ   I know that many will think this has little to do with what theology says. Very briefly, however, because it is outside the present theme of this study, I will say what this has to do with theology.

μ   God wished to produce not only a world of realities different from Himself. He could have made these realities otherwise. But He made them in such a form that these realities, even starting with the most elementary matter, behave as divinely as possible, that is, giving of themselves what they are in themselves in their own reality. Therefore reality is evolutionary in its own formal structure. But I leave theology aside from here on, because it is unnecessary for my exposition of ideas.

н   Substantivity is active by itself. This otherness in configuration has the triple possibility of being *change,* of being *repetition,* and of being *genetic.* Each of these dimensions is constitutively supported by its prior. Repetition would be impossible without change. Evolution would be impossible without a certain repetition. However it may be, let us go further to see in what way these causal dynamisms are organized upon one another.

о   Naturally, I have only just begun my explanation in a certain way. This whole system of dynamisms makes way for deeper dynamisms. I shall deal with them forthwith.

~~~~ **8**

</div>

The Dynamism of Selfhood

Introduction

I will continue the study of the dynamism of reality in its concrete structures. This is a question of a dynamism, that is, of a characteristic in accordance with which reality as such is active by itself. It does not need to be activated; it only needs something that could bring its own active being into activity. I said that this dynamism is causal: it intervenes and constitutes the functionality of the real qua real. Precisely in this measure—in the measure that it is a question of a causal dynamism so conceived—is it something that does not happen other than in and by the respectivity [referentiality] in which each of the realities of the world is constitutively situated with respect to all others. Consequently, such dynamism, by reason of this respectivity, purely and simply consists of giving of itself. In this sense, dynamism is the contrary of a change, although it is grounded in some way or other on the substratum of a change. These dynamisms—I use the plural on purpose—are, in the first place, different, but in the second, organized: some suppose the prior, all the way back to the most elementary of all, which is variation, precisely that dynamism that is basic for all the rest.

Of these dynamisms, the first in this sense is simply variation, that dynamism that relates to the inherent properties of a structural substantive system. Take, for example, the most elementary of them all, that of occupying a definite space: respectivity is here so-called space.

There is a second type of dynamism that refers not to the variation of adherent notes but to substantive structure itself: it is what I have considered under the name of alteration. By alteration I mean not the altering of the structure of a reality, but the production by this structural dynamism of another substantivity, another *otherness* [*alteridad*]. Alteration is applied to the fact of producing, not to a subject's being altered. Otherness has different possibilities, different planes. In the first place, there is an alteration by change—in other words, one or several substantivities, which produce a different substantivity through alteration. In the second place, there is an alteration by repetition, which, aside from changing elements, can have repetitions in the very structures that have acted among themselves. In the third place, and above all, there is a genesis of structures, some generated by others. That genesis precisely constitutes a phylum, a phyletic unit of realities, which occurs specially in living beings. By virtue of this phyletic unity, constituent essences are constituted into *quiddities,* or specific essences. This genesis can be achieved by way of *generation,* a normal case in all living beings—or else through something more difficult to discover but which science, with ample reason, to my way of thinking, has aimed to discover, and that is precisely evolution.

Often I have called all this genesis "evolution," not because I identify evolution with all these moments, but because evolution turns out to be the most visible and luxuriant part of alteration. This evolution naturally and without a doubt implies a mutation. It is the problem of mutations. Mutation is not evolution, properly speaking. Mutation is the factor of evolution. But I will not now deal with this distinction, which relates to science and not philosophy. Mutation, from whichever angle it is taken, does not constitute evolution. Evolution is the integration of mutation, something different from mutation. It is giving of itself in specifically new forms, from some substantivities to other different substantivities, as an intrinsic and determining function of the change of the first substantivities. Therefore I said that evolution properly speaking is not generation. How often the claim has been made, for example, that the Stoics and the first Fathers of the Church were evolutionists because they admitted the λόγοι σπερματικοί, seminal reasons![1] But this has nothing to do with evolution. It is not a question of the evolution from a seed, from seeds that flourish. Nor is it a question of an actualization of virtual potentialities. This has been the thesis of all the Neoscholastics who have wished to oppose evolution by appealing to virtual acts.[2] Rather, it is a question of something much more radical and deeper, which is an actualization, but one of *potentialities,* by virtue of which a system of virtualities is gradually produced which, in turn, will or will not function like virtualities for the species or individuals in question. Evolution is not the actualization of virtualities but the actualization of potentialities to produce new virtualities. Evolution produces new virtualities, in contrast to generation, which produces only the actualization of virtualities. In evolution, potentiality is actualized, not virtuality.

What apparently concerns no more than certain real things, for example, living things, nonetheless has a transcendental function. It is in fact that process whereby the "in-its-own-right," [*de suyo*], which consists of giving of itself, through evolution constructs new ambiences and new forms of the "self" of the "in-its-own-right." This becoming is strictly metaphysical. It relates, as I said, to the degrees of reality qua reality. It is not a question of a few degrees in the sense of an identical gradation, but rather a question of a dynamic gradation. In other words, it is about a true metaphysical dynamism in the order of reality qua reality, whereby the so-called higher degrees in some form or other are dislodged and are emergent from lower degrees.

This alteration is grounded in variation. It involves a moment of mutation. Especially for this reason, evolution justly involves a moment of change, even though it may not consist formally of change. This is one of the cases in which there is evidently a grounding of one dynamism in a prior dynamism.

Yet there is another dynamism in reality grounded certainly in the prior ones, or at least congeneric with them, and in this sense presupposing the earlier others. This is a question of a dynamism that appears in a certain type of substantive structures—those that are structurally stable. Every reality in some form or other has a moment of stability; if not, it would be purely evanescent. In short, it would not be anything at all.

Every reality implies, therefore, a moment of stability. But here it is a question of a stability that is, properly speaking, dynamic. In other words, the stability belongs to some substantivities that, in fact, through their dynamism, continue to be the same in some form or other. This dynamic stability is the other type of dynamism, which I will describe in a more precise fashion in the pages to follow.

Substantivities that are dynamically stable can be and are in fact of different types. They especially belong to two types.

First Type: Molecular Substantivity

In the first place, there is a type of molecular substantivity to which I have already alluded. In the course of evolution, in fact, different types of matter are produced. The thing is quite clear; for instance, the density of atoms ionized in the companion star of Sirius cannot be compared with ordinary molecular matter on earth, or with the state of matter such as it is in intergalactic spaces or in the structure of galaxies, insofar as they pave the way for spiral nebulae, etc.

However that may be, in these great conformations of matter, stable in a certain way, there is nonetheless not constituted the great molecular and even atomic system that is typical and proper to stability of matter on earth. Atoms on earth are normally not ionized. They are organized into a few molecules that have a certain duration in the course of the existence of the earth.

Now, I said that there are in the first place certain atoms constituted by particles. Of this there is no doubt. But it is necessary to say that the particles constituting atoms are very few among the hundred or so known particles. All these, almost all, save three or four that constitute atoms, lack stability; they have an absolutely fleeting half-life. On the contrary, an electron and a proton have a certain stability. This is where there begins to function the new type of matter constitutive of the earth. To all appearances this is merely a curiosity of physics; but at once it will be seen that this is not so. Let us, however, stay with physics for a moment. This stability is, in the last analysis, a stability of purely singular elementary particulars; in other words, they are singularities. This is clearly visible in present-day physics. There are some interactions, for instance, of electrons in certain systems. In reality these alterations pass through three phases. First, there are two electrons, number 1 and number 2, which enter into an interaction, unnecessary to describe, by virtue of a complex function of waves. In that interaction the system can no longer be divided between the two electrons.[3] It is a system comprised by the system itself. The result of these reactions is that two electrons appear once again. It might be thought that we had electrons 1 and 2 before, and now we have the same 1 and 2. But this is not the case. Previously we had two electrons and now two others. Nevertheless, it makes no sense to say which of the second two electrons corresponds to the first two: 1 does not correspond to 1^1 nor 2 to 2^1. It is a little like adding or subtracting units from the number 12: which unit is subtracted from 12 to obtain the number 11, or what is added to it to get 13? This lacks any sense. The phrase "which one" makes no sense in those problems. They are purely *singuli*: they are singles. In that case, even that lack of distinctness between the electrons is nothing to get in a stew about; it is the source of a great energy called the "exchange energy" in the structure of atoms.

Therefore it is here a question of a stability of a different kind. This is a question of "identifiable stability" once atoms and molecules are constituted. It is a stability whereby not only is it possible to say that there are two electrons and later out come two others, but also that this structure is the one that lasts, while the other structure disappears. It is *structural persistence.* Reality, in its dynamism, gives persistence to stable matter. This stability of atoms and molecules is the one that constitutes the system proper to the earth. The system, besides having these more or less stable atoms, has molecular formations, especially of the great molecules, that are relatively stable molecular formations: there is water, etc.; there are even molecules of a single substance, homopolar ones, H_2, iron, etc. But especially the complication of these molecules leads to the formation of the great molecules, which, the greater they are, the more they lose their reason for being molecules. This is evident. Why, for instance, call a molecule of insulin a molecule at all, and why not call one of the amino acids comprising proteins a molecule?[4]

If it is not desirable to call amino acids molecules, why insist at all that insulin constitutes a molecule? In reality, in the measure that molecules grow complicated, the reason for being properly molecular disappears. Whatever may be the designation employed for practical purposes, in reality the increment of molecules makes way for gigantic macromolecular substantivities. In such substantivities there appears precisely the dynamism of stability to which I wish to refer.

Second Type: The Transmolecular Structure

When I consider the dynamism of stability mentioned here, I do not refer to the molecules as the subject of motions and the subject of alterations. It is precisely the reverse: here these molecules enter as macroscopic structures, which structurally, wholly and as such, are the ones precisely involved in the dynamism of stability.

Here the structures are not those that simply endure some variation or have other substantivities coming upon them to produce a new substantivity. The activity of these great molecules is characterized because it is done precisely to be able to maintain the identity of its own structure. Here structural substantivity is not *molecular* but *transmolecular*. "Trans-" means "system" of molecules. The stability is not mere persistence. It is activity by itself in order to maintain structural stability.

Now, precisely at this point we touch upon life. It is the second type of stability, of dynamism of stability: *the structural substantivity characteristic of a living being.* It is a structural substantivity that the living being has, a substantivity of a higher type. It is clearly not monomolecular. There is no living thing that is a single molecule. In this sense it is transmolecular, as I said. These are systems of molecules, not isolated molecules nor even paired ones. Here stability does not mean mere persistence, as, for example, happens in stable particles: electrons persist in their changes from a galaxy wherein they can emit certain cyclotronic radiations. It is not a question of a mere persistence. Great molecules, macrocosmic molecules, are found not only in inner dynamism, in a dynamism active by itself, since they are real in the metaphysical sense of the word, but they are also found in a dynamism in respectivity. They are found not as something resisting the variations of the universe—that would be the case of electrons—but, in reverse, as something exerting an enormous activity precisely to persist in their own substantivity, in their own identity of substantivity. This is precisely what is proper to the living structure. Here not only does something stable exist, but there is a stability for the stability itself. This means, in the first place, that the living structure acquires in a certain way the character of an active distance, which the more alive it is, the more it separates from the rest of the universe. The activities of a living being are exercised to a great extent—I disregard the two extreme limits of this persistence, birth and death—and are largely actualized within those limits in order to maintain just its own substantive structure. In so maintaining its own substantive structure, the living being, in some form or other, wants to achieve a very relative independence—it need hardly be said—of the vicissitudes occurring around it.

In the second place, this structure is respective. Here it seems clear that the independence and the distinction are not absolute; they are respective to other things in the universe. This respectivity of the activity implies that the distinction not be one of mere passive persistence like that of an electron, but rather the reverse: that it be a dynamic equilibrium. In this equilibrium the dynamically altered structure is maintained. Therefore, its equilibrium is recovered. In other words, it is a structure that is reversible besides being dynamic.

In the third place, not only is it a dynamic and reversible structure, but by virtue of this, the substantivity acquires a very precise character in its difference with respect to the things around it. It does this by exerting that activity of dynamic and reversible equilibrium in order to keep its own structure. To be specific, it has a certain independence of the medium and a certain control over it. It goes without saying that the more alive a living being is, the more it has independence of that medium and the more it has specific control over that medium.

However that may be, the difference between a living being and things around it is not precisely a difference describable with a metaphysical definition using genus and differentia, although it has a very definite physical structure. These structures of certain molecular systems cannot continue to be what they are unless they exercise some activities in dynamic and reversible equilibrium, and unless they show independence and specific control over the medium in that activity.

Then it is well understood that a living structure is not in the first place a substantial structure. Living beings, organisms, are not substances; they are structures. They are material structures, needless to say, but structures.

What is characteristic of life is a structural quality, not a substance. There are millions of substances in every living being, even in the most elementary amoeba. A living being is not that. A living being is not one more substance, nor even a supersubstance: it is a structure.

In the second place, neither can it be said that life is a mere dynamism. In certain moments in the history of biology, it was once possible to write a bit recklessly that life is a dynamic process: thus, for instance, wrote Roux, creator of the mechanics of evolution, as it was called at the beginning of the twentieth century.[5] Yes and no: We are already seeing that this is not absolutely false, but neither is it absolutely true. If life did not have some basic structures, process would not be at issue.

In the third place, the issue lies in determining what those structures are and how there emerges from them something that, even if it is a process, nevertheless is not formally a process in its being. Therefore I said that it is not a substantial structure, nor is it a mere dynamism, but a structural dynamism: it is a *dynamic* structure.

If we now wish to be precise about stating of what this dynamic structure consists, we must face three problems:

In the first place, the living being has a peculiar position among all other things.

In the second place, the dynamic activity of the living being has a unique character.

In the third place, the living being and its life as a mode of reality deserve special attention as the properly metaphysical point of this study.

1. The Position of the Living Being among the Other Realities

Above all, the word "position" implies a locus, a τόπος [place], something in which the living being is in fact placed and installed. Naturally, the place of a living being is not a place in the way that a physical place can be. That is so, clearly, from a certain viewpoint. A cricket occupies a place exactly the way a tray occupies it. This is absolutely true, but it does not mean, however, that the character of the place of the cricket is identical to the character of the place of the tray. This will be cleared up shortly.

A living being, located at a certain point, is found in some form or another, as I said, among other living beings. Among them it is also found to be placed in a distinct way. It could be thought that it is a question of something quite obvious, that is, the fact that a living being has surroundings comprised of things around it. However certain this may be, it is neither proper nor exclusive to living beings. The electron also has surroundings; at least it has an electromagnetic field surrounding it. It is not a question of this. It is a question of the possession by the living being of something that the electron does not have: it is placed among other things, but not simply in surroundings, which are what the electron has, but in something different: in a *situation*. It is the category of situs.

The τόπος, or locus, in the first place, and the situs are the two great categories that precisely define and constitute the placement of a living being in reality. They are in no way two independent categories, since the situs presupposes a locus. Only by virtue of a place that a living being occupies can situations be defined for it. For that reason we say that things around a living being are not simply its surroundings but something completely different: they are a medium for it. It is the *medium of the living being*. The electron has surroundings; what it does not have is a medium. It would make no sense to say that the electromagnetic field is the medium of an electron. On the contrary, it would be meaningless to say that things around an amoeba are simply its surroundings. No, they are a medium. This applies all the more, as I will soon point out, the more that the same things can constitute different media for living beings in accordance with the differences peculiar to these beings.

In this locus and in this situs, in other words, while occupying a place and having a definite situation in it, a living being is not simply in the medium but is in the medium as in its own center. It has a central character. It is precisely the locus, as I have said. The electron as center of an electromagnetic field is not the same as the central character that a cricket has. For the cricket, the things of its medium are referred to it, and it is not simply found as an electron is found, immersed in a field where it performs or endures the actions of the surroundings.

The living being, in this center from which it is performing its actions, has a spatiotemporal structure. Its spatial structure refers to the fact that it is not simply *occupying* a place but further has an essential function within space (this already began to appear in the structure of space named "direction"). It is something more than a direction: it is an *orientation.* Bodies in space do not have orientation. They can have directions if there is affine geometry to define such directions, but they have no orientation.[6] (Let me leave aside what is called "orientation" in geometry, for instance, in Möbius's band.)[7] On the contrary, the living being constitutively has an orientation.

In the second place, that orientation is not any orientation whatever for any end, but it serves to put a mobility into act, however modest one wants, because even living beings most statically fixed to a corner of the universe nonetheless have a certain mobility. Space is not only a space of orientation but also of free mobility: vital space. To this is added a character of time, whereby every living being has a certain age and also performs its functions more or less with a certain periodicity.

Not only does the medium have this spatiotemporal character for each living being, but if we take many living beings together, then the medium has a different character, an ecological one: it is precisely their οἶκος [house], the house where each lives. Now, the οἶκος, the ecological structure of living beings, is essential in biology, especially in evolution. That is what allows the *association* of living beings among themselves, and also the *isolation* of some groups of living beings with respect to others. I cannot stress enough the decisive role that isolation plays in the evolution of living beings, and also the character of the region in which they are isolated.

Not only is it an ecological medium, but if we consider the totality of living beings, we find ourselves faced with a curious phenomenon: between the 4.5 billion years which, as we are told, the earth probably has been in existence, and the duration of time there has been life—some four million years—the ratio is 1,000 to 1.[8] Nonetheless, with a dizzying speed, living beings have spread over the earth—over the whole earth—and have constituted the biosphere. Not only does the medium have an ecological character, but it also has the character of a biosphere. Life, besides generation and evolution, has a mysterious but undeniable factor, which is dispersion. Life diffuses and disperses throughout the whole planet. These are more or less some of the things that it is necessary to say about the position of a living being in the universe.

2. The Character of the Dynamic Activity of the Living Being

Of the problems set out before, the most serious is the second one, that is, what comprises the vital activity of a living being within its medium?

I said before, and now I will treat in detail, that this activity develops to promote the persistence of substantive structures. It is not like the electron, which *endures* vicissitudes around it. The living being performs some activities precisely *so that* it can continue to be the same as it was before. It is a new type of dynamism, of giving of oneself. To give of oneself is not only to "predetermine" nor to actualize potentialities and virtualities. It is to *respond* adequately. These activities in persistence can be analyzed on different planes.

The first plane, the most obvious and clear and outwardly apparent, is the response of a living being. For instance, take its capability of reacting to light rays. (All living beings are so capable, because light rays, light, act not only on vision, but in twenty thousand ways on all plant life, in phototropisms, etc.) I refer to *seeing* light. The living being responds to a stimulus that I say precisely arouses a response. The living being responds to that arousal. The arousal consists of upsetting the balance of the living being. The living being responds precisely by restoring somehow, at least, in principle, in a regular and regulated way, in an adequate way, the balance of its own structures. It may fail. It can get sick and die. This will happen sooner or later to every living being. Yet however it may be, as long as this does not happen, the response to an arousal is the restoration of the balance lost as a result of the arousal. The restoration is adequate to the preservation of the substantivity in a regular way, taking it on average, and also in a regulated way. Every organism has its norm of reaction even to a small extent. Now, between the arousal and the response there is not a mere succession. Instead, the arousal leads the living being to determine its response, and this dynamic moment of *leading to* is what constitutes vital tension. The response is just the terminus into which the vital tension flows.

Let us consider that life does not consist only of restoring balance. In fact, life has an absolutely undeniable factor of creation, but if it were not for its capability of keeping and restoring its balance, no creation would be possible in the planet. The rest is empty romanticism.

This is the first description of the activity of a living being. It is independent of the medium and has specific control over it, to organize a few adequate responses with the aim of preserving its substantivity by reason of a situation that has interrupted that balance in which it was found. But no one balance is desirable, because if it were not aroused at all, the living being would die. Hence, being aroused belongs to the essential structure of a living being. What would become of the living being if the perfection of its life consisted of being inaccessible to every arousal? This would be monstrous. This living being would have died. It is best to keep this consideration in mind even when it is a question of very transcendent problems.

This is the first description of the activity of a living being: the arousal-response structure.

Not all living beings are susceptible to the same kind of arousers. It would be completely impossible, for instance, to make a mole respond to that which in another living being could constitute optical or visual sensations. The mole does not have the sense of sight. It has another type of reaction to light—that is different—but not a visual one. This means that underneath the system of arousal and response, as a primary assumption for unleashing these actions in arousal and response, there is something more radical. It is the way of coping with them, the way that a living being primarily has of how to face its medium. If we wanted to describe the life of a mole and the life of a blind dog in the system of arousals and responses, concerning the sense of sight, we would find no difference. In fact, the mole has no sight, nor does the blind dog. Even so, the difference between the two is deep: the blind dog has no response, but had to have had one previously. The mole, no. In other words, there is a primary mode of facing things that is precisely a habitude. "Habitude" is a Latinism; the Greek is ἕξις. There is a habitude. Habitude is not a custom or habit. A habitude is a way of coping with things.[9] It is a primary way of coping with them, ὅπως ἔχει [how things stand],[10] as a Greek would say. This way of coping with them is the one in which are inserted all the mechanisms of arousal and response of a living being.

On the level in which we find ourselves, these habitudes are two: the habitude of facing things in our medium for nourishment, and the habitude of facing them just to sense them. To sense is just to feel a stimulus: the biological liberation of the stimulus—I will return to this—but nourishing is something else. Every living being at least has to face the things surrounding it, as a whole or in part, for nourishment and also in some determinate cases, for the purpose of sensing them. Precisely sensing and self-nourishing are the two habitudes, the two ways of radically facing things, two ways that are not incompatible but which are different. Plant life does not have the function of sensing in the way that an animal has. Yet the animal naturally has the function of self-nourishment, as has plant life.

Now, on the part of things, there is a way of presenting themselves to living beings that corresponds to living beings' way of coping with things. In fact, to the degree things present themselves as a terminus of a habitude of nourishment, things are a *nutriment*. To the degree things present themselves as a terminus of a habitude of sensing them, they have a formality I call "stimulation" [*estimulidad*]. The whole system of things surrounding it, as a whole or in part, has the character of a stimulus for an animal.

Sensing, I once more repeat, and I shall return to this idea again, is the biological release of the stimulus, something that plant life evidently does not have. Yet this does not mean that sensing is completely foreign to the vicissitudes of sensibility. I shall also speak of this below, but for now I leave the question aside.

However it may be, in their most drastic form as polar opposites, we have these two ways or habitudes of facing things: for self-nourishment and for sensing, to which respond two respects of the things, from the standpoint of the things: "nutriment" and "stimulation."

The habitude-respect structure underlies the whole system of arousal and response and is a much deeper stratum of the biological activity of the living being. Yet it is not the final one. For it is evident that this is a description in terms of action. Now, if things act as they act, it is because they are as they are. Consequently, underneath this way in which the living being faces things, and precisely to make it possible, to determine it, the living being has its own structures. These *structures* determine the habitude within which arousal and response are inserted. Therefore, these structures, I say, imply the passage from what we would call the substances comprising it to the structure of which the living being formally consists. In the operative order it is not difficult to affirm—at least I do not find it difficult to state—that the activity of a living being, in the order of activity, cannot be distributed in an additive fashion among the elements that comprise a living being. Even the realities of physics have systematic properties that are irreducible to addition, are not additive properties—for instance, potential energy. Kinetic energy is determinable as the sum of a system, as the sum of kinetic energies of each of the points of the system; in potential energy, that is unfeasible; it belongs to the system as a whole.[11] Now, in a living being, if it did not have molecules endowed with their own activity, there would not be biological activity. This does not mean, however, that the activity of a living being is an additive mosaic of the molecular activities composing it. Rather, we can describe the order of active functions as a little like the way chemistry once described combination and mixture. A mixture is a terminus, an additive result of some substances. A combination, on the contrary, is the production of a new system. Here we would say by analogy that the joining of molecules gives rise to a whole functioning of the system, reducible neither to an additive nor to a multiplicative combination of activities of the molecules constituting it, but constituting a systematically new functional system.

Now, if we transfer this to a constitutive order, then we happen precisely upon structures composed of molecules. The more (and bigger) the molecules they have, the more they involve a certain mode of substance that necessarily has an activity consisting of a functional combination, if its structure is to persist. This structure, radical and basic, is what constitutes the substantive structure of a living being.

Naturally, no living being is the exception to that rule. We may ask, How it is possible to reduce to a system of molecular activity a dog's recognition of its master, or the pain it feels when stepped on or hit by a car? Is it true that matter has feeling? Without a doubt matter feels. This is natural. We are accustomed to a purely geometrical concept of matter deriving from Descartes,[12] and, in the last analysis, to a mechanical concept of matter which prevailed until the last years of the nineteenth century. But where is it said that matter has only mechanical properties, and not even electromagnetic ones? The matter of a dog has feeling. This is obvious. Precisely the dog feels pain. Can it be claimed that there are two things in the dog, its organism and what determines its pain? This would be absurd. That bit of matter called "dog"—that is what senses. There is no doubt at all. The fact that the dog emerges by evolution from lower strata, the fact that all life emerges, as I will soon maintain, by the evolution from something that is not life (I feel this to be the case), does not mean that evolution consists simply of *complication*. Each thing is born from the evolution of a prior stratum, that is plain. But in itself, it is formally an innovation. In the same way, a system is an innovation with respect to the properties, the elements, comprising it.

Matter senses, clearly, and in this fashion it is necessary to say that those types of complex matter constituting animal organisms have that newly originated property (from the standpoint of its being a systematic property), but, nonetheless, that it is rigorously and formally intra-material. It cannot be maintained that in the case of the animal psychic makeup, and even in the human being, to the extent of having a sensitive, animal psychic makeup, it is still a strictly, rigorously, and formally material property.

Now, these activities, thus determined and flowing into a structure of the living being, I said, constitute a dynamism that, like every dynamism, rests upon prior dynamisms. Already described in earlier pages, the two dynamisms to which I alluded at the beginning of the chapter are the dynamism of variation and the dynamism of alteration—in whose optimal case, κατ᾽ ἐξοχήν [par excellence]—we call "evolution." This is the point where the dynamism of living things is *mounted on that genetic and evolutionary dynamism.* The mounting is essential to our problem, because it means precisely life itself, because it consists, as I said, of a system of activities to preserve some structures, to preserve some substantivities, and those activities have an essential, constitutively evolutionary dimension. Since this evolution has a few determined characters, it is necessary to bring them to mind to understand the makeup of the ultimate character of this vital dynamism. Here I am going to be purely enumerative. In short, this enumeration is not rigorously chronological, but sufficiently so. Especially from the viewpoint of the nature of things, it expresses rigorous grounding, because each term is grounded on the prior one.

In the first place, there is no doubt at all, whatever its more or less unknown mechanism may be but about which important experiments have been made, that living matter stems from and is no more than the terminus of an evolution from non-living matter. In sum, the famous experiments of Oparin and others, who obtained amino acids through electrical discharges upon a medium with nitrogen, ammonia, etc., are if not evident, certainly convincing and plausible.[13] They open the door to the goal—not so remote, I think, as is often thought—of being able to create living matter in an effective, synthetic way. However, I have always rigorously distinguished between living matter and an organism, in the same way that physics has rigorously distinguished between elementary particles and corpuscles. In no way would it occur to the physicist of today to say that elementary particles are corpuscles in the sense of atoms. The proof lies in the descriptions of almost all elementary particles in wave equations of different types: that of Schrödinger, that of Klein, etc.[14] This is something completely different. Neither are they waves in the classical sense.

What are they then? We do not know. Better said, we know this much: in effect, they are entities that are elementary and whose actuation is described in terms of equations whereby they are neither corpuscles nor waves in a rigorous sense. What matters to us to say is that the particles are elementary, but that an elementary particle of matter is not formally a corpuscle. There is a distinction between body and matter. Now, I believe that we are in the same situation with biology.

We are accustomed to considering that biology begins in the cell. This is an assumption like any other. There is perhaps a prior problem, which is the constitution of living matter. It naturally may have a life very difficult to detect and to distinguish from the stages that are not life, as is evident. Therefore it is an evolution that in some form or other constitutes what I would call the "vitalization of matter." Vis-à-vis the stabilization of matter proper to the constitution of more or less stable elementary particles and molecules, passing through atoms, we have something that, I repeat, I would call the "vitalization of matter." This vitalization of matter precisely makes way for a progressive advance.

In the second place, living matter is organized immediately. What are the agents? No one can know. But however it may be, if we compare living matter, for instance, that of a virus, supposing it may be at least the detritus of living matter, with a cell, we immediately see that almost all cells have at least a nucleus besides a cytoplasm. But, as Darlington very well said,[15] a cytoplasm is precisely the field of action of a nucleus; that is, however it may be, the agents, the genetic code, etc., are accumulated precisely in the nucleus. In other words, from the pure vitalization of matter, whereby there is living matter, we have passed to something different, which is the internalization of life. Life has concentrated at least into a nuclear point that governs the basic manifestations of life.

With the internalization of the nucleus, with the nucleus, appears the cell. I mean that in a certain evolutionary stage there appears the differentiation between unicellular beings and multicellular beings. But this biological difference has not been the object of reflection on the part of the great theorists of evolution like the very well-known P. Teilhard de Chardin.[16] Yes, without doubt it is very simple to describe in grandiose terms the advance of evolution according to Teilhard de Chardin, as if in fact the individuals had nothing to do but form part of the species. It would seem that the radical biological fact of the constitution of a multicellular organism consisted just of dissociating the lot of the individual from the lot of the species.

In fact, if we consider an amoeba, the amoeba keeps dividing in two. But where is the prior amoeba? For in reality it resides in both. In other words, in the amoeba the lot of the individual is identical to the lot of the species. This is naturally so. On the contrary, if we take any sufficiently developed multicellular organism, we find that while its reproductive functions are very important, they do not even remotely exhaust all its biological activity, even in cases where genetic activity can kill. In the case of the multicellular organism, there is a radical and essential dissociation between the lot of the individual and the lot of the species. The death of a dog does not cause the disappearance of dogs from history. On the contrary, the death of an amoeba, the first amoeba, would cause the disappearance of practically all amoebas from earth. One thing is the lot of the individual, another the lot of the species.

There is a fourth degree, the appearance of meiosis and, in its time, of sexual generation.[17] Here we witness not simply the differentiation of the individual lot from the lot of the species, but the linkage of individual activity to association with other living beings, especially in the most intimate form of their possession when reproduction is sexual.

As I have said, every living being is more or less the terminus of an arousal of actions on the part of the medium surrounding it. In this sense it is susceptible to these actions, and one can say, not improperly but with full precision, that there is a certain function of sensing in all living beings. What happens is that *susceptibility* does not constitute a proper, formal release from the stimulus as such. A plant evidently is susceptible in this case, but in the last analysis it has no organic, cellular system in which its susceptible function acquires autonomy, at least in a sufficiently luxuriant way. On the contrary, in the most modest of animals appears at least something that is the acquisition of autonomy by the functions of stimulation, even in a diffuse way. Precisely because of its diffuseness I have called it "sensitescence" [*sentiscencia*]. Sensitescence is a more or less general sensitivity that can later adopt forms, different, branching out, etc. But the biological release from stimulus as such finally arrives in the form of sensitivity in the strict sense. This passes through the form of susceptibility to sensitescence, and from there to sensitivity. With this comes precisely psychic makeup [*psiquismo*]. It is precisely the moment in which we could say that there is produced in one or another form the "animalization of life." In the animalization of life, the function of sensing appears in a thematic way. Everything that happened throughout the history of animals, from the first animal with sensitescence to the most complicated of the orangutans and the first of the hominids, is nothing but an evolutionary complication of this elementary psychic makeup of every animal. In other words, this psychic makeup is the complication and development of its function of sensing as biological release from the stimulus.

The structures of life not only led to the creation of a biological release from the stimulus in the form of pure and vague animalization of life, but to something more: there has appeared a stage in which precisely those functions *centralize*. It is the *centralization of sensing*, the centralization of animal life. This is enormously important. Let us consider that through this it is possible to slaughter an animal but not a plant. A plant is constitutively a noncentralized system. An animal is centralized. The more centralized it is, the more perfect its life, but the more vulnerable. Centralization is always the seat of vulnerability. The animal, to the degree that it becomes ever more an animal, is a more centered system. In a centered system, the psychic makeup acquires more character and becomes more similar to what in the human being makes it possible to say, "I feel myself hungry" or "I feel myself thirsty." Yet the animal does not have this "myself" in any fashion: it is thirsty and hungry. The more perfect the animal, the more it resembles precisely this "myself" that we human beings have.

Not only is there centralization in animality, but there are, in addition, some mechanisms—not in every living being, but especially in animals—for preserving the *balance* of the inner medium. I refer precisely to homeostasis, the introduction of homeostasis in life. This is something absolutely essential. Without it, the living being could not preserve its structures. Homeostatic balance is something more than a balance: it is a *dynamic moment* of the activity of living beings. Certainly it is grounded on structures of balance; there is no doubt at all. Consider that the homeostasis of the inner medium is maintained precisely so that the living being needing to perform actions on a higher level than the one being considered here can count on itself in a certain way for those other functions.[18] In other words, the organization and balance of the inner medium is not a static balance but a *dynamic equilibrium* in which each of the lower phases requires of necessity the intervention of a higher phase so that the lower one can continue being what it is. The chemical makeup of an animal could not be preserved if at a certain moment the animal did not have optical sensations (at least in an integral way), or else other sensations. Plainly, that could not be. The higher function intervenes precisely because it is demanded by the lower one. Now, the higher one, for its part, can make its own move. For once it enters into action, naturally it has a much wider field than the elementary function that has set it to work. In other words, we have the lower function dynamically stretching under the higher one and also a release of the activity proper to the higher function. But the higher function could not perform its activity were it not for homeostasis, which dynamically subtends its own activity. How could we argue that without an adequate chemical reaction the nervous system could adequately function and that we would have a brain remembering things, etc.? This could not be.

Not only is there a function of stabilization in the order of activities, but this stabilization leads in fact, at least in the animal series, to something different, which is [cerebral] "corticalization" [*corticalización*]. Not only is a central axis being constituted, but that central axis ends in a telencephalon, and the telencephalon culminates precisely in a cortex.

Now, what is the function of the cortex? Neurologists have debated it a great deal. Sherrington thought that it is a system of integration;[19] Broca, that it is a system of signification.[20] Modestly I have at one time dared to think that it is neither a question of one or the other. For in fact the living being, every living being, even the most elementary amoeba, besides having some specifically determined functions, has just by virtue of its structures what I have called the "formalization" of those actions, of the way the actions are presented in the medium. I have used the example of the crab (although the example is not mine but David Katz's),[21] the crab trained to hunt its prey on a rock, but if that prey is suspended from a string on a stick, the crab feels incapable of seizing it. For what reason? In reality because the crab has not perceived the prey but the whole configuration of rock-prey. Now, viewing a different configuration, the crab does not recognize the prey within it. On the contrary, an animal superior to the crab naturally sees the prey by itself, as if cut out and independent from the rest. This is just the function of formalization.

In the evolutionary development of the nervous system, not simply have the eleven organs of sensory perception come to be created, the eleven nuances of sensitivity which we all possess,[22] but in addition, especially, there has come into being an enormous system of formalization. In virtue of this we can speak of independent things, not simply of total configurations. Now, I judge that the essential function of the cerebral cortex and of the brain in general is just to create this enormous system of formalization. By virtue of this system of formalization, an elementary stimulus received from the outer medium presents ever richer situations, the richer its inner formalization. Precisely this causes the psychic makeup, so elementary that it consists just of biological release from the stimulus, to acquire that luxuriant and complicated character that flows precisely into animal behavior. The responses that the animal gives to the arousal then change into behavior. The formalization requires the behavior for its own stability and reciprocally makes possible the richness in which is inserted the psychic makeup of the animal. On this is grounded the intrinsic unity between stability and creation in life.

In short, if we consider these stages mentioned in the advance of life, we find that from the internalization of matter to the maximum formalization in corticalization we have witnessed a progressive internalization, increasingly greater, precisely of the living being.

Now, internalization, inwardness, is proper to reality as such. Every reality, because it is real, has an *intus* [inside] that is manifest on an *ex* [outside], which is precisely the system of structural notes of which the essence of its substantivity consists.

3. Life as a Mode of Reality

What is life as a mode of reality? I narrated this long prior history precisely, in the first place, to avoid having what I am about to say seem like mere speculation in a vacuum. In the second place, I did this for a deeper reason, for I judge that, as has become evident throughout these pages, no structure concerning reality as such is mounted on itself; it is purely and simply the transcendental function that the particular dimensions of reality possess. Because living beings are *particular* beings, the *type of reality as such* represented by each of them is quite definite. It is not a question of a simple particularity but of particularity in a transcendental function, in other words, as that which determines that something is reality. Now, reality consists of being in its own right [*de suyo*]. In this being-in-its-own-right is constituted precisely the "self," of which the giving-of-itself proper to dynamism consists.

Now, if everything said above is placed in this perspective, we realize that the transcendental function of this progressive internalization comprising the evolution of living beings and the development of the activity of each is not simply any internalization whatever, merely particular, but is really the *constitution of "selfhood"* [*mismidad*]. With its activity, the living being is constituting itself precisely in its selfhood as a form of reality—and this goes beyond mere particularity. It is selfhood as a form of reality. This is precisely what is essential to a living being. Still, it must be stipulated at the outset that the selfhood of a living being does not consist of mere identity. An electron also has that identity. The electron, as long as it is not destroyed, has identity. It is the same electron throughout space and time. It is not a question of that. Nor is it a question of the living being as a kind of subject that endures the vicissitudes befalling it from without amidst all these activities. It is not a question of its enduring them, but of its *exercising them* to be able to be the *self* that it was before. Just that is the dynamism of selfhood. Selfhood is not a mere persistence, but the reduplicative and formal act in which a living being performs some actions precisely to be that which it structurally already was. The character of those structures, which are not only capacitated for that type of activity but also needed and forced to exercise it, is precisely the living structure. For this reason, in each moment of the life of every living being and of the evolution of all organisms, the evolution, I affirm, consists of nothing else but of giving of itself, of being increasingly more alive. It may be said that it can include even being less alive. This is true. But the fact remains that there are many cases, the majority, in which being less is precisely a form of being more. Let us not forget this either in amoebas or in human beings.

In the second place, this structure of the dynamism of selfhood—this is the name that this dynamism has in contrast to the dynamism of alteration—stems precisely from other structures. What happens in them? Within them it happens that the substantivity itself intervenes as a whole by affirming precisely the activity of a living being in its own dynamism as a form of reality. In this sense I say that to live is to possess oneself. To possess oneself does not mean to take a reflexive action. It simply means that the totality of one's being is normally implied in the activities it develops to be the self that it already was. Selfhood is essentially and formally an act of possessing oneself. Therefore, from the standpoint of dynamism it is the dynamism of selfhood; while from the radical standpoint, and as a form of reality, life is *precisely a self-possessing.*

Naturally, the advance of life both in the living individual and throughout the biological scale is a wholly progressive advance, and also an advance toward a life relatively (though no more than relatively) "itself," and relatively self-possessive.

In the measure that one climbs up that scale, there is more self-possession. But however that may be, within that "more"—in the measure that there is more and relatively something more of self-possession—life and evolution, the advance of the life of every living being and of all life taken phylogenetically, represent an entitative increment. A chimpanzee is more reality than an amoeba, without any doubt. Throughout its greater dynamism of selfhood and its greater selfhood, it has greater substantivity and greater self-possession. Hence, to my way of thinking, the classical theses often expressed as the philosophical characteristics of a living being are absolutely or at least sufficiently unsustainable.

For instance, the last important thesis is Bergson's that life is an élan vital. I have often said that as a boy I was impressed by Bergson's sentence, "Like swirls of dust raised by the wind, living beings whirl around themselves, carried along by the great breath of life."[23] That sounds wonderful, but is it true? This is the second part of the issue. For what is the breath of life if not the exercise of activities derived from some structures and reverting back over them? The rest is a metaphor, splendid, needless to say. I have great admiration for Bergson, but no, life is not an élan in this sense. Life has a dimension of creation (as I have stressed), but it is creation in the sense of innovation, not an *innovation* that would consist of being an "inventing" élan.

An older thesis—unless my friend Pedro Laín Entralgo corrects me[24]—held that life is spontaneity. It is Stahl's thesis of animism and Montpellier's of vitalism.[25]

Life is spontaneity. Now, this is not rigorously true in any case, not even in human life. Absolute spontaneity, where is it to be found? In the final analysis, the actions of the living being are in one form or another aroused by something that is not the living being itself—or as Aristotle would say, by the living being itself, but qua another.[26] That is clear. Actions can be aroused by virtue of . . . for instance, one's own gastric oversecretion, but in that case would the reactions cease to be limited in their spontaneity? No, life is not spontaneous in that sense.

There is an older characteristic that to my way of thinking more closely approaches the essence of the issue. This is to say that the activities of a living being are immanent in contrast with all the other actions happening in the universe, which are transcendent. For example, the collision of a billiard ball puts another in motion; chemical reagents produce reactions. Indeed, it is always a question of transitive actions in which the action does not fall back over the proper actions that perform it, under pain of destroying or changing them. On the contrary, we are told that the living being exercises immanent actions that remain in the subject, and that this would be life. Indeed, it would be life, but life very similar to that of a monolith. For one must wonder at least two things concerning this immanence. In the first place, what does *manēre* [to remain] signify in that word? Does it mean solely to persist as a passive subject? Doubtlessly, no. The subject performs its action, actions so that it can exist. Consequently, the terminus of the activity enters as already assumed in the root *manēre* of immanence. That *manēre* can serve us poorly to define life.

In the second place there is the prefix *in-*. It seems as if it were a question of a difference; hence there is a *manēre*, which in some cases is transitive and in others intransitive. But what is that *in*? (I will deal with this *in* in the next chapter.) That *in*, I here repeat once again, is a series of essential activities that spring from the structures of something that precisely consists of maintaining its own structures in the form of activity. Consequently, this form of activity and not immanence is what characterizes the essence of life. Now, the essence of life consists, from this standpoint, not of being a subject *in*, but of being an activity by itself, the active structure by itself, ordered just for giving of itself from its own selfhood.

The living being is that reality whose form of reality consists of its own giving itself its own selfhood.

Reality is active by itself. It is a giving of itself. It is a becoming. But becoming is not changing. Vital becoming is not formally a change but a giving of oneself. In life a thing changes first to be itself [*el mismo*], although it may never be the same [*lo mismo*]; second, in order to be more itself [*más sí mismo*], and third, when everything has been given, when life is so perfect that there is no more room for giving more of itself, with respect to itself there is room at least for the human being to fit into a higher possibility: that of giving itself wholly to another, and becoming in another, for example, in the phenomenon of love. (But I shall deal with this in due course.)

⌒

What I have said up to now about life as a mode of reality is sufficient as an initial approach, but in the strictest sense it requires greater precision and development.

Recall the three strata of every dynamism: in the first place, the in-its-own-right [de suyo] whereby it is reality; in the second place, the itself [sí] by virtue of which this reality is active by itself; in the third place, the *giving of itself* [dar de sí] which is the most manifest and clear part of every dynamism. Every consecutive stratum is grounded on the prior one.

The problem, consequently, of how the living being and life are a reality, the mode of reality, hinges on responding to these two questions: What is the character of that self in giving of itself? In the second place, What is the character of the giving? That is the issue.

In the first place, let us examine the character of the "self," the "self" itself.

Classical theories—many of them, at least—have judged that the self itself, proper to life, is a subject. It is a subject to whom it in fact happens that it is alive, a living being. Hence if we distinguished between the subject and its being, we would say with Aristotle that for living beings life is precisely their εἶναι, their being.[27] This expression of Aristotle's is quoted to the saturation point in contemporary philosophy. Now, whether the meaning with which it is quoted today is the one which Aristotle conferred on it is a different issue, which I leave aside. I will keep to this expression purely and simply to show how in fact Aristotle takes the living being as a subject to whom it happens, in whatever form it may be, whatever is called ζῆν, to live. It is a subject to whom life happens.

This conception is not absolutely false, how could it be? But it is absolutely insufficient for several reasons: In the first place, we are told that life is a thing that happens to a subject, the living being, the subject that is alive. But what does "happening" mean? Is that life an accident? If by accident is understood that it is not a substance, of course this is evident. But can it be said without going further that life is an accident for a living being? Is it accidental for the crab that it does what it does on a rock? At least, *simpliciter dictu* [stated with qualification], life is not an accident.

Then it could be said that life at least is a property of the living being. The living being has a property, for instance, to move itself. That is the famous definition of life that also stems from Aristotle.[28] Life is then a property that emerges from the subject. Indeed, but then it is necessary to say that this subject is already alive, and therefore self-motion emerges from it. If this is not the case, then it does not move itself; it is not that it is dead because it does not move itself, but it does not move itself because it is dead. Naturally. Then the question goes back to what being alive means. Aristotle would tell us that being alive consists of being a substance whose substantial form is precisely vitality, that is, life. A substantial form—this is the thesis of life as substantial form.

It is curious that some present-day Scholastics, Maritain among them, when speaking of hylomorphism, say that they do not wish to give biological proofs of hylomorphism, because that would be too easy.[29] But it is one thing to be a hylomorphist and another to find it very easy to resort to biology to demonstrate hylomorphism. Probably Maritain had no more information than the data stemming from the circle of Spemann,[30] whose student I was in Freiburg a thousand years ago. Spemann, with his famous discovery of embryonic organizers, had caused a great step forward to be taken in what was then rightly called the "mechanics" of evolution. This is true. But a student of Goldschmidt and of Spemann himself demonstrated that organizers organize better when dead.[31] The easiness of proving hylomorphism stays suspended once more in the very experiment that served as a basis for Driesch and Spemann.[32] But what is certain is that the living being is not a substance but millions of substances. In that case, properly speaking, the living being is a structure, not a substance. Since it is a structure, clearly it is impossible to operate with the idea of a subject, because certainly this structure has a unity, an inner unity, whose fashioning into a construct system of notes is just what constitutes all the structural wealth of the living being. This structural unity is not a subject from which precisely the structural notes spring but is something internal and also intrinsic to the system itself in whose notes it is present in a dominant and demanding way.

In any case it still remains to be seen that we be told what comprises this unity. Certainly Aristotle would not give a satisfactory answer; he would again repeat his general theory of substance, in whose critique I will not enter again. It is best, for now, to formulate a question: Of what does the structural character of a living being consist?

It could be answered—and this is the other classical thesis—that the structural unity of a living being consists precisely of *identity*. It is not a question of a formal identity. Saying that *A* is *A* is applicable to any reality in the universe: this is the famous principle of identity. It is, however, a question of something more. The identity in question has a richer and more precise character, because that identity is the one that must be shaped into the enormous variety of notes that comprise a living being and into all the dynamisms and actions that it performs in its life. Thus it has been said that the identity is precisely an achievement of life, not an assumption of life. Identity is something that continues to be formed precisely like an ambiance of quiescent motions of which the living being consists, and which we call "identity," because all those motions converge to constitute that heart of hearts of a living being, which we call its "inner selfhood."

In one or another form this was the thesis of Fichte and Hegel.

Fichte, from a standpoint purely of the ego, formulated his principle of identity in a more or less dynamic form at the start of his *Wissenschaftslehre,* his doctrine of science, of the absolute science, philosophy.[33]

Hegel, in all his metaphysics, is operating constantly with the *Selbst*—with the "self"—but as a result of the folding back precisely of being over itself.[34] The self itself would be a character, a kind of character of a quiescent motion that, without ceasing to be motion, folds back over itself instead of dispersing. Better said, it does not fold back over itself, but its folding back constitutes the selfhood of itself, its own unity. Now, this has always seemed to me difficult to sustain.

In the first place, life is not something that constitutes the living being by itself, in its dynamic vitality, but conversely, the living being is reality in life. It would be necessary to stress the moment of reality *before* the dynamic moment, the moment of the living being. Now, what needs to be said is in that case it is absolutely false to think that the same, identical reality of the living being is the result of its life. This is completely capricious. The selfhood of life does not consist of the quiescence—however much quiescence may be desired, and however wonderfully describable, I do not argue—of a series of vital motions, which in their quiescence elaborate something like the ambiance wherein they continue to be quiescent. They are something like stationary waves, as physics would say. Indeed, all this is magnificent to say but false. It is simply not so.

Certainly there is a quiescent motion in life, but it is because life is the motion of a something that is structurally "itself" and that precisely for that reason can confer that character of selfhood and that character of quiescence upon vital motions. The self itself, the αὐτός, is not the result of life but a principle of life.

So much more unsustainable does Hegel's thesis turn out to be the more it cannot be forgotten that the living being can be as identical as is wished, but that what is certain is that in no instant of its reality is it always the same. Now, where is selfhood then? Where is identity?

Vis-à-vis these two theses, which I do no more than state and critique rapidly and fleetingly, I want to affirm that to my way of thinking, selfhood, that which constitutes the mode of reality proper to a living being, implies two moments.

First Moment — The self, the self itself, as I have just pointed out, is neither subject nor mere identity, but consists of something much stricter and more rigorous: of being always the self [*el mismo*].

This selfhood is not a passive selfhood. In other words, it does not consist purely of being a subject [*subjetualidad*], which stays stable throughout some vicissitudes, but it is a selfhood dynamic in the strict sense. It is not enough to be identical as a reality to be the self in its dynamism. This is a dynamic selfhood.

To show such a difference I have pointed out in prior pages that the rest of material realities, for instance, elementary particles or pieces of matter, are the same and stable, in other words, everything that happens to them does so in spite of their being themselves, and their sameness stays amidst their vicissitudes. On the contrary, in the case of the living being, the thing transpires in a completely different way: it has all its dynamism not by lying *low,* but *in order to* be able to be itself. I shall explain this *in order to,* which to be rigorous with my terms is not an "in order to." To be rigorous with my terms, the "in order to" exists only in the case of human life. For the truth is that in the matter of the other living beings, what must be said strictly of them is that they do what they do by being what they are. That is, they do this or the other, and in doing this or doing the other they behave in the only way they can continue to be the same as themselves. That is certain.

The living being is always the self. The radical and basic unity of the living being is the dynamic unity of being the self. The in-its-own-right [*de suyo*] characteristic of all reality is fashioned precisely in the living being into a special way of being in-its-own-right, which is just being the self. It is in-its-own-right *the* self. Precisely this is the dynamism of selfhood as another mode of reality active by itself, in contrast with mere stability. Stable things are stable in spite of what happens to them; they resist the attacks of the universe. The living being, on the contrary, is producing its vitality precisely by being just itself, not being able to be itself other than by doing in fact what it does. Here, in the first place, selfhood is consequent upon structures. It is consequent upon the αὐτός [self], not prior to it.

Further, in the second place, it is formally intrinsic to the living being. It is not something that merely happens to the living being, but something that belongs to it in an intrinsic way.

Second Moment — The second moment of this dynamism of vitality, of this selfhood, is the fact that it responds to the following questions: What comprises this intrinsic belonging of the vital dynamism, of the dynamism of selfhood, to the living being as such? What is this dynamism with respect to structures themselves? What is this "self," active by itself?

Again we find ourselves in the presence of two classical theses. In the first place there is the thesis of *spontaneity*. Dynamism belongs to the living being because it emerges from it spontaneously. Here we must work with the contrast between what is spontaneous and what is forced. "Spontaneous" means what is born from oneself because it is what it is; "forced" means what is more or less imposed by things surrounding the individual, etc. Life would be spontaneity. All its pertinence to the living being would consist of springing spontaneously from the structures of that being. What happens is that there is no living being to which this occurs, not even the human. Leaving the issue apart and limiting myself to non-human beings, I repeat that this does not happen to any living being.

In the first place, no living being develops its activity, whatever its character, unless immersed in a medium. This medium is not simply a kind of occasion for a subject to live. No, it is what is constantly upsetting its dynamic equilibrium and furthermore urging it on to a series of actions that the living being performs in that medium. These actions are not spontaneous but precisely provoked, forced, by the medium. There is no doubt about this at all.

In the second place, the living being not only has the things of the outer medium; it also has its own inner medium. The inner medium also forces it to do many things, without a doubt. How, then, can it be said that it is spontaneous *a parte viventis,* on the part of the living being itself?

In the third place, the structural moments of a living being act upon one another, and therefore the living being produces its actions. There is no living being whose structure would be like a fountain from which flows something that is life. No, to speak in concrete terms, it is a question of definite reactions mobilizing a definite enzyme, which catalyzes such a definite reaction, etc. Those are living actions in which each part, each structural moment of the living system, is precisely acting upon the others. To what is spontaneity then reduced?

The other classical, very classical, thesis, which has lasted for centuries in the history of philosophy, consists of saying that life emerges from the living being, though not in the form of spontaneity, but in the form of immanent action.

Certainly the actions of the living being aroused by its medium, by its outer medium, by its inner medium, by the interaction of the structural moments of the system comprising the living being, are not spontaneous in this sense. But surely these actions, although they may not emerge from it in a spontaneous form, nonetheless remain in it in an immanent way. Here *in-manēre* [to remain within] is a conception that is based not on the opposition between

128

what is spontaneous and what is forced but on the opposition between what is transitive and what is immanent. Transitive actions, for instance, the motion of a billiard ball that gives a blow to another and the rolling of the second ball—these are typically transitive actions. On the contrary, the living being performs a series of actions, but all those actions remain or flow back into the very living being that performs them.

Naturally, this conception of immanence, of *in-manēre,* is also rather problematic if one stops to reflect a little. It is as problematic as the ancient conception that the living being is a substance. What if it were not one but millions? Of what does the immanence of vital motion consist? For every dynamic action of the living being is formally transitive. Clearly, each one of the moments of its structural system, I have just said, acts upon the other and reacts upon it. Where is there an immanence, strictly speaking? Each of the elementary actions or the elementary mechanisms comprising a vital act is formally transitive or transient from the standpoint of the structures. It is not immanent in the sense I have just defined. But in the last analysis, it may be said that if we take at least the system as a whole, a unitary vital action in which the whole system enters, that action is immanent with respect to the system. This is true provided we are told what comprises the *manēre* [to remain] and of what the *in* consists.

What is understood here by *manēre,* by being permanent? Clearly it does not mean only persisting. This is extremely clear, because then the motion of the billiard ball would also be a vital motion, since the ball persists, and this is not the case. Nor is it a mere placement of the living being among other things, as if the other things were in fact going to flow back over the living being and give it something that it in fact receives, so that the *manēre* consisted of that reception. But the fact is that the *manēre* in itself, that staying power, has a formally dynamic character. It does not consist only of movement having one character or another but of its being in a staying state, "manent" [*manente*], though in a dynamic fashion. What is understood here by a dynamic staying power? We are not told.

The insufficiency rises suddenly if instead of looking at the *manēre* we look at the *in-* of "immanence."

The immanent aspect is not that life is in the living thing but that it is necessary to indicate the *way that it is there,* the *mode of the "in."* Now, about this nothing is said to us. Nothing is given but a merely formal exposition: the active subject of the actions is the same that undergoes the vital movement. But this does not say of what the "in" consists.

Therefore I judge these two conceptions as insufficient, and the reason for their insufficiency lies in the radical assumption from which both begin.

It seems as if the theme would become clear through the attempt to ascertain how vital motion is within the living being. But what if the opposite road were taken and it were asked, How is the living being in its vital motion? This would lead to a different perspective. Immanence and spontaneity relate, in the last analysis, to the idea that life is a thing that comes out of the living being or remains in it. But what if we tried to ask, conversely, In what form is the living being in its vital motion? Then the issue would be different. For then it is not a question of how the vital motion *belongs* to the living being, nor how vital motion *arises* in the living being, but *how the living being* belongs to the motion. We do not ask how the motion belongs to the living being.

The living being is an "itself." In the dynamism of life there formally enter some structures in such a way that it is in the selfhood of these where the structures are fully what they are. The motion of vitality, the motion of selfhood, is not limited to *coming out* of the living being and to *staying* within it, but in it and by it is how the structures continue being "themselves," some structures which are "selves."

To live is only this: to be reduplicatively and formally oneself, that is, to be *structurally* the self. The structures are in the movement. They are so for something perfectly determined. To use the expression "for the purpose of," although it may be anthropomorphic, the structures are "for the purpose of" something completely determined: for the purpose of being just "themselves," such as they are. For this reason, precisely to the degree that structures are in the vital motion for the purpose of being able to be equal to what they are, for that very reason I say that the dynamism of vitality belongs to the living being; and the living being belongs to the dynamism of vitality, in that concrete form I express by saying "possessing itself."

Possessing oneself does not mean being master of oneself; this is vague and also relatively false even in the case of the human being. Rather it consists of formally performing one's selfhood.

The living being is not something that elapses in any form. The life of the living being is not an elapsing. It is precisely a self-possessing. The living being performs all the actions it performs not in spite of being a living being, nor as if life sprang from itself, but because those structures are embroiled in motion in such a way that the actions of the vital motion consist of being performed precisely to conserve the structures. In the last analysis, it is what I have said at the start in a hackneyed but unnoticed way when I said that life consists of a dynamic, reversible equilibrium. The reversibility consists precisely of selfhood as a mode of reality that maintains its structures. Hence flow, whatever life has of flow, is precisely the way of possessing itself at every instant. It possesses itself flowingly. But life is formally possessing itself. Then it must be wondered not only what comprises the itself—I have just said that itself is to possess itself—but what makes up the character of giving of itself.

This is the second aspect of the issue.

Structures, I said, are active by themselves, and the dynamism of this activity is a dynamism for the purpose of being always *the self*. Now this activity, this *giving*, has in turn two moments:

In the first place, movement is necessary for being oneself. This movement for being oneself is what we call an adequate response. The living being performs some actions not in any way, through reactions, but, taken globally, the actions of the living being are responses to the outer medium or to the inner medium. A response is something completely different from a reaction. A reaction happens just with the collision of two realities, whatever they may be. In a response, the living being responds from itself and for itself. "Itself" is here to be taken in the sense which I have just described. Only then is there a response. To respond is to act from oneself to keep one's own dynamic and reversible equilibrium. In the measure that the response succeeds in maintaining these very structures, we say that the response is adequate. To what is it adequate? Precisely to the selfhood of itself. Giving of itself is very concretely to respond adequately in this sense.

But there is a second moment. In fact this response is in a way a change. There is no room for doubt that living beings change. Now, it is not true that life is change; it certainly is not. Life is just the reverse: it consists of being oneself and possessing oneself. What happens is that the living being possesses itself only in change, and this is something different. By virtue of this, it is necessary to say that as much as the living being is *itself* throughout its life, it is never the same. Precisely the range of adequate responses that the living being continues to give at every instant modifies it. In virtue of this, we say that the living being is never the same. The theme of never being the same is the theme of the flowing character of animal life. Living is flowing so as to be oneself. Now, the living being is that reality which cannot be itself [*el mismo*] except by *never* being the same [*lo mismo*]. Precisely in that implication is to be found the mode of reality proper to the living being.

This is the dynamism of selfhood: *giving of oneself adequately,* not being ever the same precisely and formally in order to be able to be always the self. The living being is the reality whose structures give of themselves (that is, dynamically) their own selfhood. Certainly the structures are prior. How could they be otherwise? If they were not, what I have just said would make no sense. But these structures are called "living" precisely to the degree that they can structurally give, and they have to give dynamically some actions in which and only in which these structures are possessing themselves. Already from a very early date in my books and my courses, I said that the living being is always itself but never the same. Now I add, the living being never is the same precisely and formally *in order* always to be the self. To live, therefore, is not to change but to become, to give of oneself in the strictest sense of the word "oneself."

As a mode of reality, this giving of oneself certainly admits degrees. The wealth of life throughout the biological scale is a wealth, clearly, of degrees of reality, modes of being one's own, of being oneself.

The development in this scale is a development in entitative increment. Without any doubt, a chimpanzee is a greater reality than an amoeba. It will nonetheless be said that the two are equally real. Certainly this is so if by equally real is meant that they are not nothingness. But it is not a question of this. It is a question of the fact that, if reality is constituted by a positive "in-its-own-right" [*de suyo*], the in-its-own-right of the chimpanzee is much richer and deeper than the in-its-own-right of an amoeba. In fact, all along the zoological scale, the biological scale, we continue to note the building of a greater in-its-own-right and with it, hence, a greater substantivity.

We keep on seeing it being constituted not only through a kind of gradual catalogue but through a true evolutionary gradation. For this reason, the metaphysical meaning of the dynamism of life, of the dynamism of selfhood, is the fact that reality *qua tale* [as particular] is in the process of becoming in a giving of itself of selfhood. It is the reality in selfhood from respectivity.

Nevertheless, so stated without going further, this has no absolute reality in any living being. I say "absolute," because the truth is that no living being has a plenary, a formal, substantivity. Every living being, in one form or another, is a fragment of the universe. Its own life is a moment of the whole universe. To the extent that we keep on growing on the biological scale, the living being appears precisely endowed ever more with something that approaches what is real and effective substantivity, that is, plenary independence with respect to the medium and specific control over it. Therefore, in reality, life, even the most perfect and in its most perfect degrees, in its ultimate stratum of formalization, does not rise above being a primordium of what is precisely full and formal selfhood.

It is then necessary to wonder whether evolution ends here or keeps going. Naturally evolution does not end, but keeps going. The problem that now arises is the appearance of human beings within the zoological scale.

⌒

Throughout this chapter I have considered a distinct aspect of the dynamism of the real, a dynamism that was neither variation nor the dynamism of alteration, already examined in earlier pages, but a different dynamism, certainly congeneric with the dynamism of alteration, which is the dynamism of selfhood. That dynamism *a potiori* [with a stronger claim] naturally receives the denomination of evolution. As I have already set out, there is a first type of dynamism of a certain selfhood, which is stabilization: the dynamism of stabilization of matter; and, in the second place, the type of dynamism of selfhood strictly speaking: the dynamism of living structures. These living structures constitute a substantivity, not a substance. They are structures in dynamic and reversible equilibrium. These structures, which are not substantial but merely structural, are placed at some location within the universe among all other things, in a definite situation. Within it they respond precisely to things around them. To this environ, which constitutes their own medium, they respond with a few responses I analyzed in three successive strata: first, the arousal-response stratum; second, the habitude-formal respect stratum; and, above all, the properly structural stratum, characterized, as I said, by a kind of functional combination in the *structural order.*

Life, so constituted, and the living being, so constituted, keep unfolding throughout history—the history of the universe—in several strata that I will now do no more than enumerate:

In the first place, the constitution of living matter.

In the second place, the internalization of living matter into the nucleus.

In the third place, the passage of the unicellular organism to the multicellular one.

In the fourth place, meiosis and sexual generation.

Fifth, animalization of life by means of the appearance of the psychic makeup.

Sixth, centralization of animal life.

Seventh, stabilization of the inner medium—a homeostasis.

Eighth, cerebral corticalization, and within it a development by specification and formalization, which is what will most matter to us for the development of the following issue.

Life is an advance from internalization of the nucleus to creative formalization precisely because by virtue of this formalization the living being creates or makes possible the creation of enormously rich situations, all the richer and more complex the greater the formalization is. This has led us, in the final point of this chapter, to consider life and the living being as a mode of reality.

The advance of life, I said, is a progressive advance from internalization of the nucleus to creative formalization. But this advance of life so described is one described only in terms of particularity, in other words, by describing in fact how living beings are. But what matters here is to consider this particularity of the living being as a transcendental function. I understand a transcendental function as the mode of reality that the particularities in question constitute. It is necessary to recall that the real, at least such as I have understood it here, is precisely what is in-its-own-right [*de suyo*]. This concept of in-its-own-right does not coincide with a merely existential concept, nor with the usual essential concept: reality is something that is wholly in-its-own-right that which it is and that which it in fact presents in its mode of being.

Certainly every reality is in-its-own-right. How could it be otherwise if that comprises a reality? In-its-own-right, an electron has a negative charge or a positron a positive one. This is indeed obvious. (I always use the example of the electron precisely because it is the simplest example.) The electron is in-its-own-right, in fact, that which it is. Other things are in-their-own-right in physics itself and have a most extraordinary fleetingness: hence any of the mesons or baryons that are recorded in the production of particles in a cyclotron.[35] But be that as it may, if the object in question were not in-its-own-right what it is, it would be evanescent and would not be anything.

Now, in the vital dynamism it is provisionally a question of an in-its-own-right taken as a dynamism, that is, *giving of itself.* The same happens also to all realities, since all of them (as I have insistently tried to set down) are active by themselves. It is the formal characteristic of every dynamism, of all causality. The in-its-own-right is, therefore, an in-its-own-right consisting of *giving of itself.* Now, what is proper and specific to a living being lies precisely in the way it gives of itself. The living being is the reality whose structures give of themselves, that is, in a dynamic way. When the in-its-own-right becomes a self [*mismo*], the giving of itself consists of selfhood [*mismidad*]. But when the in-its-own-right becomes plenary, and this happens in the open essence, that is, in the human, then the dynamism rises a degree.

134

9

The Dynamism of Self-Possession

Introduction

The problem to be studied now is the appearance of the human being in the zoological scale. Leaving aside plants and taking the animal series, we see that the advance of the evolution of life is, as I said, progressive in formalization. That character belongs not only to the arousal of sense receptors but also to the actions of the responding effectors and to the inner vital tone of the living being. In virtue of this, it keeps on creating those formal divisions that constitute the independence of things, of actions with respect to things of the medium, and of the aspects of the vital tone on the inside of a living being. (I used the example of the crab.)[1]

The animal achieves this formalization to a very rich degree. But there comes the point where formalization rises a degree and changes into hyperformalization. This happens when formalization in an animal reaches such a degree that the range of responses aroused into action is not assured by the proper structures of the animal; they do not guarantee the adequacy of the response.

In that case, the human being, a hyperformalized animal, performs a very trivial and very elementary operation, but one in which there is a fabulous innovation in the universe, which is precisely taking cognizance of reality. Hyperformalization constitutes precisely that animal which takes cognizance of reality so that it may continue the stability of the species.

To take cognizance of reality provisionally means that things are no longer a mere stimulus but present themselves as something "in-its-own-right." This does not happen to the nonhuman animal. Things are in-their-own-right and that animal is in-its-own-right. But in the process of stimulating, these things do not function as beings in-their-own-right but merely as simple stimulations as such. On the contrary, in the case of the human, the primary and radical characteristics of things consist precisely of being reality. The most trivial stimulus for a child only a few hours old (although the child, needless to say, could not articulate it thus) is sensed by the child as a reality that is in-its-own-right. As a result of this property, the *medium* changes into something completely different. It does not change into a set of things derived from a few stimulant systems but into something different: the immense, the indefinite field of reality, which is what we call the "world."

In taking cognizance of reality, by virtue of that function, the human being is not presented things as a medium but as a world. In other words, from the start the human being is radically and constitutively an *open essence,* open precisely to the character of the reality of things.[2] This essence is not enclosed in a class, hinging on the quality of stimuli, but is open, at least in principle, to the reality of things, and needless to say, open to its own reality. This essence does not give its responses only in virtue of the particularity of arousals, but gives those responses by taking cognizance of reality and of what is really happening to itself. Structurally, the human being, as I put it, is an animal of realities.

Now, being an animal of realities implies a major consequence for substantivity. Substantivity is not then limited to being something in-its-own-right, but the character of reality is lived in the actions that this living human being performs, this hyperformalized animal, this animal of realities. By virtue of what it is, reality is not simply something that is functioning in life, but something for which purpose life is functioning.

Open to itself as reality, the substantivity of the human being is not only in-its-own-right but is a special form of in-its-own-right which consists of being "its own" [*suya*]. It is not the same to be one's own as to be in-one's-own-right. All realities are in-their-own-right. Only the human reality, at least only open essences, are realities that are their own besides being in-their-own-right. Being one's own is precisely what we call the "person."

This is the true substantivity, the radical substantivity. The human being is *structurally* the animal of realities; *modally* it is "its own" reality: the person.[3] All other substantivities that I have been setting down appear in evolution as a primordium ever closer to this substantivity of the hyperformalized animal, which is the human being, which is the person. The person is an open essence. It is an essence open before all and above all to its own reality (and thereby it is a person), and it is open within that reality to the reality of the other things precisely qua real.

Therefore, openness modifies precisely the character of "in itself" that the human reality has. All other essences—I have called them "closed" essences— are closed because they are in themselves, in-their-own-right, what they are.

But the human being is open to its own character of reality. Now, this openness is not the radical part, as if the structures of the in-itself were the existential precipitate of what happens in life. No, nor is the openness a kind of problematic addendum that happens to the human living being. Rather, openness is a *structural modification of structures that the human being, human reality, possesses in themselves.*

In fact, take the case of intelligence, which in the final analysis is the radical expression of this state of being. Intelligence is something that the human has in itself. Mine is different from others', and others' differ from mine, etc., at least in number. Saint Thomas thought that everyone born has qualitatively the same intelligence, and that each is distinguished only numerically, and that the other differences come to each from the body. Be that as it may, he attributes the difference to other factors like education, it is clear.[4] Saint Thomas could not attribute it to the third factor, which is precisely history. Once these intelligences are constituted, they are evidently a property of each of us. Yet, by virtue of that property we are open precisely to *everything* that we are not ourselves.

Intelligence is *one* note of what the human is "in itself." But as a transcendental function, this note opens us to the *totality* of reality qua reality.

Precisely as a transcendental function we have intelligence as an open essence, completely different from closed essence. Now, in this open essence the opening is a *modification* of the structures the human subject, the human reality, possesses in itself. Human reality is something in itself that in itself is open. Openness, consequently, represents and constitutes a *mode of the in-itself.*

Now, this means that when open essences arise in the bosom of the universe, in the radical respectivity [referentiality] comprising the universe, it is a mode of arising that will be a modification of the mode of how closed essences arise. It is a *modification of that evolution,* but strict evolution. It arises through a definite evolution. This evolution does not consist simply of a passage from the stability of matter to a reality that acquires a selfhood in this evolution. It is something more radical: it is a selfhood that continues being the same but settles smoothly into being a person. Here it is a question of the passage from selfhood to the personalization of life.

This personalization, this being a person, consists precisely of being one's own. If I may be allowed the clumsy expression "one's own-ness" [*suidad*] to make myself understood more rapidly, I shall say that the problem to be faced is just that of the dynamic and encompassing transition from selfhood to "one's own-ness" or self-possession. This is the *dynamism* of self-possession.

To treat this problem it is necessary to face two issues: the first is, How does an open essence arise in evolution in the bosom of closed essences, in the intrinsic and formal respectivity of closed essences? The second is, What is the structure of the dynamism of self-possession?

First Question: The Evolutionary Origin of Open Essence

It is an undeniable fact—we all know it, clearly—that the human being appears in fact as an evolution within the zoological scale of humanoids. These are divided into two branches: some pongids, which pave the way for the great present-day apes—the chimpanzee, the gorilla, etc.; and the hominids, which are not yet human, which became extinct, but in their day gave way precisely to human beings.

The human being thus originated has evolved for a long time, for almost two million years, within the earth's chronology.[5] This development has four basic stages, as is well known.

The first stratum of development is problematic. It is problematic to know if in fact the australopithecines are human or not.[6] It is not incumbent on me to resolve the issue. Whether the australopithecines or the *Homo habilis* of Leaky are in fact the first human beings, after the hominids, or whether they are merely hominids, is something that paleontologists will possibly find out someday through research.[7]

But the other three stages are surely strictly human.

The first is that of archanthropus, archaic man.[8] To the second belong, for instance, the pithecanthropus of Java,[9] the sinanthropus,[10] etc. In the third place, there are the paleoanthropoi,[11] for example, the pre-Neanderthals, Neanderthal man,[12] Mauer's jaw,[13] etc. Finally comes the neoanthropus; the neoanthropoi are human, *Homo sapiens,* properly speaking, with their various varieties: Cro-Magnon man, Grimaldi's man,[14] etc. What is important here is to point out several things.

First, in these evolutionary stages—let us call them that—what is achieved in each is *really something more than varieties* of a single species. They are human species, to be sure, in the sense that I have here defined the human being as an animal of realities having intelligence. In this sense these four types belong to the human species. But does this mean that the four stages are nothing but varieties? That would be capricious to maintain. The varieties are given within a type. To be precise, I believe that if they are not species (as they certainly are not), they are something more than mere varieties. They are *intrinsically different* types of human beings. These types are qualitatively distinct.

They are qualitatively distinct, in the first place, because of their somatic structures. Naturally, the cranial volume, the structure of the cerebral convolutions, the form of their dentition, etc., are not quantitative differences, but for the biologist, and very rightly, they are intrinsic qualitative differences. In addition, though, these differences are psychic. I judge that they are psychic precisely because I have defined the animal psychic makeup precisely in terms of formalization. Now, the qualitative difference of the somatic structures formally imposes a qualitative structure of the psychic makeup, at least the sensitive one, of these human beings. Furthermore, this goes beyond the sensitive. Evidently they have, by virtue of these structures, a different *forma animae* [form of soul]. It is not conceivable that a pithecanthropus would do what a Neanderthal man would, nor that a Neanderthal what a neoanthropus does. There is certainly a genetic step, a transitional step, whose factors (here irrelevant) biology will have to ascertain but which constitute qualitative intrinsic differences, both in the somatic and in the psychic spheres. Not only are they qualitative differences, but also each of these differences, each of the stages, comes from the previous by genetic means and by strictly evolutionary means. Each is a transformation of the preceding. All are animals of realities, intelligent too, but the fact of their being intelligent does not mean that they are rational or that they are to the same degree. In reality the rationality that a pithecanthropus has is minimal, just as is minimal the rationality of a newborn child a few weeks old. Nevertheless, it would be a great error to believe that the child does not exercise its intelligence until its seventh year, for instance; this is absolutely stupid. Intelligence is one thing, and reason as a mode of intelligence another. Therefore, to define the human being as a rational animal is really to say very little. What must be said is that the human being is an animal of intelligence, that is, an animal of realities.

Now, the serious problem is not that of interpreting genetic evolution, that is, the evolutionary genesis of these four stages of humankind. The serious problem lies in primary, radical hominization. How is the human phylum constituted through evolution? We observe the scission between pongids and hominids and within the hominids. But how is the hominization of the hominid constituted so as to change it into a human being? Here two issues must be carefully distinguished.

In the first place, there is the generic question: when the human being appears in the zoological series, is it an evolution? It must be thematically answered that it is, without qualification. The human being, the human phylum, is a rigorous and formal evolution of the hominid, just as the hominid is rigorously and formally an evolutionary branch of all humanoids. Of this there is not the least doubt as long as evolution is understood just as I have here understood it, as the *appearing of specifically new forms, intrinsically determined by precisely intrinsic and formal transformations of that from which the evolution is produced.* There is no room for doubt that changes of the hominid, precisely of the hominid and of no other animal form, univocally determine the appearing of the human. No one could think that a human being could be born from the evolution of a bird. This would be capricious. The human being in the last analysis appears from the evolution of echinoderms.[15] For echinoderms have given the line of vertebrates, and within the line of vertebrates has arisen a branch, which is birds, with scant evolutionary power, and another branch with much power for evolving, which is mammals. From there, in rigorous succession will appear human beings. There is a strict evolution in which all somatic structures are determined precisely by the change of structures, from which is born precisely the new phylum.

In the second place, there is an evolution as far as psychic sensitivity is concerned. No doubt it is precisely transformations of the psychic makeup of the hominid that determine the appearance of the whole rich psychic makeup constituting the human being. First, this holds as concerns sensitivity. It is easy to say that the human being has "a" sensitive life. But these are empty words. It is like saying that the human being has a head. But between the head of a chimpanzee and that of a human being there is a huge difference. Analogously, what psychic sensitivity lies in question? A very precise psychic makeup, one that is the rigorous, formal change of the animal psychic makeup once possessed by the hominid, from which the human phylum is born.[16]

There still remains the other aspect of the psychic makeup. All evolution is innovation in some sense. The innovation (as it undeniably is) of the intelligence in the zoological scale is univocally determined by the changes of the whole series. For in fact the intelligence does not enter into play and does not even appear as a reality until the moment a hyperformalized animal cannot subsist except by taking cognizance of reality. Intelligence, as a consequence, has a biological function before all and above all. Precisely, it stabilizes the species. A species of idiots would not be viable. Intelligence is a biological factor of stabilization of the species, as well as a biological factor of adequate response in each individual.

The mechanism of evolution is a completely different issue. The mechanism is so different that whatever the evolution of the species strictly reveals (up to where science can speak strictly on these themes) leaves as a problem in the dark precisely the mechanism of evolution in every species.

What is the mechanism whereby birds are born from reptiles? Many tests have been made with X-rays, gamma rays, experimental gene mutations, etc., but the results have never been satisfactory. One thing is evolution; another, the mechanism of evolution. They are two completely different things.

Now, when speaking of intelligence entering the zoological scale as an innovation, what is meant, to my way of thinking, is that this innovation must have a different causation. From what? From those elements constituting the respectivity of the world. These elements, generically taken, can be called the "All." They are an All, constitute an All. Only insofar as this All makes way for as much as happens within it, in some form or other it is necessary to put in this All that giving of itself whereby we say it is nature but *natura naturans* [nature producing naturally].[17] Now, what type of causality does this All have, this *natura naturans,* in order to produce precisely the appearance of what is radical innovation in the human being?

That it is radical innovation is undeniable. An intelligence is absolutely, essentially irreducible to the senses, not by reason of somatic complications but for intrinsic, formal reasons. The formality "reality" will never emerge from a complication of realities as stimuli.[18] Being a stimulus never reaches reality as such. An innovation is here at hand. By that I mean that intelligence appears through a *new dynamism of the All.* What is precisely that type of causality?

I myself, often upon explaining this issue, have always insisted on the fact that the example of hominids undergoing hominization offers a case of a required causality. In effect, if the human species in those genetic transformations needs to be a lasting species and intelligence is an innovation on the part of the innovating element. Therefore it has to be a requirement on the part of the human animal. Clearly this is so.

What happens is that this is always a penultimate consideration. Rigorously speaking, it is necessary to say so. It is penultimate because in truth the cosmic All, within which this innovation happens, will need to perform a distinct act of causality to produce an intelligence. The causation will have to differ from the one that was produced to vitalize matter and each of its evolutionary stages. This causality is effectual causality, not merely required causality. The All exercises effectual causality precisely in the production of intelligences and of the human psychic makeup. The innovation does not lie in the exemption from effectual causality of the appearance of the human psychic makeup. It lies in the fact that this effectual causality, on the part of *natura naturans,* is not the same, or at least not a prolongation merely transforming the causality with which that *natura naturans* has produced living beings prior to the human. However, since all of them in short stem from a single dynamism, which is just the dynamism of the cosmic All, of *natura naturans,* it is necessary to say that the human being is a moment of that dynamism of the All and of *natura naturans* in the rigorous sense of the terms.

Certainly this causality is not an addendum, something simply added on to animal evolution. On the contrary, it is a continuation of animal evolution, the required fulfillment of a hyperformalization that would not succeed in achieving stability except by innovating with intelligence. But it is necessary to say, further, that this action of the All, this causality, is just an *intrinsic* causality. In other words, it does not operate from without, but is precisely the reality that in its own respectivity makes what we call "intelligences" emerge. Certainly if we could visually witness the minutious development of germinal plasma from conception until when it performs, after being born, the first more or less intelligent act of a child, we would see no interruption at all. We would see how intelligence flourishes precisely from its structures. This is not a vague metaphor. The scientist having no reason to go into these questions may say that, strictly speaking, intelligence arises precisely from animality and in animality. Now, if this belongs to the competence of science, what does not belong to its competence is to say whether or not intelligence is essentially different from sensitivity. This is another issue. But what I say here is that the new causality of the cosmic All is a causality intrinsic to what came before, it is an inner causality.

For in fact the origin of open essences is just the fulfillment of all that has been the origination and development of closed essences comprising the universe. Evolutionary dynamism concerns the All; it is respectivity active by itself. The origin of open essences lies in the All. In the final analysis, it is the same All that in the first place is to acquire precisely its inner selfhood in closed essences, and it is the All that is opening itself precisely to something different, to being "its own" as a transcendental function. Therefore open essences are a modification of closed essences.

Here evolution achieves a new type of respectivity: respectivity "in openness." (I already know some reader is frowning, because it occurs to me to say that the psychic makeup is a product of the All. Naturally. What I have not said is what the All is. This is a different issue. But it is not my issue. Here I am doing metaphysics from within the world. I have no reason to concern myself, naturally, about objections crossing the furrowed brow of some reader while reading what I have written. But resolve the objection as one may, it will always be true that that cosmic All is what produces the human psychic makeup.)

Open essences are a modification of closed essences, and this is an evolution in which reality enters a different stage. It is a new respectivity, one "in openness." As a transcendental function, this elevation means *in the first place* that reality opens to itself, to its own character of reality. In other words, there is an evolution toward the transcendental function to which reality, insofar as it is reality, is open in one form or other to reality.

In the second place, this openness happens in each of us, in each person. It would be capricious to argue that the All of reality was a kind of great ocean of reality that goes on evolving somewhat à la Hegel.[19] This is completely capricious. Psychic makeups and intelligences are rigorously personal, each is "its own," each in a limited way, but authentic and real. Reality precisely opens toward itself in its character of reality. In this sense it is not a question in this evolution only of the self-opening of reality in its transcendental aspect, but of that opening happening in a personal form. It is the personalization of life.

In the third place, I say that this opening has its own dynamism. It is precisely the dynamism of self-possession [*suidad*]. Reality, upon becoming "hyper-itself" [*hipermisma*], inexorably becomes "its own" [*suya*].

In evolution reality has become "self" [*misma*], and in the evolutionary line this selfhood becomes decurrent, causal, and formalized. One more step, and life becomes *hyperformalized,* and therefore *hyper-self.* In transcendental form this evolution is the advance of reality that becomes self and hyper-self.[20] But of what does this dynamism consist?

Second Question: Structure of the Dynamism of Self-Possession

The advance of life does not end in the animal. The animal keeps on integrally enriching its life, both in its psychological aspect and in its somatic aspect. Its life is enriched not only by a relatively sparse specification of qualities that the animal can perceive but especially by the different grades of formalization. In virtue of these grades, things present themselves as being more or less independent of others or else as forming autonomous units for the animal, though always as stimuli in form.

Now, the moment arrives in which life, in its progressive advance, becomes hyperformalized. In this degree of hyperformalization, we find a great difference when we compare it with the formalization of the animal, even the richest. In the animal, however rich the range of adequate responses it can give to a single arousal by reason of its formalization, in principle the adequate character of these responses is more or less guaranteed by its structures. On the contrary, in the hyperformalized animal that is the human being this does not occur. The human being, to give an adequate response, has to perform a *different* operation, which amounts to taking cognizance of reality. Here a note proper to the human animal becomes active, of which there is no formal presence in the animal series: intelligence. Intelligence is the human capacity to face things qua realities, in contrast to what happens to the animal, even the most formalized, that has access to things only as stimuli. Reality and mere stimulation are the two great formalities.

Naturally when I speak of the formality of reality, I do not refer to the human being as being a kind of itinerant metaphysician. It is not a question of that. I refer to the fact that the most modest of the stimulations that the human being receives is, at a certain level of personal existence and reality, sensed and perceived as a stimulating reality or a real stimulus. By reason of this, I say that the human being is an animal of realities.

As an animal of realities, he is a new essence by virtue of his intelligence. Certainly this new essence is born in the bosom of matter and as a function of matter, with matter here understood to mean concretely the essences of animals. But there is no doubt at all that in this case, as in all cases of evolution, there is an innovation, and this is the most radical case: it is a qualitative innovation with its own dynamism.

I will analyze this dynamism in four successive steps.

First Step: The Open Essence Is a New Type

The first step is based on considering how an open essence is in fact an essence of a new type.

Structurally, the open essence, the human being, possesses a note, which is intelligence as a capability for apprehending things qua realities. Naturally this is an absolutely new structure. However many turns and complications we could give to the order of stimuli, we could never succeed in making a stimulus over into a reality. In the same way, however many turns could be given to a sound, never will it succeed in being presented as a color. This cannot happen. There is, therefore, an essential difference between the human essence, which possesses intelligence, and animal essences, which, as rich as they may be, nonetheless do not. This does not mean in any way that there is interruption and discontinuity. The mere fact that the human being begins sensing reality as a stimulating reality indicates clearly enough the total, integral continuity that the human essence has with animal essences.

Modally, this structure, which is a new structure with respect to animal structures, that is, a structure possessing among its constitutive notes one that is intelligence, implies a unique mode of dynamism. This unique mode of dynamism, on which I will concentrate later, will serve to reveal still more deeply the special character of the structure for which that dynamism is a dynamism.

In the first place, it is a question of an open essence. Open to what? For in one form or another the animal is also open, open to stimuli (and this certainly does not happen to plants). But the human being is open to the character of reality. In the first place, to what reality?

I go back to my point of departure: taking cognizance of the situation. The first thing that taking cognizance of the situation requires is considering where the one taking cognizance is located and what the real character is of the situation posed to it. That to which, *primo et per se* [first and by itself], the intelligent essence lies open is just its own character of reality. In this openness to its own character of reality is congenerically given the openness to the character of reality of all real things qua reality.

Viewed as a particular, this open essence has a note that animals do not have: intelligence. Consequently, it would seem that between the human essence and the other essences there is no more than a merely particular difference. That is not so. For every essence considered as particular has a transcendental function; that is, by the mere fact of being the essence that it is, it determines a mode of reality, a type of reality. Determining a type of reality by its particularity is proper to every essence. In one way or another it is a transcendental function. But in the case of intelligence this has a complication. In fact the human being, by virtue of intelligence, is a *mode* of reality, clearly, as an orangutan or a chimpanzee can be one. By virtue of a note that is its own, intelligence, a type of reality is constituted.

As an essence in itself, the human essence as a transcendent function determines a type of reality, the reality proper to an intellective essence. But what is unique lies in the fact that this type of reality is not only the reality *proper* to intelligence, but is the *reality of everything as such*. For intelligence, open to its own reality, is for that reason open to *reality as such*. The transcendent function of intelligence embraces every reality *as such*.

In the transcendental function we find, then, that open essence is precisely a type of reality: that type of reality in which reality *simpliciter* [without qualification] and *as such* enters really into itself or opens to itself.

Hence the peculiar situation of the human living being.

The human living being, like animal living beings, begins by being *placed*, though not set-in-place [*in-colocado*]. For it to be set-in-place, it would have to be a completely different type of living being. Not even angels escape from being somehow placed (although this is merely a guess). The human being, the living human animal, the open essence that is the human being, is in fact placed. Placed in what or among what? That is the problem.

When we return to the animal, we see that it is in fact placed in a medium within which there is a series of things that stimulates it in a more or less rich and complex way. Certainly the human being shares this property with the animal. The human being is placed *among* things. But the things in which the human being is placed in reality are present to him not only in their definite particularity, insofar as they are stimuli, but also insofar as they are reality. This means that in spite of being placed *among* things where he is placed and installed at the same time, the human being is *in reality*. This is something different.

The animal is situated and placed among things. Human placement with respect to the things is not the same; the *among* belonging to things has, in the case of the human being, a very precise transcendental function: it places the human being *in* reality. Hence the medium, as a transcendental function, acquires a completely different character: it is not a medium, properly speaking, but a *world,* that is, a system of realities qua realities.

The life of a human being, I repeat, like that of all animals, consists of *possessing itself.* In other words, it does not consist precisely of the emergence of vital motion from some structures, but just the reverse: the structures implied in vital movement may be in such a form that these structures cannot continue being the same unless they perform or bring about a series of actions whereby the substantivity of the structures really is always retained and preserved. In the human being we always find the same structure. It certainly consists of self-possession exactly the same as the animal. It performs actions needed for keeping the substantivity of its structures. But, since the human being is what it is in reality, placed precisely *in* reality, consequently the human being achieves self-possession not only in the sense of keeping individual structures intact, but in a different sense: it maintains itself in the sense of preserving and defining the substantivity allotted to it as a reality in the midst of reality. This is something completely different and new. Therefore, self-possession does not mean simply to continue being the self, which is what happens to the animal, but *being one's own reality.* Human substantivity is eo ipso a person. "Person" means just being "one's own" [*suyo*]. It is not simply being "in-one's-own-right" [*de suyo*]. In-their-own-right are all real things: being real consists of that. But only reality open to its own reality is the reality that reduplicatively and formally is not only in-its-own-right but is its own as well.

Using the expression "self-possession" [*suidad*], I shall say that self-possession, self-preservation and self-affirmation as self-possession, is just the peculiar mode of self-possession of what comprises being a person. Hence it is possible to say and must be said that reality in the zoological scale, when it becomes hyperformalized, becomes hyper-self. This *hyper* means in this case to become one's own. It is the passage through the hyper-selfhood of selfhood to the self-possession of which the person consists. Selfhood passes to self-possession. This self-possession certainly has at least three constitutive forms.

In the first place, since the human person finds itself simply with one or several things, this person is not only surrounded by things that arouse it in a certain way, it also has that small coefficient that the animal lacks, which is the *myself.* It feels *itself* in good health, it feels *itself* ailing; it is the form of the *myself*—personally itself. Many languages, Greek for instance, express it in the middle voice. English well translates the middle voice with the word "myself" by saying, "I have bought *myself* an apple," "I have taken *myself* for a walk," etc.

That *myself* represents just the middle voice, which is the primary and radical way with which the human being is formally its own in the acts of its life.

Yet the human being does not simply exist among things, but as soon as its world gets organized (or at least the things composing this world), the human being feels itself the center of them. Just then that "myself" turns into something different, which is a "to me" [*mí*], constitutively based on a "myself."

When those things not only are those real things, but the human being confronts the real things qua realities in the totality of reality, then it acquires the character of an "I" [*Yo*].

The "I" is grounded on the "to Me." The "to Me" is grounded on the "Myself." Each form supposes the prior. This unity is not a stratified unity, but a dynamic unity. Each one of the moments dynamically subtends the following term.[21] There is a moment in which the "myself" cannot feel itself to be a *myself* except by knowing itself and feeling itself to be a *to me*. The *to me* cannot, in a certain moment, be itself except by being subtended in the form of "I." Each term or each moment dynamically subtends the following term.

These three moments consequently have a primary and radical unity. The unity consists of being the unity of a *second act*: it is the *reactualization of my own reality* qua mine in each of the acts that I perform as a reality in my life.[22] This reactualization is the *being of the substantive reality*. This being, expressed in the "me," in the "to me," and in the "I," is not my reality but the actuality of my reality in each of the acts of my life. It is not a being set in independence of the reality. The being of substantive reality consists of reverting by identity to the reality of which it is the second act. That reversion in identity is what I have called "intimacy" in the metaphysical sense.

The progressive advance of life as an internalization flows, in the open essence, into an intimacy—something lacking in animals. Hence, self-possession, which consists in the animal of continuing to be the self [*el mismo*] by doing what it must do, in the case of human intimacy acquires a new nuance. The animal is only the self by never being the same. This is certain, for life consists of it. Now, in the open essence *the* self is the person. The acts that it performs not only attest to the human being as a subject producing them, but there is something deeper: in fact these acts are its own; here the moment of self-possession [*suidad*] intervenes. They are, consequently, subsequent moments of the substantive part of its own being. With this they configure the being of the substantive part. I not only speak but am articulate. The being of the substantive part is precisely the "I." It is not the person; it is something different: the *personality* that it is acquiring.

So as not to confuse concepts, I decided to apply the name "personhood" [*personeidad*] to the person in the sense that I have used the word up to now. On the contrary, "personality" [*personalidad*] is just the figure of being of the substantive part that this person is acquiring in the inexorable exercise of the acts of its life.[23]

Personality, I say, is the figure proper to my being, but to my being as reverting in fact over the essential structures of which it is the second act. The open essence is the person; as a consequence, it includes in one form or another that moment of the second act of reversion by identity to the first act: the personality insofar as it is precisely the second act, the intimate act of the person, of the *personhood* in the first act.

Therefore self-possession is not simply, in the case of the human being, continuation in being the self and never being the same; rather, it is concretely the continuation of being the person by configuring itself anew as a personality at every instant.

The person cannot be what it is (in the case of the human being) except by personalizing itself, that is, by giving of itself as a person something that is a personality. The dynamism of self-possession [*suidad*] is nothing but the dynamism of personalization.

This is the second step; what is this dynamism of personalization?

Second Step: Dynamism Is Making Possible

Human beings perform the acts of their lives with things, with other human beings, and with themselves. This "with" (*with* things, *with* the other human beings, *with* myself) is not an addition, an extrinsic relationship added to human beings in the exercise of their lives. That would be absolutely capricious. It is something much more radical. The "with" is a formal structural moment of life itself, and therefore of human substantivity in its vital dynamism. Respectivity is not a relational addition to each thing in respectivity, but is the inner, intrinsic, and formal structure of each of the substantivities. In the same way, analogously, the moment of the "with" is an intrinsic, formal moment of the structure of life, and therefore of the human dynamism as such. But human beings not only perform actions with other things, with other human beings, and with themselves, but they perform their actions from themselves. The *with* is a formal structural moment of substantivity as life. Yet the problem always remains open as to what that "me myself" is as something "from" which I execute my life. Naturally the "from" is not a relationship extrinsic to me myself. Nor is it a structural moment of my substantivity as life. It is something much deeper. It is a formal structural moment of the "me myself" as such.

Hence the dynamism of personalization implies these two dynamic aspects: First: personalization from the viewpoint of the "with."

Second: personalization from the viewpoint of the "from."

That something with which human beings precisely make their lives and perform the dynamism of self-possession [*suidad*] is something that has a structure of *meaning* with respect to the person and with respect to the life that each human being performs with things. It is a *meaning*.

Precisely because it is a meaning, things acquire a unique character as meaning with respect to life. *In the first place,* they are, they provisionally have the character of *insistences.*[24] They urge on the human being, who cannot avoid performing a vital act. *In the second place,* not only can the human not avoid performing a vital act, it must also perform it by having recourse to those things and to the self in the manner of resources. Resource-insistence is the first formal structure of meaning as such.

Now, reality must not be confused with meaning; they are completely different things.

When we perceive, for example, some walls, certainly these walls have, if we are in a house, the character of a room. But this is not primary. In perception, a reality in its naked reality, qua reality, is what is really perceived. It is quite a different thing that at any moment and by any mechanism—I need not go into detail—this reality has a meaning. For example, its being a "lecture hall" has nothing to do with naked reality. The naked reality of this room acts through its notes, and in them there is no character of a room. There is a form, there is a weight, there are some colors, some electromagnetic vibrations, a density of matter, etc., and therefore it is naked reality for what it is. The moment of reality as such never includes being a room. The moment of reality as such of a knife does not imply cutting, but does imply a blade, a certain density, etc., yet by no means the act of cutting, for example, at a table in order to eat.

For this reason I have always distinguished between *naked* reality—among the things that I call "naked reality"—things that have reality purely, and "meaning-things" [*cosas-sentido*]. Meaning does not shunt the reality-thing to one side, although meaning and reality-thing may completely differ from one another. Those walls of my example are completely indifferent to constituting a room in which someone is present. On the contrary, those within them are not indifferent to the real properties of these walls, without which there would clearly be no room.

Consequently, there is a radical difference, but such that meaning is constitutively mounted on real properties.

I am going to consider that meaning from two angles: one, facing the human being for whom it is meaning; the other, facing naked reality.

From the angle facing the human being, I said that the *with* does not constitute a relational appendage added to the structure of life and the human being, but is an intrinsic, formal, and constitutive moment belonging to that individual as a living being. This means that essentially and constitutively life is life *with* . . . things. Things, insofar as they are meaning-things, are something *that* constitutively belongs *to* the life for which they are meaning-things.

Just this being a "note-of" (in some form or other) is what I have called a "construct."[25] That basis upon which meaning is constituted as such-and-such a meaning for the human being is just the quality of being a construct of naked reality with the life of the human.

Meaning is the construct of reality with human life.

Now to take the case from the other angle, on the side facing reality, naked reality, to be sure, I have already said that it is a matter of complete indifference to naked reality whether or not it is a meaning-thing. This is evident. That a mountain hollow is a cavern and a room for a human being is a matter of indifference to the geological phenomenon. But if the human being with pretensions of making artificial things sought to make a door out of smoke, that could not be done. This means that not all things possess the same capacity to have a definite meaning. In addition, it will be a problem to ascertain whether every thing, because it is a thing, in fact has any meaning. This means that in naked reality, despite the complete independence and difference of meaning at least from naked reality, nonetheless, once a definite meaning is posited, evidently, it is the reality that either has or does not have that meaning. This is just what I call the "condition": the capacity reality has for being constituted into meaning. Naturally, the condition in a construct form belongs to things—it is theirs; they are things that *remain* in a definite condition when the human wishes to perform definite actions in life.

Meaning is grounded constitutively on condition.

Insistences and resources are grounded precisely on the condition, that is, on the capacity that reality has for being constituted into meaning.

But the condition is not sufficient for there to be an action. For with the same things that surround us, each having a meaning and all in a certain unitary sense, we could all do very different things. In other words, it not enough that there is meaning for actions of life to be determined. With the same things it is possible to do different things, different actions.

Now, the different actions that could be performed with the meaning-things surrounding us in each situation are provisionally what we call "possibility." There are different possibilities: the possibility of getting together to talk, the possibility of dancing, the possibility of being quiet while reading books, etc. They are possibilities. On the subject of these possibilities I say it is useless to attempt to empty the concept of possibility, as great inventors of labels would tend to do by precisely distinguishing ends and means. Possibility is something radical. There can be no difference nor constitution of ends or of means in the midst of a possibility. Possibility is the primary, radical structure within which there can be finality and mediation. Consequently, on my adhering to the notion of possibility as such, I will try to answer the question, What are those possibilities?

Aristotle, I repeat, spoke of possibility, of δύναμις, in two different senses: on the one hand, δύναμις is the potency, the capacity that someone has for acting upon another qua other.[26] In other words, if he acts on himself it is insofar as he is different from himself. But Aristotle added in a different passage that there is another meaning to the word δύναμις, that is for instance the one referring not to the potency that one has of acting upon another, but to the character of a reality that is only potentially contained in another reality.[27] One example is the oak tree, which is not actual while there are nothing but acorns. Another example is the life of mammals, which was not actual in the Precambrian era yet nevertheless there were genetic potentialities for producing them.[28] They were in potency. They were δυνάμει ὄν [a being in potency].

Are these two meanings of the word "potency" sufficient to apprehend conceptually what possibility is, the possibilities of a life? In what follows I will point out the reasons for their insufficiency.

In the first place, when we speak of possibilities—I face the problem head-on without looking sideways at Aristotle—we find that that word is always used in the plural. In other words, there is never an isolated possibility. For even were there only a single possibility, one could opt for accepting or rejecting it or else for committing suicide. In other words, possibility always implies a plural moment: a plurality of possibilities in a single situation.

In the second place, for these possibilities to be possibilities they have to be possibilities not simply of doing such and such a thing, *insofar as such,* but of doing such and such a thing *insofar as real,* that is, insofar as I am defining a reality. It is in relation to reality as such, in which all possibilities are constituted, and only in this relationship. The animal can have a gamut, a more or less rich keyboard of keys that it can play for a response. These are not possibilities. Possibilities are possessed only by human beings, because human beings face reality as such. This is also precisely because the multiple possibilities acquire the status of possibilities in view of the reality as such of which each human being consists, and which that human being affirms in the acts of his life.

Now, given that they are plural, that several possibilities fit in the same situation, and furthermore that they are possibilities in relation to reality and not simply in the particular, to say more concretely what the possibilities are it is previously necessary to answer two questions:

First: What is the object of those possibilities? That is the question.

Aristotle speaks of the δυνάμει ὄν [a being in potency] in the example cited, or of the δύναμις as an active potency. But in both these cases Aristotle always contrasts potency with act. It can be said that this contrast is obvious. This is certain whenever it does not turn out that the concept of "act" is ambiguous. What is meant by "act"? In the case of any living being—a dog, a cat—not only in the case of a human being, what is meant by "act"? Plainly, the act would be the actuation of a potency. This may be so, but what is called a potency in that case? The capacity for producing a definite act? That is, we once more enter into a vicious circle, and to get out of it we would have to say concretely, for example, that a potency is the capacity that the stomach cells of a cat have to digest whatever comes inside it, etc. That capacity is divided into each of the cells, and in each of the cells into each of the structural moments comprising the cell. We would then hold that potency in the Aristotelian sense is referred to the act as a determination of a potency in this very concrete sense I have just recounted a bit descriptively. They are the potency of acts. It would be all the same in this case to call these acts "functions." The act proper to a muscle fiber is to contract, given its spiral structure. I suppose that since the time of Szent-Györgyi, who discovered it,[29] this conception probably has not changed much. Plainly there is dehydration, and the fiber contracts in a spiral, and this is a muscular contraction. This is the act of a potency.

Now, there is another sense of the word "act" in which there is no allusion to acts taken in this sense, which would be functions—for example, the function of muscular fiber to contract under certain conditions in a definite way. No; there is an allusion to the act in the sense of action—for example, a dog fleeing or giving chase, a man walking or running away to escape something. These acts surely are acts, but in the sense of actions. There is a *deep difference between an act and an action.*

Action is composed of all the functions and all the acts, but in a different form.

With the same functions that come into play when breaking into a run to escape a threatening danger or someone pursuing us, with those very functions it is possible to take a walk. There would continue to be certain muscular structures, the nervous system would go to work to impose a certain transmission of the stimulus, a certain rhythm, and certain self-reactivating circuits, etc., the same in one case as in the other. Nevertheless, these are different actions.

An act is not the same as an action. An action is a functional system, a functional system of acts, a system in the strict sense. It is what makes the Aristotelian concept of δύναμις [potency] insufficient to apprehend possibilities. For the object for which the possibilities are possibilities is not an act but an action. As a result, the concept of δύναμις has to undergo a modification on the rebound.

In fact, the second question to which it would be necessary to respond is, Whose are those possibilities?

The Aristotelian conception reappears: the δυνάμεις [potencies] are precisely the δυνάμεις that emerge from a substance considered especially as a substantial form. (It would evidently be a matter of indifference whether we took prime matter instead.)[30] Actions do not emerge from the substance in that form, but actions are proper to the whole substantivity. It is the whole animal that structurally and systematically enters into each action. In the same way that its substantivity is a structural unity of the notes composing it, so its actions are a functional system of acts that each of those functions performs, and each of its actions is constituted by its systematic unity.

Possibilities are possibilities for certain complete actions proper to the substantivity as such.

Actions are dynamic systems. This indicates to us that *what should be understood by "possibility"* is not exactly a system of δυνάμεις, of potencies emerging from a substance to act on another reality or on itself considered as other. Neither are these potencies potential being, δυνάμει ὄν (in this case reality does not enter into potency).[31] It is a question of there being something completely different and more elementary: *substantivity itself and its situation as a resource for its actions.* The idea of resource is what formally constitutes the character of possibility as such: the resources that substantivity finds in each situation. I refer to resources of things, *in the first place,* and to resources for actions, *in the second;* I repeat: the subject exercises them *from itself.* This means that its own nature intervenes as a resource for some possibilities in a very definite form. Its nature is not a system of natural givens that it possesses but something different: it is a system of gifts on which it counts. Precisely the complete system of resources is constituted in the form of gifts from my own character and from the resources that things present. They are resources for some actions that are actions of a substantivity. For a substantivity, precisely that situation of availability that reality has with a view to taking action is just what formally constitutes the formal reason of possibility. Here it is not the δύναμις [potency] for the act or function, but it is my own personal substantivity as a resource for my personality.

This has been the second step, that is, the definition of the possibilities of open essence with which the dynamism of self-possession unfolds.

Third Step: Causal Openness to One's Own Personality

The third step is that of entering somewhat into this dynamism.

With these possibilities of human substantivity the person opens causally to its own personality. How?

This question "How?" unites different dimensions.

In the first place, *the dimension that faces the things themselves.*

With things constituted as possibilities, as resources, every possibility implies a dynamic moment whereby, insofar as it is possibility, it does not simply urge the performance of an action—that would be a derivative thing—but something deeper and more radical. In fact the possibilities are limited and furthermore circumscribe the range of actions that the human being can perform in a given situation, undeniably forcing the human to opt for one of them. Now, this force that possibilities, resources, impose on the human being has an absolutely concrete name: it is power, *Macht* in German. It is a *power*.

Power is not of itself an efficient cause.[32] As an efficient cause, seemingly the nutriments or the things surrounding us have their physical efficiency in the form of gravity, in biophysical form, etc. Further, they have a causality of a completely different order, one related to the line of possibility. They are power.

While causality, understood in the sense of a causality we would classically call "efficient," as I have considered in previous pages, is the *functionality* of the real qua real, here we find we have the dominant character of the real qua real. The dominance of reality qua reality is precisely, to my way of thinking, what constitutes a power, *Macht* in German. It is a different thing from a force, *Kraft* in German.[33]

Certainly this functionality of power, as I have just pointed out, cannot be a potency in the Aristotelian sense of the word. But it is rigorously speaking a power. The difference from causality is based precisely on what I have just pointed out: it is not a question of something proper to reality as such, in its naked reality, but to the character or function of dominance that it has *in this case* with respect to this open essence that is the human being.[34]

Every possibility is a possibility in relation to reality as such; every power is inserted just within the reality considered as a power, whence arises, naturally, the power of the real. Therefore I said that in the final analysis there is nothing exempt from the condition of being in some form or other, or exempt from being able to be constituted in meaning. For what the meaning of all meanings is, the construct of all constructs, and the condition of all conditions, the power of all powers, is just the power of the real qua real.

The human being is moved, determined, always by the power of the real qua real. This power, because it is what it is, is an *ultimate* power. Further, it is a power that in fact constitutes the ultimate and supreme resource of every reality that *makes possible*. Further, it urges on the human being, it is *urgent* about making him perform some actions, that is, about his having to choose a concrete system of possibilities within the power of the real.

In the second place, what I have said applies to things, resources with which the human being is going to perform actions. But will these be performed on the part of the human being? For it does not suffice that the resources are present.

Dynamism on the part of the human being is a strictly dynamic causality with its own structure. It is what I call "appropriation." Causality in relation to possibility is appropriation on the part of the human being. Human beings appropriate some possibilities and undo others. They bring about an appropriation. Therefore I do not use the word "volition," because if it were a question of will, as I have said once before, I would have to say that what formally constitutes the terminus of a volition is the appropriating or nonappropriating of certain possibilities.[35] If one wants to use the word "volition," so be it. But in a rigorous and strict way, causality on the part of the human being vis-à-vis the possibilities that realities offer the human on the part of the real is just the causality of an appropriation.

Now, in the third place, that appropriation of possibilities has a consequence: in this appropriation is how possibilities are actualized in things and realities through the intrinsic power the possibilities have. My appropriation confers power on a possibility, and annuls (or at least leaves bracketed) the power of possibilities not appropriated but rejected. As a consequence, there is a moment in the appropriation whereby the power of the possibility takes possession of the human being, and that is *empowerment*.

In causal appropriation, the human being has power and is constitutively empowered by what it does. The actualization of possibility has a form, which is empowerment. Now, this actualization is certainly the actuality of something that in fact is proper to the naked reality, the substantivity of the human; and in this sense it could be said that it is only a *fact*. However true this may be, if by "actuality" is meant the actuality of a possibility, then the thing changes its aspect. I have said that possibility is not precisely potency in the Aristotelian sense of the word. If we apply the word "fact" to the actuality or to the act of a potency, we cannot apply the same word to the act of a possibility. We will call it something else; I have called it an "event" or a "happening." An event or happening is not the same as a fact. Human life is not composed of facts but of events. Certainly there are many facts in human life, but they do not constitute a moment of life if they are not reabsorbed in the form of events.

The person is not its own except in the empowerment of reality through an event. Reality becomes the person's in the second act, in each of the substantivities, through empowerment.

Fourth Step: The Empowerment of Possibilities

The fourth step consists of clarifying how in fact the dynamism of personalization is the empowerment of possibilities. The dynamism of self-possession is the *dynamism of personalization* through empowerment. I will explain.

In the first place, there reappears here the dualism against which I defended myself at the start of the chapter, the dualism between structures of the naked substantivity of the human being, and the human being's subsequent act, the second act, the being of its substantive part.

I said that certainly the being of the substantive part is not independent of reality but to the contrary: reality reaffirms itself in its being in the form of intimacy. But now I must add that, in turn, the reality of the human being inexorably flows into the affirmation of its being.

Hence, first, personalization *does not leave structures outside itself,* but absorbs them into a selfhood. To be specific, the human being, like any animal, is never the same. But this mode of not-being-the-same is absorbed into something subsequent. The unity of the being of the substantive part is absorbed, in the case of the human, by a being of the substantive part that has the form of an "I." Selfhood is absorbed into self-possession. But this being of the substantive part is always and only a subsequent act. The subsequent quality of the being of the substantive part is just the dynamism of selfhood, just as selfhood was based on the dynamism of change, and this dynamism on the dynamism of variation. Nevertheless, just as in the case of an animal, in this dynamism the human person is never the same.

Now, in the second place, the question is this: What, formally, is this "not" of "not-being-the-same" of a human person in its personality?

That empowerment, that appropriation in which empowerment happens and the event is constituted, is what constitutes the personal response of the human being in the acts of its life. That empowerment has to choose in one form or another among definite possibilities that the resources offer it. It even has to have begun, in some form or another, to invent which things could be done with those resources.

Hence empowerment implies precisely a dynamic moment prior to the empowerment as such, which is the projection, the project. *Every possibility is an inchoate project.* Now, in the project there is something which, for the moment, is not real, something unreal. To say that the human being constitutes a form of reality that cannot be precisely the self, that cannot possess itself as a person except by becoming personalized, is tantamount to saying, consequently, that human beings, in many dimensions of living, cannot really be what they are unless they pass through the detour of unreality. (I have said this many times for many years.) It is a dynamism in which the human is real by making the detour of unreality in the configuration of personality.

Yet there is more. This dynamism, I said, is the constitution of a gamut of possibilities. But the human has appropriated a possibility and consequently has remained empowered by it. For instance, a human being can decide to be a shoemaker, or a professor, or a stonecutter . . . the human has been empowered by these possibilities. This empowerment not only is distinguished from a *fact* for what I have said, that is, for being the actualization of a possibility as opposed to the act of a pure δύναμις [capacity], but as far as the dynamism of the person as such is concerned, there is a deeper, more profound difference.

In the final analysis, every reality, I said, is emergent. Realities are in emergent respectivity, with one coming out of another. They emerge from whatever will give of itself, and, as a consequence, the reality that is going to give of itself has a capacity—I call it δύναμις [capacity] in this case—for producing something that will give of itself. This is certain, but in the case of the human being, in the case of the possibilities that I am examining, the thing is more radical. For the possibility is grounded on reality, though only insofar as this reality possesses "condition."[36] In naked reality human potencies, δυνάμεις, are grounded. In reality as a condition human possibilities are grounded. But while δυνάμεις [capacities] "spring" from reality, possibilities must be determined by the human being. For this reason human beings are not limited to making an act out of some preexisting possibilities for action (for then the human would be nothing but a heap, a system, a series of facts . . .), but rather they begin precisely by determining for themselves the possibilities to be made into acts. Human beings produce the possibility of reality before producing the reality. Precisely this resembles divine Creation. Therefore I have written from time to time that human life is quasi-creation.[37] It is a quasi-creation because it consists, rather than of producing reality, precisely of producing the possibility that is going to be actualized in the actions of its reality.

The dynamism of self-possession is the dynamism constitutive of possibility as such.

Therefore the *dynamics precisely of this dynamism of self-possession are the dynamics of the project.* The dynamics of the project do not consist of a succession of acts in which different potencies continue to be actualized by virtue of the previous fact. Quite the contrary, it means that, when the human being is empowered by a possibility, once the possibility is constituted, and once the production through quasi-creation has taken place of the eventual endpoint comprising the actuality of that possibility, those actions take place. Yet in the human being, even though actions may be things that have already been, they are not, however, completely past. They decant in the human being a system of resources of which the human can take hold.

Certainly in the historical dimension, human beings of today are not what medieval people were and what the Greeks were—there is no doubt—but are what they are thanks to the resources they have received from the Greeks and the medievals. The Middle Ages and Greece last in the form of a resource, in the form of a possibility. *Therefore the constitution of the resources from the event is something basic in the dynamism of self-possession.*

Personality is in fact being formed through this progressive constitution of resources, and the moment will arrive when the human being has no resource but one: to accept precisely what has been, for which there is no longer room for other possibilities: precisely the hour of death.

Meanwhile, the dynamics of possibility, the dynamism of self-possession, consists precisely of continuing step by step, moment by moment, to hammer out a personality by means of the resources that substantivity itself presents to us. The resources are in great measure inherited from previous situations and formally consist, as resources of our own substantivity, of being possibility in the order of actions we are going to perform, and which, once performed through empowerment and appropriation, leave the "I" in a situation of being a resource upon which to mount its ulterior vital moments.

In the last analysis, the *personalizing course of open essence* is not variation in the rigorous sense. As becoming, not even variation is pure passage from being to non-being or from a being in one way to a being in another.[38] Variation consists, I said, of giving of oneself, of giving of oneself the adherent notes that are "predetermined" by the character of one's own substantivity.

The course of open essence is not a change, either. In fact there can be many chemical changes in the bosom of the human organism—it is not a question of this. But for actions, all these changes are absorbed into the human being in the form of resources on which the human relies for performing actions.

Neither is the course of open essence an evolution.

Neither is the personalizing course of open essence a making of the self. In no sense is this so. An animal is also a self while it is alive, and not for that reason does it have a personality. No. It is really a making one's own, a making one's own that is not a change, but a giving of oneself.

Certainly there is no giving of oneself of any substantivity that does not imply a moment of change; I have already said that. But becoming does not consist formally of change. Becoming consists of giving of oneself. Change is something without which substantivities cannot give of themselves. They give of themselves in different forms in accordance with the character of these changes.

Becoming is not changing, it means giving of oneself.

In the case of closed essence, it is giving of oneself in the form of pure virtuality, that is, in "predetermining" in the substantivity the gamut of adherent notes that it can have. Earlier I said about local motion what applies here too: it is a matter of indifference to this glass in what place it may be; this, however, is only relatively true. It cannot be in all places, but what is essential to it is to be someplace.

Every substantivity has a definite gamut of adherent notes. As a consequence, it has some virtualities to be activated in change. Here it should be understood that occupying a place and changing place, formally considered, is not precisely a becoming, since becoming is the giving of oneself of a substantivity occupying now one place and afterward another.

This, however, is not the case of personalization. Neither does there take place in personalization what I said does in evolution. As against what might often have been thought, evolution is not simply a virtual act in which some potencies are being actualized in a different form in a virtual act throughout history. It is something more radical. Evolution is the constitution of some potentialities that, needless to say, constitute the gamut of virtualities available to the living being for its life, once it is constituted as a living being, as a new species. Evolution is constitutively potentiation. Evolution is not in mutation but in the integration of mutation: the reptile, which cannot survive except by virtue of a certain mutation, that of becoming a bird. It is precisely giving of itself in potentiation. It is not changing, but integrating the mutation in a giving of oneself. Neither is it the wealth of responses of the living being to different situations in accordance with the way its system is formalized. Here it is not a question of responding. It is a question of something previous, which is precisely the *constituting* of responsibilities. In the case of the human being, the giving of oneself does not consist either of having a system, or of actualizing virtualities, or of a system and a dynamism of potentiation, or of a dynamism of response—of systemic response [*responsion*]. It is something different: it is a *dynamism of making possible.*

Making possible is not a step from potency to act, but the active constitution of possibility as such.

Open essence, like all essence, is active by itself. In the case of open essence this activity by itself is activity of personality.

The person is personalized by itself—it cannot help but be personalized, and on its progressive enrichment, on the entitative increment of personalization, is based the only way the person has to preserve itself as a person, that is to say, precisely to be its own, to take possession of itself.

It may be said that this is a kind of anthropology. Yes it is. But I would have to say that this is not an anthropology *simpliciter* [without qualification] for a very clear reason. Anthropology, qua anthropology, that is, qua the structure of human being, precisely concerns the particularity of the human being, the being of the human as such, as distinguished from the chimpanzee or the amoeba. Here, however, I have taken the human being as a form of reality, which is something different.

As a matter of fact, reality as such is not a kind of gigantic sea within which float real things—a little the way the ancient Neoplatonists believed: *prima rerum creatarum est esse,* the first thing that God has created is being, and later within being there continue to appear things that are as in an ocean of being.[39] It is not a question of this. Reality does not have any reality except in concrete, real things that are real. Reality is not reality except *in* things. But in things the real part of them is precisely reality—what they have of reality.

The dynamism of reality itself, as reality that opens itself to itself, is here the only matter of any importance.

In the person what is important is not human vicissitudes whereby the person continues to constitute itself in the form of personality throughout its life. No, it is something more radical, and apparently more innocuous, but at base much more decisive, that is, the person as a form of reality. *It is reality in itself that opens itself to itself in the form of self-possession, that is, in the form of person.*

Further, what has been called the "transcendental order," the one comprising reality, is thought to be at least the correlate of a very abstract concept. Now, this is false. It is not that this concept does not exist, let me be understood. But *formaliter* [formally], the transcendental order, the transcendental function, is not the correlate of a concept: it is the real structure of things qua real. It is precisely the mode of reality that their particularity determines in each of them. Consequently, from the transcendental viewpoint, the determination of each of the particularities is precisely expressed as a transcendental function by some characteristics proper to this transcendental order. This means, in second place, that the transcendental order is not a priori with respect to things that have being. This is one of the great ideas that have inertly gravitated over philosophy for centuries. The transcendental order, they say, is *prior to* things that are real; yet this is absolutely false. There is no more reality, precisely, than the reality of each thing.

It may be said there could be other realities. I reply, well, just consider the limitation and the problematic quality of all research of the transcendental order. Far be it from the metaphysician to display the Satanic pride to claim to know beforehand all that must be known of the transcendental order, while needing only to apply it to poor human beings who strain their brains century after century trying to know what light is or what nucleic acid is! No, that is capricious.

The transcendental order is just the transcendental function that particularities have and which human beings must epagogically keep on discovering at great length through their research.[40]

Then it may be asked where general metaphysics stands. I would answer that it stands nowhere. For general metaphysics does not exist. There exists nothing but metaphysics as science and knowledge of the transcendental order.[41] What is called "general metaphysics" would be seeing reality insofar as coming from God and from a First Cause.[42] But this is a completely extramundane consideration. In an intramundane way, the transcendental order is what I have just said. Dynamism consists of something that relates to the transcendental order: it is modes in which reality constitutes itself and opens itself to itself, modes in which reality qua reality goes on giving of itself. That constitution of reality is precisely dynamism.

Dynamism is one of the intrinsically constituent moments of the transcendental order as such.

~ 10
The Dynamism of Living Together

In the preceding chapter, I was concerned with the dynamism that I call "dynamism of self-possession," that dynamism in which and in accordance with which reality makes itself its own in each person who exists.

Human realities are persons, first because to live is to possess oneself, and here it is a question of possession *in* reality, not only among things but in reality as such; it is precisely a making reality one's *own*; this is what formally being a person means.

I have also said that this self-possession, and the basis and way in which one becomes one's own in this self-possessing, have an essentially dynamic character. It is a question of a dynamism that, to put it in a generic way, consists of the person's ongoing self-configuring as a personality, as a being of human substantivity.

In dealing with the dynamism of personalization, I said that this dynamism must be understood in the first place as the turning of human beings to things, to other human beings, and to themselves, "with" all that makes their lives. The word *with* refers at the same time to human beings, to things, and to oneself; with oneself the human individual makes his life. This "with" with which the human being makes his life is not an addition, a relational appendage extrinsic to life, but something that intrinsically belongs to life itself.

Yet, in the second place, human beings perform their acts from themselves. The "from" is a structural moment not of life but of something deeper: it is a structural moment of the "to myself." Hence the dynamism of personalization comprises two aspects: dynamism as "with"—the dynamism of making possible—and dynamism as "from."

The unity that there is in life *with* other things, *with* other human beings, and *with* oneself constitutes what I have called the "construct" state of life, a construct in accordance with which things, human beings, and my reality have *meaning* for my life. Yet at the same time they could not have this meaning if the realities that things and other human beings are did not have the capacity to constitute meaning, that is, if they did not have a *condition*. Now, by virtue of its naked reality, which is the presupposition of all I am saying, reality has a condition, and in that condition meaning is grounded wherewith things are no longer naked reality but meaning-things, and in those meaning-things are anchored what we call "possibilities."

Possibilities do not enter in an explicit and formal way into the concept of Aristotelian δύναμις [potency] because that being, the ἐνέργεια, the act for which the δύναμις is a δύναμις, is not, as Aristotle somewhat ambiguously maintained, the act of a potency. It is instead something sensibly different, an action. If it is rigorously true that acts require *potencies,* here actions naturally require possibilities, which get hammered out over the course of life. These possibilities reveal things to us as *insistences* for hammering out, for elaborating our personality, and as *resources* available to us just for making our personality. Upon those resources is based the formal character of possibility as such. The way human beings actualize those possibilities is designated an appropriation on their part; in other words, human beings make them their own. In taking possession of a possibility while discarding others, there exists a more or less free choice. In that choice and as a result of it the appropriated possibility takes possession of the individuals. An empowerment takes place. In it, the actualization of those possibilities is not simply a fact as the actuality of a *potency,* but an actualization of *possibilities,* that is, a *happening* or an *event.*

I have also set out in a synthetic way the character of this whole dynamism of self-possession. I pointed out, moreover, in the first place, that it is necessary to keep in mind that human beings, by their animal component, have an essentially and constitutively *fluent* character. The human being is a flow, a flow in which it is never possible to be the self [*el mismo*] except just by never being the same [*lo mismo*].

The human being can never be a person except by self-personalization. This self-personalizing is an always not-being-the-same in every instant of personal existence. The way of being one-self [*el-mismo*] by not ever being the same is to configure precisely one's own being, the being of one's substantive reality. This being assimilates biological selfhood. This configuration, moreover, comes into being by means of a project that operates through appropriation and empowerment of possibilities. Here is what making possible means: the very dynamism of self-possession.

The human person is a person such that it cannot be itself unless it configures its own being. In that configuration there occurs precisely the *selfhood* of the *self* of the human person.

Now, in the measure that this is an appropriation, it means that the configuration of a person, of a being of the substantive part in the form of "I," in the form of a personality, is something that represents a rigorous *innovation*. This innovation is freedom. The act of freedom is an innovation. It is new because it is not simply an act that previously did not exist—this happens in all orders of the universe. But it is new because it is an act that never happened before, because before happening, the possibilities for it to happen have been determined by the human being itself.

Freedom is radical innovation, radical because it falls back on the very position of the possibility. Therefore in a certain way it can be called "quasi-creation." From this viewpoint the free appropriation and empowerment of possibilities is precisely a radical innovation. This character does not get abolished even in the theological context, because in that context I have several times explained that human freedom is just the secondary cause of a divine innovation, of a divine initiative.[1]

The dynamism of self-possession is precisely not being able to keep being the-self without configuring the being of one's own substantivity. Therefore in the strictest of terms this dynamism is restlessness, inner disquiet [*in-quietud*]. It is precisely the transcendental function of the flow. Restlessness is inserted wholly into the transcendental order. It is inner lack of quiescence as a mode of reality with regard to being.

If all reality, from the standpoint of its actuality in the world, is a *realitas in essendo* [reality in active being],[2] in the case of the human person this *in* of the *in essendo* [in active being] is precisely *dis-quiet*. The dynamism of self-possession is purely and simply the dynamism of innovating reality restless in being.

Before taking on a different aspect of the dynamism of personalization, essentially related to the previous one but constitutively different from it, I come back to the point of departure.

I said that all human beings make their lives "with" things, with other human beings, and with themselves. In this aspect, the "with" is a structural moment in the life of the human being and, therefore, of the dynamism of personalization. But that is not all. For human beings perform their lives "from" themselves. This "from" is a formal structural moment of the substantivity of human beings, not only as performers of their lives but also as "themselves." What is this "themselves" whose formal structural moment is the "from"? What is being "oneself"?

Being oneself immediately means being a person; I have already said so previously. On this horizon, the oneself is the reality of each person as one's own. Therefore the oneself is a oneself in reality as such and with respect to reality as such. Yet the oneself has a more complex structure. For it is a oneself not only with respect to reality as such but also with respect to other human beings. Now, in this dimension the other human beings do not perform the function of being something "with" which each one makes personal life. Human beings in fact do not limit themselves to being with other human beings, as they are with the sun or with mountains. Every human being carries within, in the "self" and *by reason of that self,* something concerning all other human beings. This "something" is a structural moment of the "to myself." Here the other human beings do not function as something with which I make my life but as something which in some measure is I myself. Only because this is so *a radice* [from the root], only for this reason can human beings afterward make their lives "with" other human beings. The "to myself" "from" which I make my life is structurally and formally a *to myself* with respect to the others.

Then there appears another aspect of the dynamism of personality that is not the mere dynamism of making possible, or better said, that is the dynamism of making possible in a different form. Other human beings, rather than realities with which I make my life, are realities with which I am *living together.* Only in this living together am I myself in a concrete form. The "to myself" is a "to myself" in living with others. The "to myself" is that "from" which I make my life.

Living with others is not simply an *interaction.* An interaction signifies, in short, something extrinsic, or at least consequent, to each of the beings reacting among themselves. Thus, evidently there can be a reaction, for instance, between hydrogen, sulfur, and oxygen to form sulfuric acid, H_2SO_4.[3] But this is plainly not the case here. Living with others belongs to the structure of each human being. In other words, human beings essentially live with other human beings, that is, from themselves. As a consequence, the dynamism that I must address here is the *dynamism of living with others.* I will do it only from the metaphysical viewpoint, needless to say. Anything else would be a theme completely foreign to my purpose in these pages.

The dynamism of living with others presents different aspects. Basically I am going to reduce them to two.

First Aspect: Society

Every living being, to the degree that it belongs to a genetic phylum, is intrinsically oriented at least toward other beings of its own phylum. A biological and genetic orientation is constitutively given by the fact that its constituent essence is made specific, that is, belongs to a phylum, and consequently traces a genetic line of the same name from progenitors to engendered beings. This is not merely a contrived consideration external to this problem. For, in effect, by the mere fact that any animal, a living animal, is in a phylum in this condition, in a certain way it *bears within itself* the others—others from which it has received its own specified essence, and others to which in some form or another it is going to convey that essence.

As a consequence, there is a primary orientation by virtue of which the animal has "received from" and "communicated to"; if it spoke in an anthropomorphic form, it would say that it is just something receiving and communicating "in itself." It is in itself in opposition to the others, those *others* from which it has received nature, or a substantive structure, to which it is going to convey, or can convey, its own.

Every living being is oriented, therefore, from itself. Its genetic character is not adventitious to it, not an extrinsic relationship, but belonging formally to it. The truth is that what happens to it as an animal is not my major concern here, but I use it only to say that it is an unavoidable stratum of the problem of living with others. It would be something else, for instance, to think of a kind of angelic living with others, of some angels with others; and so far as we know, never has any angel begotten another. This is not the case of human beings.

This genetic orientation is essential and constitutive to the problem. It happens that it is not sufficient for what we call "living with others," because what occurs to the animal is what I have just described, the same as occurs to human beings; nonetheless, animals do not live with other members of their species, while human beings do. This living with others is radically distinguished from the orientation to which I have just alluded because human beings, as open essences, have intelligence. They behave with themselves in the form of realities, and they behave with other things in the form of realities. Consequently, their orientation toward others, which constitutes them in being "themselves" and by which they have an essence or substantivity communicated to them, and communicated, in turn, by them to others, is precisely an orientation in the form of reality, originating from oneself, from one's own reality *qua reality*. Precisely this keeps others linked, in some form or other, to each living human being in a way that is not mere genetic orientation but strictly living with others. This living with others constitutes not simply a more or less related multitude, linked by sentient structures like instinct, etc., but constitutes that peculiar unit in reality which we formally call a "we."

Without any further commitment, and without making an issue of any kind of sociology, I call this "society." (I know that community and society are not the same, etc., but for my present purposes this is not relevant.) Living with others has this first dimension that is precisely living with others in society. Now, it is necessary to inquire with a bit more precision into what comprises living with others in society.

In the first place, this living with others in society is something more than a relationship among individuals. This is true not only in view of previous considerations, repeated and applied exactly to human beings living with others, but, in addition, living with others is not even something expressed in interindividual terms. Interindividuality is really one thing, but living with others in the sense of a society quite another. For this living with others, this social character, is not the result of an imitation or repetition of a contribution and an adaptation—thus it appears, for instance, in the thesis dear to French sociologists like Tarde.[4] But as another French sociologist said, repeating Hegel (although the repeater was Durkheim),[5] seemingly nothing except what is social in its own right is imitated. As a consequence, it cannot be said that what is social is an individual phenomenon or an interindividual one.

Yet neither is it possible to say just what Hegel and Durkheim maintain, that society is something substantive. Society is in no way a kind of substantivity, much less a kind of substance. All these conceptions à la Hegel and Durkheim in some form or other consider society somewhat like a kind of great human substance of a more or less collective order or character.[6] Now, this is completely false. To be sure, society is irreducible to a mere relationship between individuals in an individual or interindividual form, but it is no less false to claim to make society into something that has a full substantivity. As a substantivity, society does not have full substantivity; it is only a moment of the substantivity of individuals. Since the substantivity of individuals is a structure, it must be said that society consists of a structural moment of individuals among themselves.

Society is not a *substance* but a *structure.*

Now one may wonder what this structural moment of human substantivity may be that deserves to be called "social."

I foreground the fact that it is a question of a *habitude,* strictly speaking. Of what habitude is it a question?

The word "habitude" does not mean in this context a custom, a habit. In reality customs are habits because they are habitudes, and they are not habitudes because they are habits and customs. A habitude is a way of coping with things: it is abstracted from the mode of coping with things. In this sense habitudes—which a Greek would call ἕξις, the way of coping with things—have nothing to do with custom. A habitude is certainly something that can be engendered by a custom. The repetition of acts can engender a habitude, a habit in the sense of a custom. Yet there are habits that have to do with being—for instance, the rot that a door or the wood of a door can have if left exposed to the elements. This is a habitude, as a Scholastic philosopher would very rightly say. It is a ἕξις, as a Greek would say.[7]

A habitude is a way of being antecedent or consequent to the way of coping with things. I say that society is a structural moment of human substantivity with the character of a habitude. This habitude consists of being related to the others, not any way at all but *insofar as they are others*. This is to say, including their character of otherness in the proper affection. There is then a ἕξις [habitude], that, in my view, specifically constitutes being social; that is, being affected by others *insofar as they are others*. This moment of each human being's substantivity, according to which the stated substantivity is in the form of a habitude affected by others insofar as others, is precisely being social. Naturally, being affected has the same meaning actively as passively. I am affected by the others, or I affect the others. It is necessary to take the phenomenon of habitude in all its parts together, because this is precisely how it exists in reality.

In the second place, I have used the expression, "affected by others but *insofar as others*." This "insofar as others" is essential to the problem. For I am not saying, "to others insofar as persons," but, "insofar as others." In other words, the substantive structure, the structural moment of being social as a moment of substantivity is characterized by depersonalization. The dynamism of personalization implies paradoxically the dynamism of depersonalization. Those others are affected insofar as others, not insofar as other persons. Otherwise, we would have something different, very removed from what society is: a communion of persons. That is different. Being social as such implies the others precisely qua others, that is, in depersonalized form.

This habitude is the seat of a *power*. In fact, as a structural moment of my own substantivity having the characteristic of a habitude, society exercises a kind of influence over me that is just a power. In this way is constituted the power of what we call "we," from the particular standpoint.

Now, as a transcendental function, this means that a community is constituted particularly. A community in what? In reality. That is, in the final analysis as a *transcendental function we here find that reality has become something common*. Reality insofar as common is precisely the transcendental aspect of reality as such insofar as it is constituted into being social.

Precisely because it is a question of reality in common, qua reality, I say that each individual finds himself with this reality insofar as this reality is public. Being public is the character of the encounter that each individual has with a reality that is reality in common. Precisely there is where the difference culminates between the human species and living with others in human society. The species, in the final analysis, is a phyletic, genetic unity of some individuals with others as concerns the schema of their quiddity. Yet in the case of human society, the thing is completely different. It is not reality specified in a phyletic and genetic form; it is precisely *reality as such, made common*. Hence the collectivity, human society, does not at all resemble what would be the unity of the species. The unity of human beings in society is not comparable to the unity of human beings in a species.

This making common is effected precisely thanks to the dynamism of depersonalization. This is so because in the person reality functions insofar as it is one's own. But here it is a question of a reality precisely insofar as made common. Therefore there is no dynamism possible except depersonalization to make reality into reality in common. This depersonalization in the habitude of otherness is the *dynamism of making common.*

In this sense society is the structure of reality in common. But there is another aspect of living with others that needs attention and does not consist of society.

Second Aspect: History

Let us consider what happens to each of us in the society in which we live. Human beings and the society they form, to which I belong, too, are something that forces me, that *urges* me to adopt certain attitudes, to perform certain actions, while offering me in turn a system of *resources* in order to be able to perform these actions and to constitute—what? Precisely the proper figure of the being of my substantive reality.

Now, from this viewpoint, all other human beings and the society constituted by them to which I belong is not simply a living with others; it is a system of possibilities for the life of each individual and for the social structure itself as such.

This is the second viewpoint in which it is necessary to be situated to consider the dynamism of this construct.

This system of possibilities, it is plain, does not refer only to the possibility that other human beings offer qua human beings but also to what these human beings have made or done. One finds oneself with a system of buildings, a system of conveyances, some Greek temples, etc. We find ourselves with all kinds of things that, as moments of a social structure, constitute a source of possibilities, I repeat, for the life of each individual and also for the very life and stability of society. This system I have just mentioned has as such an even more precise character that must be defined with rigor. The fact is that this system of possibilities is not present in any way whatever, as if it were a question of a bright idea that occurred to a human being and from that idea the individual found a system of possibilities. No, human beings cannot begin to recognize this system of possibilities integrally. Who can recognize in a clear and distinct way all the possibilities in a determined social moment of individual existence? This is capricious. What can be said is that this system of possibilities is in itself formally defined. That definite system defines the presence of society in the life of every individual and the possibilities of the insertion of each one in the life of society. To the degree it has this definitive, defining structure, it rigorously deserves to be called a "body."

The body is before all and above all the defining ambiance of some actions or of some activities. It is not necessarily something that fills the ambiance, as happens with matter. Precisely for this reason the system of possibilities of which society consists is from this standpoint not only society but has the character of a body. It is a *social body,* that is, the system of social possibilities. Naturally the character of body, *bodiliness,* in connection with other human beings is a bodiliness grounded precisely on social character. The contrary would be absolutely groundless, at least to my way of thinking.

This character of body, hence, is grounded on the social structure. This grounding rests, once again, on a condition, that is, the capacity that the social structure has to be constituted as meaning and as a source of possibilities for the life of each individual and consequently for the social structure itself. Now, as a system of definite possibilities forming a body, strictly speaking from the standpoint I am treating, society is what should be called a "world." The fact is that the concept of world indeed has many dimensions that I am not going to analyze one by one here. I will say for the time being that there is the world in the sense of *my* world. Each individual has his world, it is plain. The world in which we are moving here—a classroom—is quite different from the world in which any frivolous person can move if devoted to . . . whatever it may be. In short, they are different worlds. One thing is my world, the world of each individual, and another is what stays outside, entrusted to others. Yet this world is the system of possibilities of my life, and each of us mounts these possibilities on the things and human beings that surround us.

Now, the world has a *second meaning.* It is precisely *our* world. In other words, a system of possibilities that form a body is *our* world. In that case everyone does not have his own world, but precisely the reverse, all those of a society, in a determined moment, have the *same* world.

Naturally there is a *third sense* of the word "world": reality in respectivity [referentiality] as such from the transcendental viewpoint.[8] This, however, remains off limits, at least for now.

The world to which I here refer is just *our* world. We human beings find ourselves in the social body that, before all and above all, constitutes our world.

This world is constituted by a system of possibilities given precisely to the human being, with which the human being finds himself. And this dynamism, the dynamism unleashed by these possibilities of the social body, is completely different from the dynamism unleashed by social structures qua social. Precisely if the latter is the dynamism of making common, the dynamism of the system of possibilities of the social body as such is something completely different: it is precisely history.[9] If history is the actuality of the possibilities of the social body as such, it is necessary to pose four questions:

In the *first place*, what is the *reality of the social body* qua body?

In the *second place*, what is and *how* is the dynamism of this body?

In the *third place*, what is the *formal character* of this dynamism?

In the *fourth place*, what is the *metaphysical* character of this dynamism?

These are the four questions I will succinctly consider in order.

1. What Comprises the Reality of the Social Body qua Body?

I have already said that the social body qua a system of possibilities constitutes a world, our world. Now, the radical character of this world is the fact that we come across it, one is born and there it is. Precisely to the extent it is there, it should be said with regard to living with others that this world constitutes a system of possibilities, something that is there. It is a τόπος [place], a place in the broadest sense of the word, not only in the physical sense. The world is constitutively and essentially a topical state [*topicidad*]. It is just a τόπος [place]. By this I do not mean that the world is a system of commonplaces [*tópicos*], as is usually said. I mean that commonplaces have come to be commonplaces for a reason: for they are there, for they are just in a τόπος [place]. If the commonplace in the bad sense of the word, in the pejorative sense, is what it is, it is more or less derived from something more radical, which is the character of τόπος [place]. This is the topical character in the most radical sense of the word, of topical state [*topicidad*], which the world as such has.[10]

Human beings, who do no more in all their acts than refer constitutively to the world in which they exist, are human beings who move constitutively in the commonplace as such. They may or may not know it; they may hide it better or worse, and also at the final hour perhaps it will be impossible to be absolutely commonplace. That is another issue. Yet to the extent we refer to the world, we change into topical beings, because the world is in itself an essentially topical state [*topicidad*].

A topical state is something that is there, certainly. Yet this being there has a constitutively dynamic character. For it is not being there like a Doric column, but it is a system of possibilities. Then this means that the τόπος [place] and the topical state are essentially dynamic. They are a system of possibilities.

Possibilities for doing what? For the life of each individual and for living together with them all. Now, the dynamic character of this τόπος, by virtue of that dynamic character, is expressed in three concepts:

In the first place, that τόπος, which is the world, is there, but in the form of a principle, of an ἀρχή. It has an originative [*árquico*] character. Human beings resort precisely to that character to take positions in life, at least to the extent that they let themselves be carried along by their world or accommodate themselves to it. The world is a series of more or less floating principles, constituting the τόπος [place] and the ἀρχή to which each one does or can refer in each action of one's life. The world has a originative character.

In the second place, the human being finds this ἀρχή [principle] and this τόπος in their originative character. In Greek, "I find myself" is τυγχάνω. For instance, τῆς πόλεως παρούσα τύχη [the present lot of the city] is the state in which the city in fact finds itself.[11] The world, as something that finds itself, is τύχη, meaning the state in which it finds itself. But the state is found somewhat by chance; that is, τύχη [chance], a word that precisely for this reason has meant luck, fortune. Now this character of τύχη is undeniable. The human being has the good or bad luck, irremovable of course, since it cannot be modified, of having fallen into a determined world. This, without a doubt, is absolutely irremediable, immovable. Not even Jesus saw himself exempt from this condition. In that distant world, centuries ago, Jesus lived in Nazareth and Bethlehem, in Israel, in a determined moment of history. The world has a character of τύχη, of luck, which befalls each one born.

The world does not simply have originative character and the character of τύχη, of luck. But further it has a third character that does not assimilate the totality of the human person but that in the dimension of the world is precisely what determines what the human being can do and give of himself in the midst of a determined world and a determined society. Is it precisely μοῖρα, destiny.

The character of originative principle, the character of luck, and the character of destiny are the three dynamic dimensions of which being-there consists, of the τόπος [place] of which the world as such consists. The topical character of the world is originative, it belongs to τύχη [luck], is "tychistic," if you will[12]—and it belongs to μοῖρα [destiny].

This is the reality of the social body, a constitutively dynamic reality.

2. What and How Is the Dynamism of This Body?

The problem is now to ascertain what comprises the character of this dynamism. It is the second issue of the four here posed.

In the first place, we should say that precisely because the world as a system of possibilities is a body, what each of its inhabitants does by undergoing depersonalization is precisely to incorporate himself into that body. It is the *dynamism of incorporation*.[13] Everyone is willy-nilly incorporating himself into the moment of his history. How can it be maintained that anyone is outside history? It could be said that someone is not submerged and lost in history, but that is a different issue. That the human is *in* history, there is no doubt. Even the Gospel says, "I do not ask you to free them from the world"—they are not of the world—"but rather free them from the evil one."[14] In other words, they are left in the world. The contrary would be a kind of utopia: u-topia, οὐ-τοπία [no-where], which has no τόπος [place]; they would be outside the world and outside reality.

The human being, therefore, in depersonalization is not only constituting a "we" in the community within the social structure but is furthermore incorporated precisely into what this community has as a body and a system of possibilities.[15] As a consequence, to inquire about the character of this dynamism is only to inquire how that incorporation is brought about. This incorporation is not an act that the human being can freely choose. It is possible to choose more or less—that belongs to another context—but plainly the human being, in a structure with other human beings, is nonetheless not sealed off as an individual. Yet, however that may be, what I am going to say here is absolutely unavoidable for the human being.

In the first place, the human being makes this incorporation because he is submerged in a *tradition*, sheltered in a tradition, *traditio,* παράδοσις. Tradition does not consist of transmission, because there are many transmitted things that perhaps may not function as traditional. Reciprocally, there can be tradition without there being a transmission, strictly speaking. This may seem paradoxical, but it is true. If one by tradition receives an object with determinations throughout history, and if one fine day in century X the conditions of this object are examined, it is possible to discover in it what was not discovered centuries before. If that search was crowned by success, the object still remains a tradition, traditional. It is not necessary that there be transmission for there to be tradition. Tradition is reactualization, and in this case reactualization as a system of possibilities.[16]

For what a society was in one determined moment of history has ceased to be real. What once was no longer is. But it survives by having granted us at the present moment the system of possibilities that constitute in a defining way the social body in which each of us lives. Tradition does not relate to the transmission of realities, because it is neither transmission nor does it belong to realities. Rather, it relates precisely to the reactualization of possibilities as such. For example, the Acropolis is there as a transmitted object. Yet its being a transmitted object does not constitute tradition. As a traditional object it is something that a society at a determined moment has produced, created, and delivered to me, and I observe it from a certain viewpoint as a system of possibilities that perhaps I am not going to repeat. Those that belonged to the Bauhaus would protest—they protested in fact—against the repetition of Parthenons.[17] It would be a mere mechanical transmission and would not constitute a tradition.

In the second place, the human being, constituted *in* tradition, has an *aspiration*. I do not refer to aspirations in life, but to aspiration in the sense of *ad-spirare* [to breathe in response to], in the most etymological sense of the word. In fact, the human being receives a system of possibilities and in one form or other appropriates, will appropriate, some of these possibilities, perhaps will reject others, perhaps will modify many of the rejected ones and even the accepted ones as well. And that is precisely an *ad-spiration* with which the present of a human being is constituted.

There is a third moment that is neither tradition nor aspiration but *conspiracy* ["breathing together" in Latin]. I am not speaking here of political conspiracies, well understood.[18] I am speaking of the moment of the *con* [together], according to which all aspirations of each of the individuals, with a converging or diverging character, have a moment just of conspiracy, a dynamic moment without which there would not be a possibility of incorporation and society would not exist as a social body. This is precisely the dynamism of history. The human being, incorporated into a system of possibilities received through tradition and dynamically actualized in the form of conspiracy, in history, this human being becomes incorporated particularly into the community in virtue of what he is. This means that the subject of history is precisely the social body as such.

The community is not the result but the principle of history. It would be an enormous falsehood—one that in the last analysis would date back to Hegel—to think that what we call "society" is a product of history.[19] History is a product of society, if one wishes to speak of product. The contrary notion is as capricious as thinking that the nature of the human being is the product of the human being's life. This is absolutely capricious, it goes without saying.

Society is not a result of history, but is a principle of history. The social body is the formal subject of history. To put it more clearly, the subject of history is materially the social structure precisely for what has been said. The truth is that formally in that social structure what constitutes the formal subject of history is its character as a body, its bodiliness.

By means of these three dimensions of tradition, aspiration, and conspiracy, incorporation comes about, that is, the connection, the concomitant construct, essential and dynamic, of the human being in history.

3. What Is the Formal Character of This Dynamism?

It is necessary to say what the formal character of this dynamism is.

Here it is essential to do away with some positions step by step. For one can fall more or less easily into using inadequate concepts.

In the first place, it could be thought that what I have just explained is a mode of flowing of human life, that it is a flow. History would be a *flow*. This is absolutely capricious, because history is not a flow. The life of each human being is a flow. History does not flow. It is something completely different. One cannot claim that history is a kind of great élan vital of collective consciousness that flows the way individual consciousness flows.[20] This also is absolutely capricious. Nor can it be said that history is simply a becoming, if the word "becoming" is given the double meaning usually given to it.[21]

In the second place, thinking that history is a *development* is a thesis that one could present, and usually in two different forms: compared to biological development, history would seemingly be a kind of great tree that springs from some modest seeds to be found at the start of history.[22] This is completely false and capricious. I will explain why. There is a rational theory that also relates to another conception of development, which would consider that it is not a question of the development of a biological seed, but of the development of an absolute principle comprising spirit as such. That was Hegel's thesis: a dialectical development.[23] But no matter whether the dialectic of the spirit or a biological seed, it would always be a question of a development, and this is what is constitutively false and impossible.

Is it possible to say that every human being alive today is a development out of the Cro-Magnon or *Australopithecus*? To what extent is it possible to apply the word "development" in this case without the words losing their meaning? For what is certain is that from *Australopithecus* to the Cro-Magnon there has been not only development but other things: there has been an evolution, with which I shall deal shortly. But apart from this, even taking the Cro-Magnon as point of departure, from the Neolithic era to our day, can it be said that all our societies and all our history are purely and simply a development from what those human beings were? What would have developed? Is it possible to say that our capacity for building airplanes or telephones is the development of some possibilities that those human beings had? In no way did they have them! That had potency, but that is another issue. I am not speaking of potencies, but of possibilities, and history as such consists of that.[24]

It cannot be said that history is a development. Hence it seems to me absolutely impossible to sustain—perhaps I err, but I set down what I think—the thesis so much in vogue today that consists of saying that the evolution of the human species continues in what is called history. This is not so.

History is never a prolongation of evolution. Evolution, with or without mutations, or by any mechanism one wishes, is always something that is genetic. Now, the case of history differs.

It is not the case that history is independent of evolution, but it is something different. It is a lapse of time. Naturally it is not independent of evolution; how could I say otherwise? In the final analysis, if history is taken from the first hominid, or from the first hominoid, from *Australopithecus* to *Homo habilis* [adaptable human] to our day, plainly it implies some evolutionary moments, without doubt. The australopithecine has passed to paleoanthropic man, to archaic man, to neoanthropic man, etc. All this is true, implying an evolution. But this evolution does not constitute history.

It does not constitute history because for it to belong to history it is necessary that history be in some form or other based on that evolution and reabsorb it precisely in the form of a system of possibilities for the very reality of the human beings that live it. Only then is there history. Naturally in that case evolution clearly belongs to history as all psychic and somatic structures also belong to it, as well as all the geographic conditions of each human being. But they belong to it only insofar as they are possibilities.

Evolution and development operate purely and simply on the concept of reality. Now, history, to my way of thinking, is mounted on the concept of possibility, which is something different. Therefore history is an actualization of possibilities. The past bequeaths a system of possibilities that constitutes the present upon which human beings mount their projects and individual lives and even social structures for the future, but it is precisely this: a bringing to birth and sealing off of possibilities. That is what formally comprises history. The rest is a vehicle that could transport history and which, reabsorbed into the form of possibility, belongs to history itself. This is, however, something completely different from what a development is, that is, from the act of certain potencies, to say it with precision. Here it is a question of the actualization of certain possibilities.

For this reason historical dynamism is neither flow nor development nor evolution. It is something different: it is purely and simply a *time lapse*. It is a time lapse in which possibilities follow their course, some broadened, others reduced, some annulled, others changed—whatever one wants. But history is just a system of actualization of possibilities, not of actualization of potencies. For this reason, if the actualization of potencies as such is a fact, history is not constituted by facts but by events, which would be the actualization of possibilities. Naturally, since this actualization occurs precisely in a fact, it must be said that reality itself is at once a fact and an event. But it is a fact for a reason different from the reason for which it is an event. In the same way, the actions of a person are personal and natural, but the reason they are personal differs from the reason they are natural. This dynamism, the primary formal character of historical dynamism, is precisely de-realization.

The human being is incorporated into history in a depersonalized way, and history follows its course precisely in the form of de-realization with tradition as a system of possibilities. This is why society has the character of *insistence* and *resource* for the actions of each human being and for social structures themselves.

Now, let us not think that these possibilities and the dynamism of actualization share the character of possibilities and their actualization in the life of every individual. This would be completely false. The human being—each individual one—selects a system of possibilities and configures the being of his own substantivity precisely in order to be able to continue being a person. Insofar as we are persons we find ourselves forced to personalize ourselves to be able to keep on being the same persons. Nothing like this happens to history. History plainly lacks selfhood in a radical sense. History is an open structure, not in the metaphysical sense in which I used the word before,[25] but certainly in the sense that it is an open structure with regard to the type of world. History is completely open to the world. It makes no special effort to preserve structures on which it lives precisely in the present; it will be able to change them at a future point, to hurl them through the window, but always by operating on possibilities that it has received. The possibilities for revolution in the twentieth century are not the same as in Alcibiades' time.[26] History is open to a type of different world, something different from an open essence in the abstract sense of the word.

4. What Is the Metaphysical Character of This Dynamism?

The metaphysical character of historical becoming is the last of the questions that history poses.

Hegel maintained that the subject of history and its formal, entitative character consists of being objective spirit in contrast to subjective spirit.[27] According to Hegel, subjective spirit would definitely consist of the spirit of each individual, and that would culminate, as he says, in self-consciousness, in the consciousness that each individual has of himself.[28] Objective spirit is something different. It would have to be precisely a structure whereby the subjective spirit ceases to be subjective and there is born precisely that other form as a second stage, which is the objective spirit.[29]

An objective spirit does not leave unattended the subjective spirit of each individual.[30] But Hegel says with a brutal phrase that the individual is not preserved in history, in objective spirit, except as a memory.[31] One wonders if this conception of Hegel's is acceptable.

Now, the first thing that needs to be said, to my way of thinking, is that the so-called objective spirit is not spirit but τόπος [place]. It is completely the contrary of spirit; it is precisely a τόπος, of a topical quality.

In the second place, this τόπος is characterized by not being a reality in itself, but just the reverse, by being purely and simply a system of possibilities and nothing more.

Third, this system of possibilities, the fact remains, is not objective. In reality, it is something different: it is an objectified system of possibilities.

It is objectified because it is placed in a community with others and consequently has the character of a body from the standpoint of the "we." To use the word "objectified," we will say that the world is an objectified system of possibilities. Yet in no way do these possibilities, this world, constitute an objective spirit, which would be a phase between subjective spirit and absolute spirit.

These possibilities are grounded in an ultimate possibility, in an instant possibility, which is precisely reality as such. The world in this case is the world in its metaphysical character: as respectivity of the real qua real. To this respectivity of the real qua real is related *primo et per se* [first and by itself] the historical dynamism as dynamism of reality and not simply as the particularization of such a determined history. For reality in fact is by itself, as I have tried to present it, a dynamic reality. It is not simply a case of its "having" a few dynamisms proper to itself, but its character consists not of being activity, but of being dynamic. It is something that, if given the conditions whereby it can produce its effects, produces them by itself. It needs no activation of any order, but simply the one to which the activity is applied. It is active in itself and by itself.

Now, this means that the respectivity that constitutes the world of real things qua real is precisely a respectivity of what is dynamic. This does not mean in any way that the world is a kind of dynamic substantivity that acts by itself. Rather, each of the realities comprehended in the world is in constitutive dynamic respectivity simply by the fact of forming part of the world, that is, of the respectivity of the real qua real.

The world, consequently, is a world dynamic by itself. This means that the world, reality qua world, is constitutively historical. Historical dynamism relates to reality by constituting it qua reality. History is not simply a happening that occurs to some poor realities, the way gravity can occur to material realities. On the contrary, it is something that relates precisely to the character of reality as such. For this reason, metaphysically speaking, historical dynamism is purely and simply the dynamism of world-making [*mundificación*]. This requires explanation to avoid misunderstanding.

In the first place, this does not mean—I have just pointed this out—that the world is a kind of great entity, or a great human being, a big man continuing to grow over the course of time. This is what Hegel claimed with the thesis of the historical individual reduced to a memory. It is certain that individuals do not enter history as persons. But they enter in a depersonalized way, and not as individuals, but precisely for the things that they have done in history. The declaration of war at a given moment can certainly be the free action of a person. There is no doubt at all. But this does not form part of history. What forms part of history is the declaration of war, not the freedom with which a determined ruler declares it, for this is something in his personal life. In this sense history is depersonalized, as I have just pointed out. This does not mean that individuals are nothing but stages for a kind of historical structure superior to the individuals, with the individuals preserved purely in this mnemonic form. This is absurd.

What I mean is precisely the contrary: individuals, precisely qua persons, do not form part of the world but surely are in the world. Since historical dynamism relates to the world qua reality, and qua world, the person as such does not form part of history, the person is in history but does not form part of it.

From every vantage point, history is never an ultimate reality of spirit; it is a penultimate reality, not with respect to absolute spirit as Hegel thought, but with respect to the personal spirit of each person. When I say, therefore, that historical dynamism is the dynamism of world-making of reality as such, I do not mean that the world goes on making itself in the course of evolution or of development or of the time that has led dynamically to the opening of human history. It is not a question of this.

The world has been a world ever since there has been reality, because reality is respective [referential] by constitution. In this sense the world is not an object of world-making. What happens is that the respective character of the world in its dynamism and in its properly mundane activity as such does not become transparent and function as such except precisely in human persons. In human persons, world-making means that the world is formally and reduplicatively world, that is, what in a direct and purely material way was already there before there was history. It is world-making in each person. In this sense it is the world-making of self-possession. In this alone is where that metaphysical world-making that comprises history takes place.

Human beings are submerged by the construct state in a social structure with a dynamism of communication and in a social body with a dynamism of history, which is a dynamism of world-making. Therefore, in the final analysis, they are always inclined to make their own lives and to take possession of themselves in the same way that evolution has not annulled in any way the lot of any living individual. The final pivotal point of the dynamism of a human being is precisely the dynamism of the human being's own self-possession. The human being may be immersed in a society in a depersonalized, communal, and historically reduced way, but that depersonalization constitutes no more than a phase. For what end? For an objective spirit? No, for the human being's own personal spirit.

History and society are made for the human being, not the human being for history and society.

The dynamism of history is radical in this sense but penultimate, a dynamism of world-making. It is the concern precisely of reality as such in the same way that it has been the concern—as I have shown—of the making possible that constitutes human life, of the making potential that constitutes evolution, etc.

Now there still remains to be considered in a synthetic way these various dynamisms that have appeared in the course of these pages to clarify what the unity of all of them means within the world and within reality.

Part 3

Reality in Its Dynamism

11
Dynamism as a Mode of Being in the World

Introduction

In this study treating the dynamic structure of reality, I first explained what was meant by reality and, in the second place, what was meant by dynamic structure. I developed, in the third place, the different dynamisms of reality. Presuming all that, I now must return to the point of departure to establish thematically, and with greater rigor, what the dynamic structure of reality is.

To that end, of the many problems that dynamism can pose as dynamic structure, I am going to concentrate in this chapter on two very radical and very basic ones.

The first problem is the following: dynamism is certainly a structural moment of things, that structural moment, or one of the structural moments, perhaps the most radical, whereby things are *in the world*. It is the manner of being in the world.

To my way of thinking, the manner of being in the world is not what Aristotle sought: a kind of τάξις [order], of substances already there and only later set in order.[1] Rather, their manner of being in the world is a dynamic one, absolutely dynamic. The second problem is to ascertain, if dynamism is the radical manner that things are in the world, what then comprises the intrinsic unity between dynamism and the very form of reality qua reality? This manner, I say, is constitutively dynamic.

I say that such is the manner of being of things in the world. I have used the word "manner" while alluding to the way of being of things in the world. "Manner" is perhaps a bit trivial sounding. It implies the same idea as another word, which is less so, though more ambiguous because it has, naturally, a tradition (and in philosophy traditions are sometimes deadly): the *form* of dynamism. I say this because the word *form* should not be assigned a technical meaning that would not apply in this case.[2]

The problem posed is the form assumed by dynamism qua dynamism, that is, the very form that reality, in its dynamic moment, is in the world.

I will treat this problem in six points. This form of orientation seems suitable to me for the progress and exposition of this theme.

First Point: On the Problem of the General Form of Dynamism as a Form of Being in the World

What is this form?

Reality is always emergent. All things are in some form or another emergent by virtue of dynamism. This is precisely the dynamism of the real, as I have pointed out. Now, it is an undeniable fact that all things emerge, though, to be sure, at their moment, in their time. The general form of dynamism is apparently time. Things emerge now, in a now, a before, an after. Time is present to us in a form (a word, I repeat, nontechnical in this case). I will say why I do not use the word in a technical sense: time is the general form of dynamism.

Time, as the general form of dynamism, is what responds to the question *When?* All reality is in some place, it is in a *where*. All reality emerges and is emergent in a *when*. This may make it seem that a great parallelism exists between the two things. In fact, it has often functioned in this way over the centuries in the history of philosophy.

It seems to me that this is completely erroneous for the following reason: Scholasticism canonized this homology between the *where* and the *when*. For the word responding to "where," it spoke of *ubicatio* [location, from *ubi*, "where"], and for the word responding to "when," it invented a harsh but very expressive word, *quandocatio*—a derivative of *quandoque* [whenever].

Naturally the problem of the *where* and the problem of the *when* are not so homologous, because although the structure seems from certain viewpoints formally more or less homologous, in reality it is very different.

Kant understood that time and space are two forms that are not homologous and coordinated, but that time is above space. Kant said that we have all the phenomena of the physical world that are in space, but they happen in time, one after another.[3] Now, mental phenomena all follow one another, but they are not in space. Hence time is the universal form of reality, both physical and psychic, while space is nothing but the form that would relate to nothing but physical phenomena.[4]

That this is so seems to me absolutely unsustainable.

Certainly time and space are not two forms that can be coordinated; but they are not two forms that interact with each other as Kant thought. I will explain why further on.

Thus, the general form of dynamism is time. Having established this, I move on to the second point: what is time?

Second Point: Description of Time

At this point I seek to do no more than give a description of time. The description is not simple to make.

Time, what we call "time," has different structures. Here I group them the way I did in the previous chapter.

1. In the first place, to use spatial vocabulary, time has a kind of *topological (chronological) structure*. Topology is a geometric science that actually studies the full set of things simply by reason of their position with respect to each other. Clearly in time there are no things in space, but there is a connection of the moments of time with each other. This is a certain connection. In this sense I call that structure "topological." With this explanation, I hope the reader will understand to what I am alluding.

Now, the topological structures of time—though this may seem a contradiction in terms—are at least three in number.

a. The first is a property already spoken of since Aristotle, the *continuity* of time.[5] I take it now as a purely general title for what I am about to say.

This continuity of time has different aspects:

In the first place, time—and this is the most common thing that can be said about it, but the most real—is a *duration*. Time is a kind of line that lasts.

In the second place, time *has parts*. It has a *before*, it has a *now*, it has an *after*,[6]—or if one prefers, a present, a past, and a future—and one could think that those parts of time resemble those of space. But this is not true. For the ultimate part of space, in infinitesimal analysis, is the point, which is not spatial, although it is related to space. On the contrary, any part of time is always time.[7] Already Aristotle stated it this way, and he was right. But at any rate, time has some parts: a past, a present, and a future; or rather, a before, a now, and an after.

In the third place, these parts are linked, united among themselves. Now, time certainly appears here in the form of *continuity properly speaking*.

It is certain that some Indians, so it seems (and in seventeenth-century European philosophy, in the Cartesian Geulincx), maintained that time has atomic structure.[8] In brief, time is not a continuity, but is composed of atoms of time, atoms of duration. As our friend and esteemed professor of psychology Mariano Yela has told me,[9] this has a certain psychological reality; there is in fact a kind of minimal duration in the perceptive consciousness of time in each subject. This is all well and good. There is also minimum duration in quantum physics.[10] But the problem of the consciousness of duration does not coincide—by any stretch—with the real problem of the structure of time. In short, the atomic conception of time does not seem otherwise clearly sustainable. Time—the before, the now, and the after—is not only a duration in three parts—before, now, after—but those three parts are in continuity. From the viewpoint of time, there is nothing to separate the before, the now, and the after, the past, the present, and the future. There is a kind of continuity. This continuity is properly speaking the third of the things that I needed to point out about the continuous structure of time.

Taken as a perduring [*durante*] continuity, time has still more complex structures within what I have called "continuity" in general terms. Thus, for instance, there is the problem of the *limits of time*.[11] Is time limited?

It may seem that this question is absolutely useless, for as long as we live, time is seemingly not limited, but, in the end, everyone thinks that at some time the world will come to an end. This is so, but I do not refer to that limitation. I refer to a limit from the metaphysical viewpoint. Is time indefinite in its own right? The question is put to reason. No less than the Iranians thought that time, taken in itself, is infinite. They called it *zrvan akarâna*.[12] The Greeks, who knew this conception, called it χρόνος ἄπειρον, infinite time. It is an infinite duration that has neither beginning nor end. But within it, the Iranians said, time of limited duration is inserted, and this is very extensive: *zrvan darego xvadatā*.[13] The Greeks translated this as ὁ ἀεὶ λαμβανόμενος χρόνος, as Aristotle said in his *Physics;*[14] briefly, time of long duration within infinite time. It is the time of the cosmic cycle, which according to the Iranians are the twelve thousand years that the world takes to pass through, etc.[15] This does not relate to the problem I am treating here.

Very rightly, Aristotle forcefully rejected this dualistic conception of time,[16] thanks to his *own* conception of time (despite the more than debatable character, though, of Aristotle's critique of the Iranians, as I shall now show). Nevertheless, the Iranians were not completely wrong either. Be that as it may, the problem has to do with the limits of time, more or less indefinite, unlimited time.

Finally, a different problem within the topological structures of continuity is the problem of the dimensions of time.

In fact, what structure does this duration of time have? Is it a cyclical structure? Then time would be the time of eternal return from the cosmic standpoint. This would be the cyclical conception of time.

Vis-à-vis this conception, the Semites always thought of a linear conception of time. עולם for the Hebrews does not simply mean eternity, but an indefinite time, practically infinite time.[17]

There is a third conception of time. The other Semites had it, but Israel never did.

It was the idea that time radically ends on day one of the year, and begins anew as a whole on the festival of *akītu,* of the New Year. A small part of the tradition has survived in popular mythology, in folklore, in the celebration of the burial of the sardine in Spain.[18]

We have here the problem of the dimensional form of time: *linear time* and *cyclical time.* Continuity is a duration in three parts: past, present, and future; time has a continuity properly speaking; it is unlimited in its direction, and further it is dynamically linear because nowhere is to be found the idea of the eternal return.

b. The second topological structure of time is not continuity but ordering. The three parts—before, now, after—have a certain order. In fact, although it may not be temporal but spatial, it is always possible to mark two points in a continuum and to say which comes before and which comes after. The continuum, from that point of view, is ordered. It is possible to establish a certain structure of the ordering of the parts. Before and after, then, do not mean before and after in time, but before and after in ordering: we say that one point is structurally after another, or before another, yet not in time, but in the sense of order. It is first, it is second, it is third . . . this does not mean that the points follow each other in time. It is merely an ordinal concept. This does not mean that the continuum, because it can be ordered, can ever be "well ordered." That is a theme of mathematics.

For some time Zermelo was famous for his theorem that the continuum can be well ordered. He understood by a well-ordered set one in which, once one element was put in place, it is always possible to say what is the following. This contradicts common sense. In a continuum, as close as two points may be, there is always an intermediate continuum: there is no point that "immediately" follows. Zermelo maintained that this could be done by means of a rational proof in transfinite analysis.[19] But this has not fared well in mathematics. There is, hence, an order of parts. I do not mention this theory of the order of parts to show any mathematical erudition—it would be absolutely out of place here—but to go on to what follows next.

c. In the third place—and here begins a difference proper to time—not only is it an ordering, but an ordering in such a way that at each instant only one of these parts exists; *nothing but the present exists.* The past has ceased to exist; the future does not yet exist. No other part exists but one, the present.[20] When the ordering of the elements of a continuous magnitude is such that priority and posteriority in the order means that the first ceases to be what it is in order to be the second, then we say it is a *flowing* continuum. It is a flow. This flow, counter to what has been said time and again since Aristotle, is not necessarily a change. It was said that flow consists of a ceasing to be one way in order to be another. Yet this is not self-evident. Take a reality, for instance, effort. Effort does not consist of ceasing to be one way in order to be another, but the past way is preserved and potentiated precisely in that second moment of effort. Without this the effort would not have its reality as effort, nor would the different moments of effort have their reality. Effort does not consist of ceasing to be but precisely of maintaining what has been in order to continue being it, and being it more and better. In this sense it would be possible to hark back here to the definition of temporal flow given by Saint Augustine: *Distensio quaedam animi,* a kind of distension of the soul.[21] Now, distension is not a succession in change.

These three moments of *continuity, ordering, and flow* comprise, I believe, what I call the "topological structure" of time.

2. Furthermore, time has other structures that are not topological. One example is directionality. In geometry we speak of an affine structure. In geometry, determining the parallel direction in a definite space is an affinity.[22]

Naturally, time has a *directional structure,* which is *unique.* It goes right from the past toward the future. In addition, it is *irreversible.* It may be that mathematical formulas that measure time imply a certain reversibility in time (in the theory of particles).[23] Yet one thing is time and another the number measuring it, however much Aristotle sought to identify both things, as I shall shortly point out.

There is, then, a unique direction that is somehow guaranteed by the second principle of thermodynamics, the principle of entropy. According to this principle, work produces a quantity of heat; heat, however, cannot reproduce the total quantity of work that has preceded it, because part of the heat has been spent in the molecular structure of that very body. As a consequence, energy continues to be degraded and therefore imposes an irreversible direction on the cosmic process.[24]

3. Third: Naturally, time has measurable structures: it is precisely the quantum: an hour, five months, twenty years. This is the quantum: the number that measures it; it is a *metric.* For this purpose a unit of measurement is necessary. A certain periodic motion has always been taken as such a unit, and with that periodic motion duration has been measured by introducing a measur-

able structure into it: it is a quantum in the sense I have just stated. It is a question of number in the sense of a *numerated* thing, not of the *numerating number* of the motions of things.

In this aspect, time makes way for chronometry.

Nonetheless, the *placement of things in time* is another problem. It is not purely a problem of chronometry. We are very accustomed to calling this "chronology" and nothing more, but this is not true. There are many moments of placement in time that have nothing to do with chronometry. For instance (to take only a few at random), in the first place, simply mere respectivity [referentiality] is relevant: one thing happens before or after another. This may be time, but I am not saying that it is. It may be time, but how much is not indicated. How much is it necessary to wait from the first to the second for there to be time?

But independently of that, there are moments in time, for example, the καιρός, the opportunity, which is also a temporal moment. How can it be said that this hinges on chronometry?[25]

In the third place, something concerns us more closely, and it is age. In fact with the quantum of time comes age. But age does not necessarily coincide with the quantum of time. In any case age, as a biological time, is not reducible to the temporal parameter, to the *ft*, the function of time, which mechanics introduces into its equations.[26]

There is yet something more: the moment at which something occurs. I said before that all things are born in their time.

None of these ways of referring things to time, of being in it, have anything directly to do with chronometry.

Chronology, the reasoning of time, is something more extensive than chronometry. To be sure, it does or can imply at some moment a chronometry, but before that it is a topology in the sense described previously, and an affinity, and an irreversible and continuous direction of the past through the present to the future.

Now, after making this purely descriptive description of time, the point arrives when it is necessary to inquire *what* time *is*, strictly speaking. The question is justified not only by the emphasis I have placed on the word *is* but by the very considerations I have just made.

I have in fact said that there is a before and an after, an ordering. Then it may be said that time is already there. But no, time is not there. The before, the now, and the after that I have pointed out are a before and an after in ordering: first, second, and third. In no way does this mean that those parts are comprising a flow that is time.

The before and the after, which Aristotle himself causes to take part in his famous definition of time, ἀριθμὸς κινήσεως κατὰ τὸ πρότερον καὶ ὕστερον, the measure of motion according to the before and the after,[27] is not a vicious circle. For the before and the after of which Aristotle speaks are the before and after of ordering; they are not the moments of time in the sense of a present, a past, and a future. That would be a begging of the question too stupid to attribute to Aristotle. Yet, be that as it may, this duality of the before and the after demands that we rigorously pose the problem, then, of what time is.

Third Point: The Essence of Time

The essence of time is the issue that I would like to enter.

The *classical theories* have shown their conception of time by appealing in some form or other to the different moments of time.

For instance, I have often cited the classical conception of Aristotle. Aristotle notices the fact that neither the past nor the future has reality.[28] The only reality is the one that the now has, the νῦν. What is certain is that this now is not at rest but is a now that will immediately be a past, and the future that does not yet have being will be a now, etc. Aristotle says that time consists of nothing but the *intrinsic mutability of the now.*[29] The now, to say it in technical terms, would be a flowing now, *fluens* [flowing]. It is not a now at rest. It is not like points that are there in space. The now changes, and that change, that *res fluens* [flowing thing], is precisely what time would be. The measure of that time, I repeat, would be precisely an ἀριθμός, a number, according to the before and the after.

But time can be understood not by taking the present but the past as the point of departure. Then the present is, in reverse, an emergence from the past. Time is really the past that is pushing toward the present and really bites into the present reality of things.[30] The past is not a pure past, but because of the fact of having passed, it is biting into the very structure of the present. It is, for instance, the conception, first, of Saint Augustine, the *distensio animi* [distension of the soul],[31] and later the conception that, perhaps without knowing the historical connection, nonetheless in fact has been represented by Bergson. It is what he calls precisely the *durée* [subjectively perceived duration].[32]

To avoid confusions that the word "duration" could introduce, I take the liberty of naming this "tension" instead of *durée*. It is a tension. For, in fact, the example that Bergson gives is: time is not a succession but is like an elastic point made of rubber that stretches,[33] provided that it does not break! This "provided that" cannot be forgotten.

Time, then, is this tension that bites into things, and as can be seen, the present is precisely something that preserves the time that has led to it.

3   Yet time can be understood from the third moment, from the future. Then the future is not simply what does not exist, but something that is being announced as being *soon to come* [*por venir,* Spanish, from *porvenir,* future]. The "soon to come" is not simply what does not yet exist, but what is coming to exist, it is *Zu-kunft* [German, future].[34] It means what is going to come. In this sense Heidegger says that the essence of time is *making the future*. It is being a project in which is determined a future that is coming; it is precisely a "soon-to-come" [*por-venir*], a future. And this soon-to-come, which in its moment will be an already come and a past, crosses precisely at the moment a human being plans the project of individual life and constitutes what we call the present. Time is the time of the project, of projecting and planning.[35]

Nonetheless, none of these three conceptions turns out to be absolutely satisfactory. The three hold part of the truth, naturally. But this does not mean that these conceptions satisfy me. They do not satisfy me for the following reasons, which I am only going to enumerate so as to enter immediately into the problem.

In the first place, let me begin with the third conception, time determined from the *Zu-kunft* [future], as *Zeitlichkeit*, as Heidegger would say, temporality.[36] Heidegger starts from the fact that human beings project their lives. This is this issue. Can it simply be said that the project and projecting of life is a simple fact? Is it not rather an intrinsic, an inexorable need that human reality has to project in order to be able to live and not simply let itself lapse? Yet even letting oneself lapse is the result of a project: the project in fact of doing nothing but letting oneself lapse.

The fact that the projecting quality of life rests on itself is a postulate. That postulate cannot be admitted because it leaves the question unanswered as to why human beings have to project their lives inexorably. Moreover, they must project their lives inexorably, certainly because each life is a *dynamic tension*.

This leads us to the conception of time as a tension. For human beings, projecting their lives is an inexorable need grounded on tension. I will say why afterward.

Now, about this conception of time as the tension underlying the projection of the future, I must say it does not satisfy me in an adequate way either.

In the first place, tension in itself is not time. Tension is a structure of real things, of some real things. There is a thing—call it as one may—human spirit, human reality, human life (in sum, it matters very little to me what noun is placed there next to the adjective "human")—that has a property: tension. It has it as it can have the property of being dismayed or the property of having passions. It has a tension. Now, this is not time. Time is something else.

Time would be in any case an intrinsic moment of that tension. Which moment? We are not told. This leaves unanswered the question of the structure of time.

Then it will be necessary to go back to the first conception: time as a change. Time would be the structural, temporal moment of tension: it would be precisely what there is of variation, what there is of change.

Very well, and yet, I repeat, change *simpliciter* [without qualification] is not the seat of time. In effort it cannot be said that there is a change in the sense of succession. There is an increment, as we well understand; for that reason a human being is striving. But actually in effort nothing is done that was not, in the strictest sense. Yet in a certain way, yes, and in another way, no. In any case, clearly, change *simpliciter* is not time.

But, further, duration as temporal property is not change. It is not in any way at all. And I will say why. Duration is something much deeper than change.

Hence it seems to me that it is necessary to refocus *this reflection* on the problem of time by recalling certain things anew.

In the first place, the basic phenomenon for understanding time, from where I stand, is not change or flow (in tension or non-tension) but is something much more elementary, yet much more universal: it is precisely *giving of oneself*. In the dynamism of giving of itself is precisely where the problem of time is inserted. It is a giving of itself that requires time. It is not flow or change. Nowhere is it said that giving of itself is a flow or is a change. The giving of itself of the dynamism, the dynamism as a character of reality active by itself that consists of giving of itself, is precisely, as I see it, the basic phenomenon on which it is necessary to center reflection if one wants there to be time.

In the second place, as a structural moment of what we call "giving of itself," time is a moment that *belongs to a reality in its respectivity with others*. To maintain, as the old physics does (and I call "old" all physics prior to the year 1916), that time is a type of great dynamic line in which things exist is as false as saying that space is a receptacle of things. Reality is spacious and is temporal but is neither *in* space nor *in* time as in places where things can be placed. Time is a temporality, but as a respectivity: it is the time of some things with respect to others.

It is a respectivity. And, as a consequence, since this respectivity of the real qua real is precisely what I have called "world," it turns out that time constitutively relates to giving of itself in its moment of respectivity, that is, giving of itself in the world and within the world to things insofar as they are in the world. I use interchangeably, to simplify my exposition, the expressions "giving of itself" and "flowing." They are not the same, as I will be *quick* to point out. But it may turn out to be clearer to use both in somewhat synonymous fashion.

Given this supposition, time is not formally a giving of itself. For greater clarity I will say that neither is it simply flowing. Flowing, like giving of oneself, is a structural moment of the dynamism of the real qua real, but in itself it is not time. In the same way the flowing of a river forms part of the intrinsic reality of the water current, but the flowing is not the river. This is not time, properly speaking. Time is not in giving of itself nor in flowing.

From the merely respective point of view, with respect to the world, time is present in that flowing and in that giving of itself. This is certain. Yet time does not consist of flowing and of giving of itself, but of being-there flowing [*estar fluyendo*] and being-there giving of oneself [*estar dando de sí*].[37] This is the issue. This is where time is. Time is not flowing, but *being-there* flowing. It is not giving of itself, but *being-there* giving of oneself, provided that we be told what comprises that *being-there* and what makes up giving of itself or flowing where it is. Only then will we be able to say what comprises the ultimate structural essence of time.

In the first place, what is that being-there?

Certainly, being-there is an actuality, the actuality of the real. Otherwise, there would be no possibility of speaking of a being-there. This is so. But here the being-there under examination is not simply being, the way a thing is real by contrast with not being anything at all, but it is a being in respectivity, in the respectivity of some things with respect to others. That is the actuality of the real in the world. Now, the actuality of the real in the world is precisely what I have called "being" [*ser*]. Being is not reality, but the actuality of the real in respectivity, in the world. I explained this at the start of this study, and I briefly call it to mind once more in this final part. Iron does not have a substantive being and nothing more. The properties stated as belonging to iron are not the being of the iron, but are the iron itself purely and simply, ferric reality. The being is a kind of affirmation, I shall say in an anthropomorphic fashion. It would answer to something as if the iron, in the ensemble of the things in the universe, said, "What I am is iron." Just that is the being of what is substantive. It is a second act.[38] It is an actuality that presupposes actuality, naked actuality, the actuality *simpliciter* [without qualification] of something that is reality. Being is precisely a subsequent actuality of that very reality, precisely in respectivity.

In the measure that reality is actual in that respectivity and formally in that respectivity, we say precisely that it has being. Therefore being has a certain active character. In saying this I do not refer to what Leibniz maintained, that reality is *vis*, that it is force[39]—this seems completely capricious to me—but I refer to an active character in the sense that I have just stated: a kind of reactualization or reaffirmation of the reality of a thing in the respectivity that constitutes the world as such.

The dynamism of giving of itself, or of flowing—as being actual in the world as such—that is the being [*ser*] of giving of itself. There is where time is present.

It is a being-there giving of itself. And the being-there to which I here allude is not precisely a form of reality, but the actuality that the real has in the world, and, as a consequence, being.

Hence time, against what Kant maintained,[40] is not in any way coordinated with space. Space is a structural, respective [referential] moment of things among themselves. Time is not something that implies space. The fact is that it is a completely different thing. It is the actuality of all things, of their giving of themselves in the world; hence it is something that concerns being, it is a mode of being. That is formally time.

Time transcends space but not because it assimilates it, as Kant said,[41] but for these other deeper reasons; for time is a pure actualization, a pure actuality, the actuality of giving of itself in the world, the being-there, in fact, of *giving* of itself in flow.

For this reason, even though I may immediately come back to the matter, it seems to me an absolute mistake to connect being and time as Heidegger does.[42] Being is not grounded in time, but just the reverse: time is grounded in being. It is precisely a mode of being.

Time with respect to dynamism is something similar to what I said to illustrate the difference between being and reality, the difference between the light and the light-source.[43] If by "light" is meant the clarity that any focal point sheds around itself, and if we then call "being" the actuality of the things in that light, then it must be said that being-there hinges on reality, hinges on there being a light source. It may be that the clarity itself serves me in at least a conceptual way to be able to see retroactively the gleam in the clarity it sheds in its environ, something contrived and ultimately false. But if there were not something brilliant in itself, there would be no clarity. If there were no reality, there would be no being. Now, time is with respect to dynamism what light is with respect to the light source.

Time is the actuality of being, that being present in the light of something that happens and that happens precisely as a dynamic moment of reality, which is what would be precisely equivalent to the light source.

Time is the *being* of dynamism.

Yet this is not enough. It is necessary to say here what this mode of being-there and this mode of being is for there to be time, so that there may be time. Can it be said that this being is being-there flowing, or being-there giving of itself, taking the flowing, taking the giving of itself, in all the many modes of dynamism? All these modes, are they time precisely in the measure that they constitute giving of itself or in the measure they constitute flowing? I do not think so, even though plainly there is something of that in time. But that is not what formally constitutes time.

Time is not flowing being. It is something different. Forgive me for the somewhat absurd expression: it is gerundial being. It is being-there *giving* [*dando*] of itself. It is being-there *flowing* [*fluyendo*]. In the gerund is where the character of time is located, not in the flowing and in the giving of itself. The actuality to which time responds is precisely gerundial actuality: to be-there giving of itself. Here "gerundial" is not taken in the acceptation proper to linguists, who distinguish between gerund and gerundial; I do not refer to this. I take gerundial in the common meaning that I am using. "Being-there-giving" is plainly a gerund. I take "gerundive" in this sense.[44]

Now, time is not flow but gerundive quality, it is *being-there giving*. The manner of being that consists of a gerund formally defines the consistency of time. Even if it were instantaneous, it would still be time. Precisely for that reason, because it has that gerundive character, every thing is born in its time, precisely because it is emergent. It is there being discharged [*dada de alta,* as from a hospital] into reality in a certain way. And there is where time is to be found.

For this reason I can consider retrospectively what I have stated with respect to the three interpretations of time as a function of the past, the present, and the future. It can be seen (at least according to what I have modestly thought about this theme) that time is none of the three parts; it is neither the before, nor the now, nor the afterward. It is not the past, nor the present, nor the future, but the least that must be said is that it is the unity of the three moments, as is natural.

What is this unity? It is not a unity in process. There is not the least doubt that the world is in the form of a process. But the process is in the same situation as flow: it is not what constitutes time but is something one of whose moments is time. It is not useful for understanding time. The unity of time is not that of a process.

Nor is it a question of a kind of *assimilation of the three moments,* of a kind of Hegelian synthesis.[45] Naturally, Hegel saw in this synthesis the opening to eternity.[46] As if time were a kind of hidden eternity, he said that necessity is a kind of hidden freedom.[47] These are dialectical constructions. Time is time and time alone. Let us not complicate it any further. As a consequence, it is not a question of unity in process nor of a unity through an act of surpassing by elevation—as Hegel would say[48]—but precisely of a *gerundive unity.*

It may be said that this is all well and good, but with the condition of being told into what time is inserted as a *gerundive unity.*

Time is neither in the before, nor in the now, nor in the after. Time is something completely different: the essence of time is the *always.*

No reality, even what may be in change, what is in its dynamic moment of changing; no reality, although it may be flowing, in its dynamic moment of flow; none of these realities would deserve to be called "time" if we did not say that time is certainly present in a limited segment of being in which it is precisely changing, flowing. The change must have a certain changing stability in its being precisely for there to be time, a *mora in esse* [pause in being].[49] Now, "stability" is what we call being "always" with respect to the three moments of what is stable. The unity of time is not the synthetic unity of past, present, and future, but the unity of stability of these three moments, the *pause* in the being [*ser*] of the being-there [*estar*] giving of itself. Only for this reason I call it "always." If we apply the name "being always" to this pause, to this essential structure of being-there giving of itself, then that comprises precisely the essence of time. The "always" does not mean that there is always time; this is false. Instead, while reality is giving of itself, it is always passing away, it is always coming to be (future), and always moving into the present. The essence of time is precisely in that "always" of gerundive character.

Hence something more must necessarily be asked. Time is precisely an always being-there giving of itself, precisely gerundive being, the gerundive being in that species of always, of a segment of being. Since time is not independent but is a structural moment of dynamism, it must be asked if there are different modes of time.

Fourth Point: The Modes of Time

The modes of time form an issue about which I wanted to think in this study of mine.

If time is taken as the actuality of dynamism in the world, the modes of time are essentially modes of being, that is, of the actuality of things in the world. The actuality may have different modes.

In the first place, all reality (I have written it before and therefore do no more than allude to it)[50] must have a certain stability in one of its dimensions. A thing that was essentially unstable and evanescent would be nothing. As minimal as it is, it must have some stability; however brief, stability in the end. If not, not even time would exist; time would disappear. Now, to say that something is stable means that it has a kind of inner consistency, a certain kind of solidity. I call it "hardness" in a physical way. The actuality of the hardness of something in the world, that is, the being of what is hard [*duro*] is precisely *duratio, duration*. Duration is not Bergsonian tension. Therefore, when I mentioned Bergson's example to explain what the *durée* [subjective duration] means, something like a rubber string that is stretched, I added, "provided it does not split."[51] Just there is the moment of solidity, of hardness. This is duration.

The moment of stability is absolutely essential for the phenomenon of duration. It is not tension, but a certain mode of "being-there being" [*estar siendo*] within stability. While it is, it just always is. That actuality is what comprises duration.

One mode of time is duration.

There are other modes of temporal being. In fact, reality can float within change. Actuality in the world, in this sojourn, is something different from a duration: it is endurance [*perduración*]. It endures and persists beneath the changes that keep on occurring in the world. Time is then a time of endurance, not simply of duration.

This may seem at this point a thing expressed very roughly. Perhaps it is so, but unfortunately this is what has weighed upon the mind of philosophy and theology whenever eternity has been considered. Eternity has been thought as a kind of great monolith around which there occurs, by divine decree, the rush of things, and it remains like a motionless post amidst the current. This is not a metaphor. All Thomists who have studied the problem of the coexistence of time and eternity have resorted to this famous and ill-starred example of the post.

Eternity is not that. It is not endurance in this sense. It is an inner, intrinsic mode of Divine Reality, which lives in a *plenary* way but not in a *monolithic* way, which is something different.

The second reality, the second form of temporality, of time, is endurance.

There is yet a third to which I have alluded already several times, *flowing* duration: it is a mode of time. But it is no more than one mode of time. It is unnecessary for there to be flow in order for there to be time.

Finally there is a different duration. It is *duration in effort,* duration folding back over itself to be itself. Now, if this is so, if there are different modes of time, if time has different modes, then one must wonder whether time has no unity.

That is the fifth issue that it is important to consider here.

Fifth Point: The Unity of Time

Time, radically considered, has a diverse character. In an ultimate and radical way, every dynamism has *its* time, its own, its proper time as a mode of actuality in the world, as its mode of just being-there giving of itself. Just for that reason each thing emerges *in* its time and belongs to a time which is intrinsic to it, proper to each one of them, for it is the dynamism of this reality and not of any other. This is not only true as concerns the human being, of whom it can be said that each one has his own proper human time. This is true as concerns every reality. In no way can it be said that physical processes happen in *one* time alone. This is true only of chronometry, something different. Yet each physical process has an intrinsic time, an intrinsic, essential mode: precisely its time, its own mode of time.

Nevertheless, despite this fact, time has a certain unity. What is this unity?

It might be thought that since we have times, let us make an abstract concept of time. Yet the unity of time is not conceptual. Here Kant had a clear vision of the problem.[52] Neither time nor space is a conceptual unity. I leave space aside; now is not its moment. Time is not a conceptual unit. It is something more: it is a real unit.

Every moment of time, each fragment of time, appears to us, as Kant said, just as a fragment of something that is precisely unique. Precisely because it is unique it is not conceptual. Therefore Kant said it is an object or, better said, the form of an intuition.[53]

Time is an intuition. Kant called it a "pure intuition." Here I dispense with the reasons he might have had for calling it "pure."[54] An intuition of something is unique, but as a form of the presentation of things. It is not something that intrinsically relates to the very structure of things.

Now I do not think that this is time either.

Time actually relates to the very reality of things. It is one of their structural moments, and consequently it is a question of a real unity: it is neither a conceptual nor an intuitive unity. It is a real unity.

Now, this then means that all dynamisms of real things are nothing but one dynamism: the dynamism of *reality*.

This singular *reality*, what is it?

Every dynamism is dynamism in a respectivity. Every reality is active by itself in this respectivity. Within this activity by itself is where its inner, constitutive dynamism is constituted. Now, this respectivity has an extremely concrete character: it is precisely what I have called "world." Hence the unity of time is the actuality of the dynamic respective unity of reality as such in the world.

Then I can look to a part of the universe for a very definite operation, which is measuring time. Physics has been exemplary in this mode of considering time. Yet let us not forget that Bergson was right when he said that in place of time what physics takes is the imprint of time on space, the trajectory. Time, then, functions like nothing but a parameter. Here Bergson was indeed right, without any doubt.[55]

Nonetheless it is possible to do something different, which is not to homogenize time by playing a bit underhandedly, taking local motion, and making time a parameter of mechanics. Indeed, superior things can be done with time. For instance, the periodic motion of stars in the solar system can be taken to measure time and to confer on time a certain metrical unity. Now can this be done without further ado? Is it possible to do it alone in a way *simpliciter* [without qualification]?

All Einstein's physics is mounted on the idea that time as measure behaves precisely as a measure for space: purely and simply as a dimensional parameter, whereby events that are simultaneous in one system of coordinates can be successive in others.

It is impossible to establish the universal metrics of time in such a simple manner. However, be that as it may, this is an affair of physicists and watchmakers. The unity of time is the actuality of the dynamic unity of respectivity in the world as such.[56]

Finally, then, the last issue to be wondered about is how one can be in time.

Sixth Point: How One Can Be in Time

Up to now I have dealt with time, but since time is the actuality of giving of itself peculiar to each thing in the world—this precisely comprises time: the being-there giving of itself—it must be asked how one can be in time, how one is in this actuality.

This is a false question if the word "time" is taken in Newton's sense to which I alluded before, as well in the sense of all physics since the years of Buridan.[57] In other words, with time conceived as a kind of great continuous line, things are in time as they are in space. But this is completely false. In the same way that things are not *in* space but are only spatial, things are also not *in* time, but are temporal—as I have already said. As a consequence the problem of the modes of being in time is the problem of the modes of the temporality of things. To say that reality is in time means that reality is temporal.

Now, it is possible to be in time in many different manners, just as it is possible to be in space, as I said, in many different ways. For example, one can occupy it. Occupying space means that, at each point of surrounding space, I can make the outer surface of the body occupying it correspond one for one. This is an occupation of space: filling it. Yet it is possible to be in space in other manners. Take for example space as limit that defines the field of action of something that in itself does not occupy space. The Scholastic philosophers already said this, as I pointed out at the appropriate moment. It is possible, then, to be in space in different ways, by occupying it like Christ in the sacred Host, *circumscriptive* [commensurately] or *diffinitive* [integrally in every morsel], taking space as definition of one's field of action.[58]

Now, although these may not be the two manners of being in time, there is at least a homology in the question. To be specific, it is possible to be in time in different manners. I can distinguish at least three:

In the first place, it is possible to be giving of oneself, but within the other. This is an extremely curious manner of being in time. For in that giving of itself, nothing happens to the donor, but it happens to the recipient, wherein the donor experiences a becoming. "Becoming in another" is a being-there giving of oneself in another. Consequently, it is a mode of being in time that is in a certain mode *to be-there constituting time.*

An example of what it is to become in another is the case of love. I was saying how in love there really is no change, but it is precisely the becoming of the lover in the beloved, even though the lover undergoes no intrinsic alteration.

There is a second mode of being in time, which is not giving of oneself in another, but giving of oneself and flowing—note again the interchangeability of these words—*flowing precisely into oneself.* This then is a kind of *occupation of time.* In fact, then, time relates to the intrinsic reality that flowed. If we imagined, as physicists usually do with such glee, that we plot the fourth coordinate of the universe in a line and mark the before, the now, and the after there in points—the chronotope of Minkowski[59]—then we would have to say that the reality that flows temporally has a kind of occupation of time: it is in time in the sense that it flows. It has some parts that succeed one another or implicate one another, or preserve one another, etc. This is a mode of being in time very similar to what occupation would be in space.

There is, however, a third mode of being in time. It consists not of becoming in another, nor even only of occupying it by flow, but in a different mode: *relying on time.* This means taking time as a synoptical structure and not as a flowing structure.[60]

As a synoptical structure time is something on which the human being—this only appears in the human being—in fact relies in personal life, counting on time.

This synoptical structure of time is not independent of the flow. The human being is a flowing being, besides having a presence or a synoptical apprehension of time. The human being does not have a *knowledge* of time, but at least a perception, and I dare say an apprehension of time in its totality, to take the word in all its breadth. This is to count upon time.

On the unity of these two moments, the flow and the reliance on time, is based the inexorable root and the formal structure of what we call a "project." The human being projects because as a flowing reality the human being is counting on the totality of time. Therefore, inexorably, counter to what Heidegger maintained,[61] the phenomenon basically underlying human time is precisely flow.

That flow makes the human being inexorably have to project, having time for projectivity. The projectivity is not mounted upon itself as if the flowing duration were the precipitate of a projectivity that rests in itself. This is not so. To explain what I mean, I used the example, from the spatial viewpoint, of the runner. The runner lucky enough not to be blind is not only taking a succession of steps in flow, but in addition sees the entire visual field, and from the vision of the entire visual field is determining each one of the steps being taken. This happens with time.

The human being has an intelligence. Without it there would be no time on which to rely.

The human being has an intelligence, one in which this flowing has two different dimensions: on the one hand, as a psychic act, it is submitted to a flowing, precisely like everything else: like human sentiments, and volitions, and life as a whole. It is a flowing of acts in an undiscerned way. Each act with respect to the other flows into the unity of the rush of consciousness. This is true. But, on the contrary, what happens with that unity is that intelligence sees precisely its own flowing reality, and relies on all reality as such, and consequently opens up to the totality of the field of the real in its flowing character. It is synoptical time. This vision of the whole field of flowing reality reacts upon the present moment in its flow, and this reaction is precisely the pro-ject.

The human being has this unitary, radical structure of flow and projectivity precisely because of being sentient, fluent, and open to the whole of reality because of being intelligence.

In fact, because of being a *sentient intelligence* the human being has this inner metaphysical unity between time as flow and synoptical time as projectivity.[62] This is purely and simply human time. Human time is precisely time as the proper possibility of the human being and of this human life as such. Therefore the human can model that life by relying on this synoptical character of time and can do it in very different ways that evidently transcend metaphysics. But some of these modes must be enumerated to clarify what I am explaining.

Let me address the project in the first place. I have just said that the human hammers out such *projects* precisely for that reason. Yet there are other structures that apparently at least relate more to time and would not be given without this intrinsic unity between the flow and the synoptical structure of time. For example, there is an "awaiting the opportunity to do something" [*dar tiempo al tiempo*, literally, "to give time to time"].

It is necessary to await the best chance to do it. This is undeniable. Here time functions twice: from a synoptical viewpoint, which is precisely "it is necessary to take time"; and later it is necessary to give—precisely it is the giving of oneself, the being-there giving of oneself. This intrinsic human unity that constitutes the unity of human time is what allows there to be waiting for the best opportunity to act.

There are other modes of relying on time, one of which is, for example, to "while away the time." Among the many things that human beings can do on earth, one of them is to amuse themselves with something unimportant. Someone is waiting, whiling time away.

There are other dimensions; for instance, the human being devotes himself to "passing the time." This is evident: it can be done and is done.

It is possible to "waste time." And it is especially feasible to "recover time," it goes without saying.

Yet none of this would be possible if there were not an intrinsic and radical unity between time as flow and synoptical apprehension of time. In all these phenomena here set down, time is underlying as a possibility and as power.

Now, this power of time can be interpreted in different ways: a classical way of sensing the power of time—without calling it "power"—appears in the Vedas and the Greeks.

The Vedas have a famous phrase, *Kālah pácati bhutāni, kālah samhárate prajāh:* time is that which is cooking, that which forms all things, and that which once they are formed drags them away.[63]

The Greeks said that with time we keep drawing nearer precisely to the end of things and reality. The power of time would essentially be a devouring power: devouring κρόνος, a destructive and devouring power.[64]

Personally, I think the contrary: *time is always and only a time of self-fulfillment: it is just being-there giving of oneself.*

Naturally, there is a moment of complete loss. But it is not because time has devoured us, but, in reverse, because the fact is that our reality, frail in itself, has devoured the time in which it is giving of itself. That is a different affair.

It is not time that devours reality, but reality that devours time. Time is devoured by reality.

Time is purely and simply the worldly form of dynamism as a giving of itself. As a consequence it is not something that can be an agent of the destruction of the world, but just the reverse, it is something that can be destroyed when the world, for other reasons, gets destroyed through its inner, its intrinsic fragility. If that is correct, if the power of time refers precisely to reality as a giving of oneself, as a dynamism that gives of itself, then it will be necessary to say what the internal unity is between the very structure of reality and its dynamic moment.

Having arrived at this point in my study of the dynamic structures of reality, I now pose the problem of the dynamic structure of reality in a unitary way.

Dynamism, I said, is precisely a moment and a mode of how things are there in the world. Further, it is something that intrinsically belongs to them qua reality. In conclusion, being there in the world dynamically is the general form of dynamism.

Dynamism consists of giving of itself. Hence things are *there* dynamically in the world giving of themselves. The being-there-giving of oneself is just the form in which dynamism is in the world.

What is this being-there? The being-there is being there in the world. Since the actuality of the real in the world is just what I called "being," it turns out that being-there giving of oneself in the world is a mode of being. It is not a mode of reality but a mode of being. It is not giving of itself but it is being-there giving of itself, the gerundive actuality of giving of itself: to be there giving of itself. This mode, in a gerundive, is precisely time.

Time, therefore, is not first a mode of reality qua real, but a mode of reality in its being. In the second place, is it a mode that is not fluent but gerundive.

Time consists of being-there giving of itself, that is, in being giving of itself. If the being of what is substantive is, as I said, *realitas in essendo* [reality actively being], in this case the *in essendo* consists precisely and formally of time.[65]

Time is the entitative fulfillment of reality. As such the dynamism of reality, as actuality in the world, is temporality.

By virtue of itself, first, every reality, I said, is emergent in *its* time. In the second place, the whole world is not in time. This would be impossible. It would suppose that the world is a reality contained in another world, and thus we would proceed to the infinite. It is not a question of that. The world, because it is dynamic, in its inner structure, internally institutes within itself time in respectivity and as a moment of that respectivity.

The world is not in time, it is temporal, it *has the quality of time.*

~ 12
Reality in Its Dynamism

Introduction

Take the problem of dynamism not from a standpoint referred to how things are in the world but from a vantage point facing the very reality of the things that are. In this way is posed the *general problem of reality as dynamic.*

Above all it is necessary to remember that, from among the various dynamisms, I began by citing the dynamism of variation. Things vary. The variation relates precisely to the notes that I have called "adherent," that is, notes that are not constitutional or constitutive of the reality in question. For instance, let us mention the most trivial thing, changing place in space.

In the second place, there is the dynamism of notes that are not adherent but constitutive. This is a dynamism of *alteration,* a dynamism that is in turn diverse.

It implies in the first place substantial change, a dynamism of *substantial change:* it is the constitution of new substantivities through a synthesis or an analysis of previous substantivities.

In the second place, it can be a dynamism that is not of substantial change, but a *dynamism of generation.* It is the constitution of new substantive essences by genetic means. Rather than repeating or producing a new substantivity, it is a question of bringing about an individual reconstitution of a substantivity already made a quiddity or species within a phylum.

In the third place, there is a rigorous *evolution,* which is the constitution of new essences made quiddities by the integration of mutations into the substantivity.

In these last two dimensions the constituted essence is formally *self.* It is the dynamism of selfhood. Its actions and reactions are the only way the structures of the substantivity can continue being the same. Precisely this way of being contained in a dynamism, with the dynamism as the only way to preserve the substantivity itself, is the one which defines self-possession. This is, to my way of thinking, the definition of life. Life consists of possessing oneself. As a form of dynamism, life is the dynamism of selfhood. It cannot be the self except by never being the same.

Third, in the matter of open essences [human beings], their self-possessing is a self-possessing no longer within the things around them qua particulars, as such and such, but a self-possessing in reality and in the form of reality. Self-possessing in the form of reality, possessing one's own reality in one's own way, is then precisely that which causes reality to be "its own" [*suya*]: it is precisely the *person*.

The person cannot be its own except by never being the same, exactly as any other living being, but with one peculiarity: never being the same qua reality. Therefore the person cannot be the same except by personalizing its reality in the form of the being of its substantivity. Hence the dynamism of the person is the dynamism not of selfhood but of self-possession. The dynamism of self-possession is nothing but the *dynamism of personalization*.

Fourth, these persons themselves naturally have a life in which their structure is personalized. It is a construct structure precisely with things and with other human beings. It is life as a sketch and an appropriation of possibilities. It is the *dynamism of making possible*.

Above all, those "other human beings" constitute the habitude proper to the person, which has this habitude of otherness of other human beings qua other. It is, as I said, what we ordinarily would call society, in a generic way, without entering into distinctions between society and community. Society is characterized by depersonalization, and as a consequence the reality of the social is a reality common to all persons. In this sense the dynamism of self-possession is changed by depersonalization into a dynamism of reality in common, into a *dynamism of making common*.

Finally this common reality, as the definer of human possibilities of each life, is precisely a body, hence, a social body.

The dynamism of the social body, that is, the dynamism of the possibilities of reality in common, is what constitutes *history*. Since these possibilities constitute "our" world, the world in common, the dynamism of history is the *dynamism of making a world*, world-making dynamism.

These dynamisms are consequently moments of reality as such. From this several questions arise anew.

The first is, what is dynamism? Or better put, who is dynamic? In the second place, what is its dynamism? In the third place, what is the character of this dynamism? Finally, what is the dynamic structure of reality?

1. Who Is Dynamic?

Certainly I have tried to show throughout these pages who is dynamic: real things qua real are dynamic. Here the transcendental turn of dynamism is important, not its particular turn, in other words, not the study in particular of what life is or what evolution is, etc. What is dynamic is what is real as such. This is certain, but each real thing, which is precisely what is dynamic, each of the real things is structurally and formally respective [referential] to the others. It follows that among all of them, they have a unity of respectivity.

Now, since each thing, as I have said, is dynamic, each substantivity is dynamic. This means that respectivity itself and the unity constituted by all these substantive realities are a dynamic respectivity. Therefore this world—that is, respectivity—this unity is the one that *primo et per se* [first and by itself] is dynamic.

This statement must be correctly understood. For it may be thought that I am appealing to a kind of idea of the great All, which keeps having its dynamic vicissitudes, a little the way Spinoza sought to do with his unique substance, or as Hegel seeks with his absolute spirit.[1]

It is not a question of this. In both conceptions the world, the All, appears as a great substance, as a great thing. This is absolutely untenable. There are no more things than each one of the real things. The All does not have this character of a type of all-embracing reality of which existing things are nothing but its moments. The fact is that each thing, each one of them, is constitutively respective to the rest. This respectivity is what constitutes the dynamic unity. The dynamic unity of the whole world is not the dynamic unity of a substance that keeps evolving or producing beings or particular realities within itself; it is purely and simply a dynamic unity in which all things are constituted by reason of their intrinsic and their formal respectivity.

The unity of dynamism is not formally the respectivity. But respectivity grounds dynamism in this unity. Dynamism belongs, as a consequence, *primo et per se* [first and by itself] to the respective unity of things. Only insofar as each and every thing is dynamic does it possess a dynamism. This immediately suggests the second question: what is dynamism?

2. What Is Dynamism?

In the first place, dynamism is a becoming. Of this there is no doubt at all. Yet by "becoming" changing is never necessarily meant, which would be absolutely false.

All becoming—I have given examples throughout these pages—all forms of dynamism and of becoming doubtlessly imply a moment of change. But the change is not what formally constitutes the becoming. Becoming is not constituted by change, despite integrating change into itself through becoming.

In the second place, dynamism is an *actuation*. This is certain. But the actuation is not consequent to the structure of substantivity of each of the things composing the world. It is not that—although I myself have at times written that phrase, though in much more general terms; in formal terms, it is not a connection of actions and passions.[2] For actions and passions emerge precisely from substantivity, and here the respective [referential] unity of things is not something that emerges from each and every thing that there is in the world. Rather, the reverse, it is something that forms and constitutes an intrinsically real and formal moment of each and every reality as such. To put it in other terms, dynamism is not a consequent actuation, but a constitutive one. Reality is active *by itself*. Dynamism is not a capacity for acting that acts at certain moments, but reality as such is active by itself. In the first assumption, it would suffice that external conditions were posited for reality to act. If reality does not act, it is not because it has a capacity that is disabled, but simply because it has nothing on which to act. Now, this is a completely capricious hypothesis. Reality is constituted in respectivity, and each and every substantivity is active by itself, for its own reason of reality.

Third, dynamism, by virtue of what I have said, is something formally constitutive of reality, and as a consequence dynamism consists of being able to give of itself just what reality is in a plenary mode.

Without a doubt, there is a difference to establish between what reality is as a substantive structure and what the structure is as dynamism.

The moment of primary cohesive unity constituting the formal essence and the reality *simpliciter* [without qualification] of all the substantivities that there are in the universe, that moment *in its own right* is not *formaliter* [formally] an active moment or a moment of activity. There is not the least doubt. It is a moment of reality. The primary cohesive unity relates precisely to the constitution of reality as such. This does not hinder the notes of that reality from being active by themselves. This is the second point of the issue. Dynamism does not behave with respect to essence as a consequence with respect to its principles. Dynamism is nothing but essence itself giving of itself what it constitutively is.

Dynamism, as a consequence, is a giving of itself. Change is only something integrated into the substantivity. This integration is just giving of itself.[3]

3. What Is the Character of This Dynamism?

In the first place, in this dynamism the functionality of the real qua real takes place before all else. This functionality is causality. Causality, as I pointed out at the appropriate time, is not a kind of abstract category of the mind. It is something that is immediately *perceived,* because the functionality itself is the way things vary and are implicated in real dynamism precisely as realities: that is the *causality.* This is something completely different from a *cause.* What are the causes of the causalities that there are in the world? This is always essentially problematic. But that is another issue. Here what is important and immediate is just causality. Causality is purely and simply the functionality of the real qua real. As a consequence it is not the true cause, but true causality that relates to what is the primary subject of dynamism as such—namely, the world.

True, plenary causality is in the world as such, not in each and every thing comprising the world. In a problematic way—it is a problem needing to be solved in each case—these things will be precisely causes. But causality as such resides in the radical unity of the world insofar as it is a respective unity of the real qua real.

At this point, I once again call to mind that the world is not a kind of great thing, of great substance that continues to produce causal actions. It is not a question of this; that would convert the world into a cause. I have said that the world is causality, which is quite different from saying that the world is a cause. Just as the world is not a thing [*cosa*], so it is not a cause [*causa*].

But the dynamic unity in which all dynamic substantivities by themselves are in respectivity, that unity which we call "world" as the very seat of giving of itself, is just the seat of causality as such. It is always essentially problematic to distribute the causality of the world into particular causes. It is so problematic that it is unclear whether any of the substantivities integrating the world are causes in any way. An occasionalism would be metaphysically irrefutable. It is false by congruency and by experience (that is a different affair); but in itself, it is irrefutable. It is also irrefutable that there is causality in the world. What a cause may be is a different story.

What is this causality as a moment of the world?

Every reality is respective, and in accordance with that respectivity of each, every reality is a moment of the world. Since every thing is active by itself, it turns out that in this respectivity are to be found the things giving of themselves. Now, the constitutive respectivity of a giving of itself is what I have thematically called so often "ecstasy."

Ecstasy is purely and simply the respectivity of a giving of itself. Each real essence gives of itself, and only insofar as this giving of itself is constitutively referred, respectively, to the rest of the reality of the world, each and every one of those substantive realities is constitutively ecstatic. The ecstasy is purely and simply the respectivity of the giving of itself.

Causality is a constitutive ecstasy precisely because it is the very structure of giving of itself in respectivity. From the viewpoint of cause—I use the example of the world if the world were a cause or the example of a particular cause—this means that *from the viewpoint of the cause,* causality would be a *determinant,* a functional determinant of the phenomena that occur in the universe. *From the point of view of the effect,* causality would consist of a being determined, a determinacy. The two dimensions are inseparable. Precisely in their unity lies the intrinsic unity of what causality is.

Now, this idea of determination does not mean in any way the determinism of certain antecedents and consequents. Determinism in this latter sense is the inner, degraded form of causality. First, from the viewpoint of the effect, it starts only from the determination; second, from the viewpoint of the cause, it places the cause in a relationship of temporal antecedent, which in no way is essential to causality. So inessential is it to causality that even in cases of determinisms of succession, there is plainly the unitary moment between the determinant and the determined, and that moment comprises the causation itself.

Causality is something completely different. It has an ecstatic character. Something is a cause in the measure that it is ecstatic. Now, all physical realities are ecstatic in the sense that they are in respectivity among one another in a giving of themselves. No reality is isolated from the world, from the rest of the realities of the world, but each is constitutively referred respectively in intrinsic constitution to all the other realities.

Now, there are other realities, persons, that are certainly referred in a construct state, only by reason of their lives, to the world in which they are but of which they do not form part. These persons have as their characteristic not only the fact that their actions, once performed, are univocally determined— this is quite clear—by some temporal antecedents, but just the reverse, they posit precisely the antecedents by themselves. This comprises freedom. The freer one is, the more a cause one is.

Freedom is the supreme form of causality, because it is the supreme form of ecstasy.

Yet there is more. For causality implies a predominance. The determinant predominates over the determined. This applies exactly to the very causality that there is in the world.

This predominance would certainly not exist without causality, as is quite plain. But it does not formally coincide with causality. They are two different dimensions. This dimension, whereby reality can perform the function of the dominant, not simply the function of the determinant of the real but of the dominant with respect to other realities, is just what I have called "power."

If causality is the functionality of the real qua real, power is the dominance of the real qua real.

This idea of power, of the German *Macht*, is something completely different from the Greek δύναμις [potency], and from the German *Kraft*, the force of things. Power is something inserted precisely into the very structure of the world.

Thus in fact was born philosophy.

Here I recall the fragment of Anaximander where he says that the ἄπειρον, the indefinite, is the ἀρχή, the principle of the world, from which all things come and to which all will return after a fixed time, thereby paying justice to the fact of having come out of this ἄπειρον [indefinite].[4] Now, the ἀρχή appears in three different functions. *First,* it is the *beginning* of the world, the *archaic* function. In this sense, as archaic, the past, the past of the world that disappears or that at least is not identified with any of the things existing in the universe, without a doubt certainly has a predominance already constituted over the real.

Yet in the second place, that ἄπειρον, that indefinite, is the principle, ἀρχή, as Aristotle would say, precisely intrinsic to each and every reality, which is formally constituted by this ἀρχή [principle] that it carries in its bosom and from which it intrinsically emerges and comes to be constituted such as it is. There the ἀρχή is not archaic, but originative [*árquico*]: it has the character of an inner constitutive principle.

Yet there is not only that, but—if my reference has been correct, perhaps the words do not completely agree, but the idea does—things will return after a fixed time to pay justice, δίκη. Rather than justice [*justicia*] it would be better to say rectification [*justeza*]. "Justice" is a bad translation because it always evokes a moral quality and it is not a question of that, it is just a question of adjustment, of rectification, a concept that will reappear later in Heraclitus with the name of ἁρμονία [harmony]. Harmony in Heraclitus does not mean a harmonization, but just the connection of some pieces in carpentry. For this reason Heraclitus was able to say, ἁρμονίη ἀφανὴς φανερῆς κρείττων:[5] the joinery that is not seen is stronger than that which is seen.

Now, in this sense, the rectification, the adjustment, makes things revert back to their principle, to the principle from which they came. In this sense the ἀρχή [principle] has a character that is neither archaic [*arcaico*], nor originative [*árquico*], but one belonging rigorously to an archon [*arcóntico*], an ancient Athenian magistrate. It is the supreme Archon of the universe.

The intrinsic unity of these three dimensions is what constitutes *Power.* That

Power of the ἀρχή is just what makes way, according to Anaximander, for the vicissitudes of the universe, and with whose formulation philosophy was born in the world.

Dynamism taken synthetically in the two aspects of causality and power is the causal dominion of reality qua reality.

4. What Is the Dynamic Structure of Reality?

It is not a question of coordinating causes. It is usual in books of metaphysics to say that there is material, formal, efficient, and final cause. There are causes of different character connected in the order of causes, to educe a result, which is the world. It is the old Aristotelian idea that in fact the universe is a *taxis* [order].[6] That is, it is an ordering of things that begin, each of them, by being by themselves with a determined nature and which through an action, whatever it may be, enter into coordination with one another. It is clear that that is not the point of view I have maintained in this study.

In the universe each reality is not a substance but a structure. This structure is in respectivity, consisting of intrinsic respectivity with the structures of the other substantive realities.

The world is not an ordering, but an inner and at the same time intrinsic structure.

Consequently, here it is not a question of coordinating causes but just the reverse, of seeing how the different dynamisms are organized, each with respect to the others. Of these dynamisms I foreground the fact that they are organized.

They are organized; in other words, some dynamisms are based on others as their substratum. The basic dynamism of all is just the dynamism of variation. If there were no variations in the world, there would be no place for giving of itself in the form of the other dynamisms. Even within these dynamisms of variation, probably the variation of place is the most elementary dynamism, but one that constitutes the substratum of all the other dynamisms. In any case, the dynamism of variation is the giving of itself with respect to adherent notes. These variations can relate to the structures themselves. Then we find that there is a new type of dynamism grounded in variation. For instance, take in the first place the dynamism of substantial change to which I have alluded. A substantial change is the synthetic or analytical production of new substantivities. In the second place, there is a variation of another type but grounded in substantial change: the possibility of mutations making way for beings that constitute or make quiddities of a new reality, a new species, or at least the generation of certain organisms through the genetic vicissitudes of others.

In these substantial changes, especially the genetic ones, substantivity is constituted as formally self [*misma*]. It is precisely life, life as the seat of the dynamism of selfhood.

In the second place, essence opens up, and what was closed essence is now open essence. Then self-possession, community, and the worldliness of the real are begun.

Yet these dynamisms are not only based on one another, forming a unitary dynamism, but go beyond being organized. They have a strict *metaphysical unity* of enormous wealth. In fact, dynamism consists, I repeat again, of giving ecstatically of itself.

Now, this giving ecstatically of itself does not consist of the passage from a potency to an act, either in the form of active or of passive potency. That is a much more elementary story, but one not very useful to us here, because the two terms of "potency" and "act," as I have pointed out, turn out to be very ambiguous. What is meant by "act"? Is the act proper to a potency understood as an act? Or is the action proper to a complex system of substantivity understood? And what is understood by potency?

It is not a question of an act with respect to a potency, but of something much more radical and unitary in which in fact there unfolds the unfathomable wealth of the real qua real.

In the first place, there is certainly in this dynamism, in dynamism taken in the whole universe, a *step from potency to act*. The typical case is *variation*.

But in the second place, there is a dynamism precisely by force of varying. In fact, some substantivities are produced that variation integrates, and then the dynamism relates to the form not of a passage from potency to act, but of a *development* of certain virtualities. This is the case of generation and life. Furthermore, not only is there this, but, in the third place, life by virtue of developing can make way for a dynamism of higher order, which is *potentiation*. Potentiation does not consist of the passage from the development of certain virtualities into certain acts. It consists of the production of the virtualities themselves. That is evolution.

Potentiation is prior to all virtualities and to all their acts, and even to the character of virtual act that it could have: it is just the production itself of the system of virtualities.

Fourth, this potentiation leads to a *making possible,* wherein the possible is produced before the real. As a consequence, in that case actions have the character of quasi-creation, precisely because possibilities have been posited prior to reality. This is making possible.

In that unfolding of the actuation of the potency, by passing through the development of some virtualities and from a potentiation of virtualities to a making possible of the real qua real, the complex, unfathomable dynamism of the real world pursues its course.

Each of these moments presupposes the previous one in proper order. It presupposes it not only as a particular function but especially and more importantly here as a transcendental function. For as a transcendental function, giving of itself is nothing but *innovation.*

The world, thanks to its dynamism, is in constant innovation. In constitutive innovation.

Reality certainly keeps diversifying in all its innovations. In this diversification, reality begins not by doing, but by having been there in the form of pure active character by itself. This reality continues to enter itself in the form of selfhood: it is reality as *self.*

In a second stage this reality is becoming not only self, but furthermore is opening to itself. By virtue of being *self* it ends up being its *own.* It is just the self-possession of the person.

This self-possession of the person, precisely in order to be so, must have a moment of reality, a moment which is reality constituted *in common;* that is society in the particular order. In the transcendental order, it is reality in common.

To my way of thinking, only from this viewpoint is the final aspect of dynamism comprehensible, which is historical dynamism, that is, as a type, as the constitution of a new type of world. Reality becomes a world in various types.

Here we find a kind of succession that is rather graduated and belonging to a metaphysical order in which there is continuous passage from the mere diversification of variations to a selfhood of reality that is itself, to the reality that opens in selfhood to be a self-possession, to the reality that changes into a statute of *community* and changes into a type of *world different* for each one in different epochs of history.

Now, these great stages are certainly not the stages of a great reality—I have said it several times, and I repeat it again: it is not a question of the passage of one thing, which is the great All, through all these vicissitudes. No, it is something completely different.

Each of these steps occurs in the first place *only in real things.* Respective [referential] unity is the seat of causality. In the respectivity of things, of some with the others, there occurs what I have described about reality qua reality, but *in each* and only in each of the real things.

In the second place, it not only happens in each of the real things, but it happens at the same time in millions of real things. In millions of living beings, millions of persons, millions of social forms, what I have just described certainly happens.

Third, this happens while they are being in fact what they are respectively in the world, and consequently while they have the character of time, while *being temporally in the world.*

In all these vicissitudes of reality, which more than vicissitudes are inner structures of reality qua real, what we find is just this: reality giving of itself qua reality.

This dynamic unity is the dynamic unity of the degrees of reality. I say dynamic unity because it does not seem to me that reality is a question of gradations (that is, that there are some realities more real than others). It is rather a true dynamic unity in which each reality of a higher type, in the order of reality, is mounting upon the substratum of a reality of lower order. This mounting is a dynamic subtension. In a metaphysical and dynamic fashion, each of the moments of reality that I have described subtends reality in its following moment.

Therefore, it must be said that all this dynamism does not relate to the substance but to the structures, to the substantive reality.

The reality of the world is substantivity and structure, but it is not substance.

It must be added that this reality has being dynamic as its inner moment. Being dynamic does not consist of being non-static, nor of anything higher. It consists purely and simply of being active by itself.

Fourth, this reality, active and dynamic by itself, to the extent that it is giving more of itself, is being ever more reality. There is no doubt whatsoever that it is ever more reality. This does not mean that it is a more perfect reality— that is another story. Yet undeniably, I stress, it is more reality. Without a doubt, the reality of an old man is more imperfect than the reality of a mature man, but it is more reality. Let us not forget this. In life one has ever more reality. All this dynamism of reality does not consist of anything but the fact that the reality, because it is active, is by itself ever more reality. It is more by giving of itself. The fact is that giving of itself has a precise limit. This limit is the intrinsic dynamic frailty of the real qua real.

Conclusion

In this study of mine, I did not wish to limit myself to dealing with a few isolated dynamisms that are very important in the world, each one very interesting in itself. It was important to me to show how all of them constitute an inner and also intrinsic unity, which is the intrinsic, multivalent, but perfectly clear dynamism of reality qua reality. This reality begins by existing and by doing nothing more than varying, then enters itself just by becoming the self. By virtue of being the self, it opens to self-possession, which is enacted in the form of a community and structured in the form of a world. This it does up to a certain moment and only to a certain limit, because reality is fragile, because it has a limit in its own reality.

This is the dynamic structure of reality.

Reality as essence is a structure. It is a constitutive structure, though one whose moments and ingredients of constitution are active and dynamic in themselves. Consequently, what has sometimes been said of my book [*On Essence*] is absolutely capricious. It has been said that it is a static book, a book of concepts merely at rest. I am very sorry. Rightly or wrongly, I hold precisely that in an essential and formal way, dynamism concerns essence such as I have described it in my modest, cumbersome book *On Essence*.

Notes

Translator's Introduction

1. Scholasticism refers to philosophy adopting the method and system of Christian schools that evolved from the sixth century, taught dialectic, and came to prevail during the Middle Ages. Scholastic philosophy achieved its acme in the thirteenth century but has continued ever since. The Italian theologian St. Thomas Aquinas (1225–74) radically innovated in Scholasticism by opposing St. Augustine's Platonism and Christianizing the Greek philosopher Aristotle (384–322 B.C.). Marías, *Historia de la filosofía,* 160–61.

Francisco Suárez (1548–1617), a Spanish Jesuit philosopher and theologian, was a pioneer in Scholasticism who separated metaphysics from theology. He systematized metaphysics, grounded on Aristotle, though with relative independence of him, while taking into account all the Greek and medieval interpreters of Aquinas and other Scholastic thinkers. Marías, *Historia de la filosofía,* 199.

Jacques Maritain (1882–1973), a French Neothomist, adapted St. Thomas to contemporary problems. Bourke, "Maritain, Jacques," 188.

2. The Spanish philosopher, journalist, educator, and politician José Ortega y Gasset (1883–1955) elaborated a metaphysics of human life, synthesizing in an original fashion late-nineteenth-century and early-twentieth-century German philosophers.

3. Pintor Ramos, "El magisterio intelectual de Ortega y la filosofía de Zubiri," 65.

4. Zubiri, "Ortega, maestro de filosofía," 8. All Zubiri's opinions expressed on Ortega and cited in the present introduction appear on page 8.

5. McClintock, *Man and His Circumstance,* 167–69.

6. The biographical data with chronology stem from Pintor Ramos, *Zubiri,* 9–10.

7. Ibid.

8. This I learned in private conversations with Pedro Laín Entralgo in 1989 and in the department of history of medicine, Complutense University of Madrid.

9. Orringer, *La aventura de curar,* 152.

10. Thomas B. Fowler Jr. translated Zubiri's *Naturaleza, Historia, Dios* under the title *Nature, History, God*. A. Robert Caponigri translated *Sobre la esencia* under the title *On Essence*.

As to the philosophers examined in *Cinco lecciones de filosofía* [Five lessons of philosophy], still not translated into English, the German philosopher Immanuel Kant (1724–1804) established a method for setting the proper limits and use of reason. He asked how synthetic a priori judgments used in Newtonian physics are possible about sensory data. In his *Kritik der reinen Vernunft* (*Critique of Pure Reason*), he submitted to inventory and deduction all synthetic a priori forms used in knowing nature.

The French philosopher Auguste Comte (1798–1857), founder of philosophical positivism, reacted against metaphysics with its pure speculation that overlooks facts of nature and society. Zubiri shows interest in Comte's theory of the three stages of human history: the two unscientific phases (theological and metaphysical) and the final, factual phase (positive). Zubiri, *Cinco lecciones de filosofía*, 131.

The French philosopher Henri Bergson (1859–1941) regards philosophy as an attempt to use intuition to discover the reality of the human spirit, to examine the limits of the *durée* [subjective time], and to open us to its transcendent meaning. This intuitive effort invents its own concepts adequate to the *durée* and borrowed neither from the other sciences nor from practical life. Ibid., 203–4.

The German philosopher Edmund Husserl (1859–1938), leader of the phenomenological movement in early-twentieth-century Germany, sees philosophy as the rigorous science of employing intuition to extract the essences of experience from the fact-world after barring all nonintuited interpretations. Ibid., 218–19.

The German philosopher Martin Heidegger (1889–1976) conceives philosophy as ontology, the problem of being itself, as distinguished from the (less radical) essences of Husserl. Heidegger grounds this problem on the existence of each of us. Ibid., 270.

11. Ortega y Gasset, *El hombre y la gente*, in *Obras completas*, 7:226.

12. Rodríguez de Lecea, "En la muerte de Pedro Laín Entralgo," 75.

13. Laín Entralgo, *Cuerpo y alma*, 65.

14. Ibid., 64, note 9.

15. Laín Entralgo, *El cuerpo humano*, 262–63.

16. Laín Entralgo, *Cuerpo y alma*, 67.

17. Weisskopf, "The Three Spectroscopies," 15–27.

18. Pintor Ramos, *Zubiri*, 23–24.

19. Laín Entralgo, *Cuerpo y alma*, 261.

Foreword

[The notes in this section were provided by the translator.]

1. Aristotle's *Metaphysics* treats being as substance, something withstanding change underneath appearances. But the German philosopher Georg Wilhelm Friedrich Hegel (1770–1831) treats being as becoming. See Hegel's *Phenomenology of the Spirit* and the

introduction to *The Science of Logic*, where reason makes being emerge from itself as a (rational) process, a becoming. See Zubiri, *Sobre la esencia*, 36–38.

2. The "in-its-own-right" is the set of notes constituting a reality. Zubiri, *Sobre la esencia*, 399. It is not "in itself," i.e., constitutively referred to other individuals. Ibid., 319. Nor is it "for itself," i.e., physically bonded to each note belonging to something real. Ibid., 281.

3. For Gracia, the relationship between the "in its own right" of a reality and its "giving of itself" is not a relationship of a structure to its activity but of a structure to its world-relatedness: on the meaning of constitutive (meaning, forming a system of essential notes), see ibid., 189; on "operative" as referring to the activity of a being, see Zubiri, *Estructura dinámica de la realidad*, 174; on substantivity as the radical structure of a reality, see Zubiri, *Sobre la esencia*, 87; and on respectivity (referentiality) as the quality of being a "note-of" all the other notes of a reality, see Zubiri, *Sobre la esencia*, 287–89.

4. On Scholasticism, see "Introduction," note 1.

5. *Inteligencia sentiente* [Sentient intelligence] is Zubiri's trilogy on the act of using the intelligence. The first part, *Inteligencia sentiente* (*Sentient Intelligence*), first appeared in 1980, and in the third edition (1984) acquired the subtitle *Inteligencia y realidad* [Intelligence and reality]; the second part, *Inteligencia y logos* [Intelligence and logos] came out in 1982, and the third part, *Inteligencia y razón* [Intelligence and reason], was published in 1983. The English translation of the first part is titled *Sentient Intelligence* (1999). The other two parts have not yet been translated into English.

On Kant, see "Introduction," note 10. In *Inteligencia y razón* Zubiri sets up a logical debate with Kant by completely reformulating his system of categories. See Gracia, *Voluntad de verdad*, 167.

On Husserl, see "Introduction," note 10. Zubiri, in his trilogy on intelligence, attempts to make use of phenomenology. Like Husserl's method, Zubiri's noology, or theory of intelligence, tries to avoid explaining what things are beyond direct apprehension and merely describes them insofar as they are present in aprehension. Gracia, *Voluntad de verdad*, 113. Husserl's use of the term *noesis* refers to an act of pure consciousness of apprehending essence; but Zubiri elaborates a noology to study acts of using the intelligence.

6. Zubiri's *Man and God* has the title *El hombre y Dios*. St. Augustine of Hippo (354–430), with his introspective empiricism, begins with the outside world, moves inward toward the self, and ascends toward God. In *Man and God*, Zubiri begins by treating man as a human reality, deals with reality as such first, then with its human variety, and finally, the human reality as a person that accedes to *religation*, the ultimate dimension of its reality that aims it toward the search for its own foundation, which is deity.

7. *Phenomenology of Spirit* (*Phänomenologie des Geistes*, 1807) is based on Hegel's analysis of self-consciousness and treats the Spirit as the ultimate given posited as the essence of man and human history. Hegel traces the unfolding of this Spirit throughout human history with the intention of seeking the extent to which the development of spirit is verifiable in actual history. Friedrich, *Philosophy of Hegel*, xxiv. Analogous-

ly, *Dynamic Structure of Reality* traces becoming in reality as the ultimate given posited as the foundation of man and of human history, with one changing reality mounted upon others.

Dialectics of Nature (*Dialektik der Natur,* 1927) was an unfinished work, mostly written between 1872 and 1882, by the German Socialist philosopher Friedrich Engels (1820–95), collaborator with Karl Marx (1818–83). Marxist dialectics is the science of the general laws of change. The same laws are said to govern change in human society, thought, and the outer world. Hence dialectics are presumably applicable to problems in material science (physics, biology) as well as to the social relations of science. Engel's book purported to prove that in nature the same dialectical laws operate as in history. Analogously, *Dynamic Structure of Reality* is a (structural) philosophy of becoming, applying not natural laws but a metaphysics of reality to problems in material science as well as to problems in history.

Chapter 1: Reality and Becoming

1. Parmenides (515?–440? B.C.), leader of the Eleatic school of Greek philosophy, in his poem *On Nature,* argues that the universe is eternal, one, continuous, and immobile. He distinguishes three ways of thinking: either [1.] it is, in other words, any intelligible name applies to something that exists, [2.] it is not, that is, to say that something does not exist is meaningless, self-contradictory; or [3.] it both is and is not. But if [2.] is true, then [3.] is also meaningless and self-contradictory, since it is necessary to reject all views saying that something does not exist, as this is unthinkable. Fishler, "Parmenides," 225.

2. Diels-Kranz, 28 B 6, 1 [Gracia's note. He refers to the notation of Hermann Diels and Walter Kranz in *Die Fragmente der Vorsokratiker*. The notation of Diels and Kranz, abbreviated "D.-K.," consists of a number identifying the author (number 28 corresponds to Parmenides), followed by a letter (A for the testimonies of given authors, B for the fragments of the works), followed by the number of the fragment and page.]

3. D.-K., 28 B 6, 2 [Gracia's note].

4. Ibid. [Gracia's note].

5. Ibid., B 7, 1 [Gracia's note].

6. Ibid., B 7, 2 [Gracia's note].

7. Cf. ibid., B 8, 12–15 [Gracia's note].

8. The "dialectic of being and of non-being" implies a comparison with Hegel's *Phenomenology of Spirit*. Hegel's dialectic denotes the process of becoming and passing away of being. The process, the movement as a whole, constitutes its truth. Being engenders non-being in Parmenides (as much later in Hegel), but Parmenides wholly rejects non-being, whereas in Hegel the dialectical process (thesis-antithesis-synthesis) both supersedes negation, the antithesis, and preserves it in its rise to the synthesis, the becoming. Hegel's word *Aufhebung,* applied to both processes, denotes "supersession" as well as "preservation."

9. The Greek philosopher Plato (428?–348? B.C.), founder in Athens of the Acade-

my, his own school of mathematics and philosophy, derives most of his fame from his approximately twenty-five dialogues, among them the *Sophist,* with its methodical exploration of non-being, among other themes. Bourke, "Plato," 236–37.

10. Plato, *Sophist,* 237 a 6–7 [Gracia's note].

11. Ibid., 237 a 8–9.

12. Ibid., 237 c 7–8.

13. Ibid., 237 d 6–7.

14. Ibid., 237 e 3.

15. Ibid., 256 a 11– b 4.

16. Ibid., 257 b 3–4.

17. Ibid., 241 d [Gracia's note]

18. Ibid., 258 d 2–3 [Gracia's note].

19. Ibid., 258 d 5–e 1.

20. Ibid., 256 d 7–8.

21. For Plato, the problem of being and non-being was a problem of method, which he called "dialectic," the knowledge and ability to distinguish by types how individual things are or are not able to be associated with one another: Ibid., 253 d 10–12. For Aristotle, who was concerned with practical applications of Plato's dialectic, being and non-being become a doctrine of nature, studied in the treatise *Physics.*

22. Aristotle, *Physics,* V.1, 225 a 34 (all references to the *Physics* are to the Hardie and Gaye translation unless otherwise noted).

23. On accidental change, see ibid., V.2, 226 a 26–30, in which Aristotle applies the name "alteration" to motion with respect to a quality (affection), not to the substance of something.

24. Zubiri refers to the Aristotelian distinction between substance and accident. "Substance" means essence or formal cause of something; the universal in each thing; its genus; and its subject, of which other things are predicated while it itself is not predicated of anything. Aristotle, *Metaphysics,* VI.3, 1028 b 33–1029 a 2. "Accident" means whatever is not a definition, nor a genus, nor a property of something, yet is present with it. Aristotle, *Topics,* I.8, 103 b 17–19. Aristotle distinguishes accidental change from substantial change but limits movement to substantial change. In *Metaphysics,* XI.11, 1067 d, Aristotle excludes generation from substantial change because contradiction is involved (in change from non-being to being). Zubiri, however, after Hegel, includes generation of substances within movement.

25. Aristotle, *Metaphysics,* XI.6, 1063 a 17–18.

26. In *Sobre la esencia,* Zubiri refutes Aristotle's notion of substance in favor of his own idea of substantivity. On 85–87, he notes that Aristotle attributes only to substances an essence, because only a substance is a true being. The substance, as distinguished from the accident, is the ultimate subject of predication and is permanent underneath all change. Aristotle's word for subject, *hypo-keímenon,* means the underlayer, the substratum. Zubiri, *Naturaleza, Historia, Dios,* 497.

27. Aristotle, *Metaphysics,* XI.6, 1068 a 3–7.

28. Plato held that motion to a certain degree participates in being and non-being.

Plato, *Sophist,* 256 d 7–8. Therefore Zubiri has inferred that for Plato, motion "is" becoming. Here Zubiri, following Plato, holds that non-being in a certain sense is becoming (although so is being in a certain sense).

29. Aristotle, *Physics,* III.1, 201 a 10–11 [Gracia's note].

30. Ibid., 201 b 31–33.

Chapter 2: Reality and Being

1. Zubiri's distinction between being as copulative and being as substantive stems from his debate with Scholastic philosophy in *Sobre la esencia,* 403. *Esse,* the word used by Scholasticism for "being," indistinctly embraces existence, essence, and the copulative, and Zubiri finds this too imprecise.

2. Non-Archimedean space is any space to which non-Archimedean geometry applies. The German mathematician David Hilbert (1862–1943) invented this seemingly totally abstract, self-referential geometry in 1899. It is the sum total of geometric propositions deducible from Hilbert's twenty axioms, referred to three arbitrary collections of objects, "points," "straight lines," and "planes," and five undefined relations between them. Detlefsen, "Hilbert's Programme and Formalism," 423–24.

3. Here Zubiri takes issue with Scholastic philosophy's conception of *esse reale,* real being. Scholasticism holds that not *every* being is reality, but reality is reducible to being. Zubiri, though, maintains that every being is grounded on reality. *Sobre la esencia,* 404.

4. The essence and the existence of iron are simply different moments of something previous: the reality of iron. Ibid., 409.

5. Just as reality is prior to being, so "respectivity" (referentiality) is prior to every relationship. The formal, intrinsic moment of the constitution of a real thing, whereby this thing is a function of all others, is what Zubiri has termed "respectivity." Ibid., 427

6. Zubiri applies the term "world" to respectivity in the order of universal reality as such, not in the order of particulars, to whose respectivity Zubiri applies the term "cosmos." Ibid., 427.

7. Although Zubiri may here follow classical terminology, for him there is no substantive being, properly speaking, but being of substantivity, being of what is substantive, being of reality. There is no being that is real, but a reality that has being [Gracia's note].

Chapter 3: Reality and Structure

1. Aristotle, *Physics,* III.1, 201 b 1–3.

2. Zubiri, *Sobre la esencia,* 87–88, 154, 156–61, 163, 382.

3. Aristotle, *Metaphysics,* VII.6, 1031 b 19–26.

4. Zubiri, *Sobre la esencia* [Gracia's note].

5. F. Suárez, *Disputatio* 15, § 2, 10–12, in *Disputaciones metafísicas,* 2:660–62.

6. In *Wissenschaftslehre (The Doctrine of Science),* the German philosopher Johann

Gottlieb Fichte (1762–1814) tried to base Kant's transcendental idealism on a single principle, the Self. He reduced Kantian dualisms of intuition and thinking and of knowledge and will to the activity of the "I."

7. The intrinsic, closed unity of constitutional notes comprising a substantivity, a reality in its own right, makes something "sufficient." Constitutional sufficiency is the formal principle of a substantivity. Zubiri, *Sobre la esencia*, 153.

8. For Aristotle, a substance has the character of being a permanent subject underneath all change. However, Zubiri finds substantivity irreducible to such a character. Substantivity is prior to it and therefore prior to substantiality. Ibid., 87.

9. See ibid., 193, 219.

10. On the construct state of notes, see ibid., 289–97.

11. Structure is a key concept in the present book. It is "an intrinsic unity expressed in systematic properties." Ibid., 513.

Chapter 4: Dynamism and Change

1. Aristotle, *Metaphysics*, I.3, 983 b 6.

2. Ibid., VII.9, 1034 b 31.

3. Ibid., IX.6, 1048 a 28–29 [Gracia's note].

4. Cf. Plato, *Sophist*, 257 b 3–4; see chap. 1, note 16.

5. Aristotle, *Metaphysics*, IX.6, 1048 a 33–34 [Gracia's note].

6. The German philosopher and mathematician Gottfried Wilhelm Leibniz (1646–1716) devised his metaphysics of monads, or individual cosmic potentialities, in such a way that God had to have started from an infinite realm of possibilities when he moved the universe of monads from potentiality to actuality in various combinations to produce the (preestablished) harmony of existence. Marías, *Historia de la filosofía*, 232.

7. Aristotle does stress generation and corruption, on which he wrote a treatise. However, generation and corruption of substances does not always imply passage from one substance to another. On *qualified* generation and *qualified* corruption, see Aristotle, *Physics*, V.1 225 a 12–17; Aristotle, *On Generation and Corruption*, I.3, 318 b 30–319 a 1–3; and Aristotle, *Metaphysics*, XI.11, 1067 b 21–23.

8. According to Aristotle, *Metaphysics*, IX.8, 1049 b 30, it seems impossible to be a builder without having built anything. This text uses the word οἰκοδόμον for "builder," not Zubiri's synonym ἀρχιτέκτον.

9. Aristotle, *Physics*, III.1, 201 b, 11–12.

10. Aristotle, *Metaphysics*, XI.9, 1066 a 20–21; Aristotle, *Physics*, III.2, 201 b 31; Aristotle, *On the Soul*, III.7, 431 a 6 [Gracia's note].

11. Aristotle, *Metaphysics*, XI.9, 1065 b 21–23.

12. Aristotle, *Physics*, III.1, 201 a 10–11 [Gracia's note].

13. Aristotle, *Metaphysics*, IX.8, 1049 b 4–5. "Prior" means nearer a given first principle, or according to place or to time, or to the first moving power, or to greater potentiality, or to some order. Ibid., V.2, 1018 b 9–34.

14. Ibid., IX.8, 1049 b 26–27.

15. τάξις denotes the ordering by rational spacing of individual elements, like dancers in a group or strings in a lyre. Ibid., V.2, 1018 b 26, and V.17, 1022 b 1.

16. Ibid., V.2, 1018 b 22–26.

17. On the four causes, see ibid., V.2, 1014 a 7–10. Of all causes, some are said to be in potency, others in act; for instance, the cause of the building of a house is a builder, or a builder who is building. On the concept of potency acquired through practice or study, see ibid., IX.5, 1047 b 32–34.

18. Thomism denotes the system following St. Thomas Aquinas in philosophy and theology. More narrowly, the word applies to doctrines held by a school composed mainly of the Dominican order. A distinction between potency and substance appears in St. Thomas's *Summa theologica*, First Part, Ques. 50, Art. 2, concerning the composition of angels.

19. Cf. Aristotle, *Metaphysics*, V.12, 1019 a 15–17.

20. The greater the distance between electrical charges, the less the attractive or repulsive force between them. In 1767, Joseph Priestley reasoned that an increase of distance by a given factor produces the forces between two charged bodies by the square of that factor. The French physicist Charles Augustin de Coulomb (1736–1806), whose name is used as the unit of electrical charge, lent expert precision to Priestley's proof. He suggested, however, that there were two "fluids" of electricity and two of magnetism, a theory today discredited.

21. The Scottish physicist James Clerk Maxwell (1831–79) discovered that light is a form of wave motion whereby electromagnetic waves move through a medium at a speed determined by electric and electromagnetic properties of that medium. This discovery came from the realization that changes in electric and magnetic fields around an electrical circuit produce changes along the lines of force within the surrounding space. R. L. Smith-Rose, "Maxwell, James Clerk," 573–75.

22. An antenna seen by a fixed observer emits an electromagnetic wave in the same plane with respect to him or her. The electric field, changing in time, stays perpendicular to the magnetic field and to the direction of propagation of the wave. The electric and the magnetic components of the wave nurture one another. The whole configuration moves through space with the speed of light in accordance with Maxwell's differential equations concerning induction of electric and magnetic fields. Halliday and Resnick, *Fundamentals of Physics*, 834–35, 838.

23. Zubiri puns to mock nineteenth-century science. "Filamentous" refers to the filaments deemed realities in the "net" of the universe; "phyletic" pertains to a biological "phylum," here extended to mean reality as a "type" of being; "philic" is a coined word used for alliteration and also perhaps to hint that reality lovingly gives of itself. Laín Entralgo invented the adjective to refer to Christian love; see, for example, *Teoría y realidad del otro*, 684, note 89.

24. Nineteenth-century physicists theorized the existence of a medium, an ether, for transmitting light through space. The ether contained electric and magnetic fields. But in 1905 the German-born physicist Albert Einstein (1879–1955) postulated that the speed

of light, traveling in free space, has an identical value c in all directions and in all frames of reference. If no reference frame can serve as a basis for measuring the speed of light, then Einstein's postulate eliminates the theoretical need for an ether. Halliday and Resnick, *Fundamentals of Physics*, 857. The most famous physics equation is $E = mc^2$, wherein E is the amount of energy lying dormant in a mass m and c is the speed of light. Ibid., 162–63.

25. By "contemporary physics," Zubiri means quantum mechanics. See *Estructura dinámica de la realidad*, 80. He refers to the controversy between wave theorists of light and particle theorists. Before modern quantum mechanics developed, the Danish physicist Niels Bohr (1885–1962) noted that experimental evidence on both light and matter called for a wave picture in some cases, a particle picture in others. A particle is always localized, while wavelength and frequency demand extension in space and in time. Controversy erupted in 1926–27 between the German physicist Werner Heisenberg (1901–76) and the Austrian physicist Erwin Schrödinger (1887–1961), among others, as to how to offer a single coherent and universal framework for the description of observational data. The issue remains far from resolved. Jos Uffink and Jan Hilgevoord, "The Uncertainty Principle."

26. On the respectivity of the real, see chap. 2, notes 5 and 6, and Zubiri's "Respectividad de lo real," 13–43. Reality has a formal structure that Zubiri terms its "in-its-own-right." The primary mode of that structure is its openness. Openness enables reality to refer to other realities in a respective mode. Respectivity is the second mode of the structure of reality. Openness toward the thing which is real is *respectivity, constituent* of the self-possession of the open reality, of its own form and mode of reality. Self-possession is the third mode of structure of reality. Openness refers both to self-possession and to reality as constitution of the worldliness [*mundanalidad*] of its self-possession. In taking possession of itself, a reality is more than itself, making a world. This worldliness is the fourth mode of the structure of real openness. Given the openness of the formal structure of notes constituting reality, whenever there are several real things present, each with its self-possession, all these forms and modes of reality and the worldiness constituting them enjoy respective unity. This unity of respectivity is what Zubiri calls "remittent respectivity," as distinguished from "constituent respectivity." Ibid., 40–41.

27. On the in-its-own-right, see the previous note.

28. In the 1694 study "On the Emendation of First Philosophy and the Notion of Substance" ("De primae philosophiae emendatione, et de notione substantiae," IV, 469), Leibniz attributes to all substances self-governing "active force" [*vis activa*], as opposed to Scholastic philosophy's "bare power" [*potentia nuda*], merely responding to outside influences. On Leibniz, see note 6.

29. A *quale* (plural, *qualia*) signifies a sensory universal—the redness of this rose—of which we have immediate awareness and which forms the source and confirmation of our empirical knowledge. The originator of this concept is American philosopher Clarence Irving Lewis (1883–1964). Baylis, "Neorealism," 299.

30. The relationship between being in-one's-own-right and giving of oneself appar-

ently stems from Zubiri's debate with Heidegger. In *Sobre la esencia*, 442, Zubiri writes that Heidegger, seeking an ontology, conceives understanding of being as an act in which being shows itself and does this from itself, and as a mode of being, that is, of the very thing that is showing itself, of being. The possibility of understanding being is therefore equal to the possibility of being, itself. Hence Heidegger's statement that "being gives itself in the understanding of being." Zubiri infers that this giving of itself performed by being is literally giving itself, that is, being what it is.

Zubiri maintains that reality is prior to being. Something only gives of itself, including giving its being, if that something is already real. Ibid., 446. From here it is a simple step for Zubiri to maintain in *Dynamic Structure of Reality* that things, because they are in-their-own-right, i.e., real, have an *active moment* consisting of giving of themselves. The *active moment* is the dynamism in Zubiri's title, *Dynamic Structure of Reality*.

31. In research begun in 1676 but mostly pursued in 1689, Leibniz, widely held to be the founder of dynamics in the science of mechanics, criticized René Descartes's (1596–1650) ideas of mechanics and made innovations in theories of momentum, kinetic energy, and potential energy. Marías, *Historia de la filosofía*, 230–31. On Leibniz's metaphysics of monads, comprised of active force, see chap. 4, note 6.

32. Near the start of *Philosophiae Naturalis Principia Mathematica* (*Mathematical Principles of Natural Philosophy*) (1687), the English natural philosopher, mathematician, and physicist Sir Isaac Newton (1642–1727) formulated his third law of motion: "To every action there is always opposed an equal reaction; or, the mutual actions of two bodies upon each other are always equal, and directed to contra parts." Halliday and Resnick, *Fundamentals of Physics*, 84–85.

Chapter 5: Causal Dynamism

1. *Sic!* See Aristotle, *Metaphysics*, V.1, 1013 a 17–18 [Gracia's note. Zubiri loosely translates Aristotle. To be more literal, "All causes are principles. Hence, it is common to all principles to be the first from which something either is or becomes or is known." *Metafísica de Aristóteles*, 218].

2. Leibniz's principle of sufficient reason is, "Nothing happens without its being possible for one who should know things sufficiently to give a reason showing why things are so and not otherwise." Greenwood, "Principle of Sufficient Reason," 250.

3. Aristotle, *Metaphysics*, V.2, 1013 a 24–25 [Gracia's note].

4. Ibid., 1013 a 26–27 [Gracia's note].

5. Ibid., 1013 a 27 [Gracia's note].

6. Ibid., 1013 a 27–28 [Gracia's note].

7. Ibid., 1013 a 29–30 [Gracia's note].

8. Ibid., 1013 a 29–32.

9. Ibid., 1013 a 32–33 [Gracia's note].

10. Ibid., 1013 a 33 [Gracia's note].

11. Ibid., 1013 a 34 [Gracia's note].

12. Ibid., V.2, 1013 a 35 [Gracia's note].

13. The *Dialogues concerning the Two New Sciences* (*Dialoghi delle scienze nuove*) (1636), 197, by the Italian mathematician, astronomer, and inventor Galileo Galilei (1564–1642), purports to "set forth a very new science dealing with a very ancient subject" (motion): the work starts by dealing with properties of solids before considering acceleration and projectiles.

14. In *Dialogues concerning the Two New Sciences,* 137, one of Galileo's characters remarks, "Thanks to this discussion, I have learned the cause of a certain effect which I had long wondered at and despaired of understanding." The effect in question was the difficulty of using a certain water pump in a cistern.

15. Newton's first law, also termed the law of inertia, holds that a body on which no net force acts will stay at rest if at rest, but if moving at a constant speed will continue to move at that speed. Halliday and Resnick, *Fundamentals of Physics,* 80.

16. Albert of Saxony (ca. 1316–90), the German Scholastic philosopher noted for his research in physics, subscribed to the widely held theory that a falling body acquires a quantity known as impetus when set in motion and eventually comes to rest as the impetus is exhausted. Moody, "Medieval Philosophy," 18:711.

17. Newton's second law of motion is expressable with the equation $\Sigma F = ma$, that is, the vector sum of all forces acting on a body is equal to the mass of that body multiplied by its acceleration. Halliday and Resnick, *Fundamentals of Physics,* 82.

18. In his *Treatise of Human Nature,* I, the English empiricist David Hume (1711–76) refuted classical causality on nine grounds deftly ordered and analyzed by Fowler in "The Formality of Reality," 58: (1.) an absolute distinction exists between relations of ideas and empirical knowledge, (2.) we know our ideas alone, (3.) in matters of fact, we can conceive these ideas in a separable fashion, (4.) hence we perceive no real effect of anything on anything else, that is, no causality in the classical sense, (5.) so-called causality is nothing but constant conjunction of the idea of the cause with the idea of the effect, (6.) yet we need and use this conjunction to keep in touch with the world and reason about its contents, (7.) knowledge of the external world and of its contents is problematic, (8.) constant conjunction does not serve for metaphysical purposes; a stronger version of causality is required, (9.) therefore metaphysics is impossible.

19. Kant, *Kritik der reinen Vernunft,* B 13, 5–9 = A 9, 5–9, p. 47. "A" and "B" refer to the first and second editions, respectively. [Gracia's note.]

20. Cf. Kant, *Kritik der reinen Vernunft,* B 13, 9–11. [Gracia's note.]

21. "For Leibniz, all truths are analytic in God's mind, though not for us." Fowler, "Formality of Reality," 62.

22. Kant, *Critique of Pure Reason,* B 13, 14–26, p. 9.

23. Cf. ibid., B 5, 4–8, p. 5.

24. A pure principle of knowledge means an a priori, universal principle, removed from immediate sensory experience.

25. For Leibniz no causality exists *between* cosmic substances or monads, only a reciprocity caused by God's preestablished harmony. *Within* every monad, however, Leib-

niz does find causality, which he terms appetition or desire. In the *Monadologie* §11, he actually speaks of an "inner principle" [*principe interne*], that produces changes in monads since an "outer cause" cannot influence their interior.

26. Kant holds that the principle of causality applies (with absolute validity) *only* to things as objects of experience, *not* to things as they are in themselves. Preface to the second edition of the *Critique of Pure Reason* (1787), B xxvii, 3–7, p. xxxviii.

27. Kant, *Critique of Pure Reason*, B 183, 15–18, p. 125.

28. Recall that Galileo in his *Dialogues* aspires to make a new science in which he aspires to reveal *how* things happen, not to enunciate a causal law.

29. On Albert Einstein (1879–1955), whose equation $E = mc^2$ helped bring about quantum mechanics, see chap. 4, note 24.

The Austrian physicist Erwin Schrödinger produced equations about undulation that explained behavior of electrons in atoms. These equations formed the basis of wave mechanics and allowed for the development of quantum mechanics.

The English physicist Paul Dirac (1902–84) produced equations to explain magnetic and "spin" qualities of the electron. Dirac's famous wave equation introduced special relativity into Schrödinger's equations.

The German physicist Max Planck (1858–1947) discovered in 1900 that electromagnetic waves emitted from objects did not have a continuous distribution. With the discovery, he realized that a particle containing electromagnetic waves with a certain energy could only have been subjected to radiation. Planck called this particle a "quantum." Planck's theory revolutionized physics, forming the basis of many quantum theories.

30. Werner Heisenberg's uncertainty principle is succinctly formulated as follows: the more certain the position of a subatomic particle, the less certain its momentum at a given point in time; the less certain its position, the more certain its momentum. Church, "Uncertainty Principle," 325.

31. "Metabasis," originally signifying a shifting or moving over, as of the body when walking, can also mean a revolutionary change in government or laws. Liddell and Scott, *Greek-English Lexicon*, 990.

32. Aristotle, *Metaphysics*, V.2, 1013 a 4–5.

33. Ibid., V.2, 1013 a 30.

34. Ibid., V.2, 1013 a 32–33.

35. Kant, *Critique of Pure Reason*, B 792, 7–10, p. 493.

36. Leibniz reduced the principle of causality (no effect without a cause) to the principle of (sufficient) reason (no true statement without a reason). The consequence of "no true statement without a reason" is either that a proposition is true or that it is false. If true, then, by the principle of truth, the form of a true proposition excludes any contradiction, and this is the form of the identical proposition: A = A. If false, then, by the principle of contradiction, a proposition is false through its very form because it makes the proposition nonsense. See Leibniz, *Monadologie*, §§31, 32, and Ortega y Gasset, *La idea de principio en Leibniz*, 331.

37. On sentient intelligence, see "Foreword," note 5.

38. When I apprehend something, the object apprehended not only actualizes a content but does so in its own *form.* This piece of paper seen by me presents itself to me not only as an area of off-white, but also as an area understood as stationery in its own right. The self-presentation in its own *form* is what Zubiri calls "formality." Gracia, *Voluntad de verdad,* 113.

39. On functionality, Fowler explains, "Things can be related in many more ways than can be adequately described by the deterministic paradigm of classical causality [every effect has its cause]. To describe this situation, Zubiri borrows a term (and idea) from mathematics: that of functionality. Functionality, sometimes describable only in mathematical language, is a much more general way of describing relationships among things. These relationships may be among more than two things, and may involve statistical ideas. Functional relations may or may not involve causality in the traditional sense, or Hume's version, constant conjunction; functionality is a much broader concept, capable of supporting inferences such as counterfactual conditionals which are beyond the range of constant conjunction. Furthermore, functional relationships may be—and indeed often are—statistically based, for which constant conjunction as an explanation is hopelessly inadequate." "Formality of Reality," 64.

40. Causality has to do in Zubiri with formality of reality, with *how* it presents itself; cause is simply the particular link between two events. Quantum mechanics has revealed to Zubiri the distinction between causality and cause: "It is possible that things are interrelated by determinate links, i.e., that the state of the electron in an instant of time determines its later course. But what Heisenberg's [uncertainty] principle affirms is that such a determinism has no physical meaning, on account of the impossibility of knowing exactly the initial state." Zubiri, *Naturaleza, Historia, Dios,* 333.

41. "What" is real refers to the particular thing; "its being real," to the form in which it presents itself in apprehension.

42. Occasionalism maintains the incapacity of mind and body to affect one another. Hence, all apparent causes in nature stem from divine intervention. Scott, "René Descartes," 131.

43. By "modern science," Zubiri means mathematical physics from Galileo to and excluding quantum mechanics. See note 29.

44. On respectivity, see chap. 2, notes 5 and 6, and chap. 4, note 26.

45. On the *quale,* see chap. 4, note 29.

46. Zubiri dislikes the word "active" because he means something more universal than the usual sense. For him, "active" means "giving of oneself" or making manifest one's essential properties or notes. See chap. 4, note 30.

47. On Leibnizian *vis activa,* see chap. 4, note 28.

48. Cf. St. Thomas Aquinas, *Summa theologica* I, 5, 1, in which fire is said to generate fire by its own active nature.

49. Zubiri disapproves of Leibniz's probable view of fire as a kind of burning substance, a *vis activa,* because Zubiri regards each reality not as substance but as substantivity, active in itself.

50. Zubiri's neologism *actuosidad,* which I translate as "activeness," dissatisfies him,

possibly for failing to suggest the underlying referentiality that grounds the activeness: the activeness comes from the interrelation between the *notes* of a reality and also from the interrelation between the reality and *other* realities.

51. Here Zubiri explicitly relates causality, the main theme of his chapter, to structural dynamism, the theme of his whole book. If giving of oneself constitutes dynamism, and if giving of oneself unfolds in activity, then this activity functions as causality (in the order of universals, of reality as such).

52. For Zubiri, scientific determinism, by trying to explain how things happen, starts from the *effects*, not as Aristotle maintains, from the *causes*, of events. Zubiri sees shortcomings in both approaches and tries to overcome them. He surpasses scientific determinism by tracing the antecedents of phenomena to the activities of their realities; he surmounts Aristotle by rejecting the notion of cause as underlying substance.

53. The problem of causality is transcendental, having to do with the order of reality as such and serving as a basis for the problem of cause, which belongs to the less radical order of the particular. This we have seen in the present chapter, in which Zubiri finds the production of the bell sound (from Hume's example) a function of the character of reality that the sound itself has, over and above the particular content of the sound.

54. On Maxwell, see chap. 4, notes 21 and 22.

55. By Einstein's Postulate of Relativity, the laws of physics are the same for observers in all inertial frames of reference, with no frame of reference privileged with respect to any other. All observers can assign different space-time coordinates to the same event. Halliday and Resnick, *Fundamentals of Physics,* 953–55. Hence, according to Ortega y Gasset, "event A, which from the earthly point of view precedes event B in time, from another place in the universe—Sirius, for example—will appear to come after B. There can be no greater possible inversion." *El tema de nuestro tiempo,* 235. If laws of physics try to explain the "how" of two events, then the order of the events can vary with the frame of reference.

56. According to Zubiri, *Sobre la esencia,* 467–69, every substantivity or essence is intrinsically limited. Being a plenary reality, not tolerating any reduction, describes God alone. The exhaustibility of reality as such exists within every other essence as part of it, independently of any outer cause. Zubiri contrasts a house collapsing to the wrecking ball with a house crumbling on its own. In the first house, I apprehend a causal connection; in the second, I see a reality in itself breaking apart.

57. This statement forms a corollary of the previous one. If all substantives were part of a single great reality, that reality qua essence would be intrinsically limited, flawed. Hence, how much (external) causality could be predicated of the parts, and how much inner decrepitude?

58. On respectivity and causality, see note 44 and accompanying text.

59. Medieval thought divided nature into *natura naturans,* a self-sufficient, active, creative totality, and *natura naturata,* or the (passive) nature requiring that totality as its principle and cause. Zubiri distinguishes his own conception of this twofold division from the old notion: *natura naturans* is not a great natural object, but merely a

dynamic structure in the cosmos determining the essence of natural objects [*natura naturata*]. *Espacio, tiempo, materia,* 600.

60. On infinite analysis in Leibniz, see chap. 5, note 21.

61. Aristotle, *Metaphysics,* XI.5, 1062 a 16–17.

62. In the Preface to the Second Edition (1787) of the *Critique of Pure Reason,* B xxv, 15–16, p. xxxvii, Kant holds that "space and time are only forms of sensible intuition, [and are] therefore conditions of the existence of things as phenomena only." Yet human knowledge is *always* conditioned by sensible intuition. For Kant, however, it is only reasonable to assume that things-in-themselves remain *unconditioned* by extraneous factors. Since thought is intuitively *conditioned,* it is humanly impossible to think of the unconditioned without *contradiction.* But the contradiction disappears when we admit that things-in-themselves are unknowable. Throughout the *Critique of Pure Reason,* Kant calls for this admission in multiple forms. Hence, as Zubiri suggests, Kant is respecting and abiding by the principle of contradiction, with much the same deference to that principle as Aristotle shows.

63. According to Zubiri, *Sobre la esencia,* 8, classical philosophy holds that the conceptual pair essence-existence is grounded on causation: because everything has a cause, we are justified in inquiring into the fact of its existence. However, Zubiri holds that nothing can exist without being a moment of something already constituted as real. Therefore he rejects the essence-existence distinction. I can consider a real thing either in an essential way, or else in an existential way; reality is both essence and existence. Ibid., 401.

64. Here Zubiri mocks the Big Bang theory, problematic even for the order of the particulars, but not directly relevant to the order of universals, that is, of reality as such, the sphere proper to philosophy.

65. On cosmos and world, see the doctrine of respectivity, chap. 2, note 6.

66. For Zubiri reality is structure, the actuality of a primary unity, organized into a construct system of notes. An organism, for instance, is a structural unity, with each of its features in a perfectly determined position. The organism has a respectivity belonging to the order of particulars, but a respectivity grounded on a deeper respectivity, one belonging to the order of the universals, of reality as such. This organism is a concrete mutt, but a dog in general. Hence the first respectivity (cosmos comprising the mutt) receives its foundation from the second, grounding respectivity (world defining the dog). Ultimately, the structural system of this organism is based on the formality of the notes or construct system comprising the dog.

67. On the "how," see note 28.

68. On determinism, see note 39. On scientific laws, see chap. 4, pp. 28–29.

69. Given a small light source, something opaque placed in its path has a sharp shadow. Primitive researchers inferred that light travels in a straight line—a light ray—emanating from the source. However, the more we narrow the slit through which light shines, the greater it spreads out through diffraction. Hence, "geometric [e.g., straight-line] optics holds only to the extent that we can neglect diffraction." Halliday and Resnick, *Fundamentals of Physics,* 903–4. Also, in chap. 4, note 21, we noted Maxwell's

idea of light as an electromagnetic wave sustained by energy oscillation between electric and magnetic components.

70. On process as expression of dynamism, see chap. 4, "Fifth Step."

71. On closed and open essences, see Zubiri, *Sobre la esencia,* 499–504.

72. Heidegger, in *Sein und Zeit,* §§67, 68, holds that *Dasein,* our being-in-the-world, consists of our being ecstatic "openness" [*Erschlossenheit*] in accordance with the precise unity of the instant. Through temporality we are as we are and we stand "in the being" beyond every being. Zubiri, *Sobre la esencia,* 440. However, for Zubiri, Heidegger incorrectly prioritizes temporal existence as opposed to reality.

73. Among numerous passages to the same effect, see Plato's famous parable of the cavern, dividing being from becoming, essence from generation, while privileging being and its science, dialectic. *Republic,* VII, 534 a 4–5.

Chapter 6: The Dynamism of Variation

1. "Constitutional" notes comprise the primary structure of the reality, which they integrate with other realities. Some constitutional notes are grounded on other notes, which determine them, while others are ungrounded, rest on themselves, and are not derived from other constitutional notes. They determine the whole structure of the constitutional system. Zubiri calls ungrounded notes "constitutve" notes. Zubiri, *Sobre la esencia,* 188–89.

2. Ibid., 478–79 [Gracia's note].

3. *Esse-ad* refers to a relationship between an accident and a substance, wherein the accident is not inherent to anything but is a being-toward for the substance to which it refers. Suárez, *Disputaciones metafísicas,* 37, §2 (vol. 5, 667).

4. Aristotle, *Physics,* V.1, 226 a 26–29, 270 a 27–30, 319 b 10–14.

5. Ibid., 225 b 5–8.

6. See Aristotle's treatment of locomotion as mechanical motion in ibid., V.2, 226 b 1–2, VII.1, 243 a.

7. On Maxwell's research of electromagnetic fields, see chap. 4, notes 21 and 22. On the ether, see chap. 4, note 24.

8. The kinetic theory of gases involves the approach to the kinetic energy of gas molecules at a certain pressure and temperature and within a certain volume; macroscopic properties of a gas (like pressure and temperature) are related to microscopic properties (like speeds and kinetic energies). Halliday and Resnick, *Fundamentals of Physics,* 484, 500. Thermodynamics concerns the study of the internal energy of systems submitted to a change of temperature. Ibid., 447. As to the kinetic theory of temperature, the temperature of a gas equals the average translational kinetic energy of its molecules, that is, the energy with which molecules of a gas move around in a given volume. Ibid., 489.

9. Aristotle, *Physics,* IV.1, 209 a 30.

10. Ibid., III.1, 200 b, 33–34, 225 b 2–3.

11. In *Sobre la esencia,* 436–37, Zubiri combats the conversion of space into substance

in Aristotle and Newton. The *Physics*, IV.4, 211 a, presents place as something containing what it serves to locate, but *Sobre la esencia*, 436, sees space as merely respective, referential, not a "receptacle of things." Galileo and Newton absolutize space (as the ideal space in which scientific laws apply with precision). But Einsteinian relativity denies the existence of an absolute frame of reference. Ortega y Gasset, *El tema de nuestro tiempo*, 237.

12. The "next to" is a structure whereby some points are placed next to others. This concept relies on topology, studying properties of geometric forms that remain invariant under certain transformations. In an infinite set of points, a series of subsets can be defined so that so that the meeting of several open subsets is itself a subset, and the intersection of these open sets is another subset. An open subset is the absence of a boundary as part of a subset. In topology, a space (or this structure "next to") may be either continuous or discontinuous, connected or disconnected, compact or not compact. When a set forms a whole, it is connected; when isolated into discrete points, it becomes disconnected. Given an infinite succession of points, if the succession converges on a limit belonging to a space, that space is compact; a space where the convergence does not take place is not compact. Zubiri, *Espacio, tiempo, materia*, 48–49.

13. According to Zubiri, an affinity is "a property in accordance with which at every point there exists a law whereby a vector passing through that point undergoes transformation into another vector, obtained when the first vector is displaced in a way parallel to itself. The parallel displacement can be performed in infinite ways within the same topological space. . . . Affine structures are grounded on topological space, but in no way predetermined by it." Ibid., 54.

14. The Nagata-Smirnov Metrization Theorem holds that a topological space is metrizable if and only if it is regular and Hausdorff and has a base that is a union of countably many locally finite collections of open sets. A space is regular if C is a closed set with p a point not in C; C and p have disjoint neighborhoods. A Hausdorff space is a topological space in which any two distinct points have disjoint neighborhoods. A base is a set of open sets, each one of which forms a union of sets. Nagata, *Modern General Topology*, 194–96.

15. "If I define a metric, then I automatically induce a certain affinity, that is, a certain mode of parallel transportation and a certain topology." Zubiri, *Espacio, tiempo, materia*, 57.

16. A geodesic line belongs to the geometry of curved surfaces and replaces the straight line of plane geometry.

17. The speed of light, 299,792,458 meters per second and denoted c by Einstein, marks the greatest verifiable speed in reality as such. Halliday and Resnick, *Fundamentals of Physics*, 393, 400, 543.

18. According to Einstein, a gravitational field curves the trajectory of light. In the presence of a gravitational field the trajectory of a light beam is deflected downward in a curve toward the attracting body, whereas in the absence of a gravitational field, the light trajectory displays no curve. Pirani, "Relativity," 719.

19. In quantum mechanics, Planck's quantum of "action," denoted h, represents a basic physical constant, equal to the smallest quantity of action that can occur in the

universe. In the atom after Bohr's model (with its shells of particles), "action" means the angular momentum inherent in the orbital movements of electrons. Let x = the momentum of a particle, p = its position, and δ = a spread of values centered on some given value. According to Heisenberg's quantum uncertainty principle of 1927, the product of δx and δp cannot be less than h. Church, "Uncertainty Principle," 324. An inverse mathematical relationship obtains between δx and δp. For Heisenberg, if δp is small, then there is little uncertainty in the position of a particle and a great amount of uncertainty in its momentum, that is, its action. Hence Heisenberg, Zubiri thinks, finds it difficult to determine subatomic trajectories, momentum, or action.

20. Aristotle, *Physics,* III.1, 201 a 11 [Gracia's note].

21. Ibid., III.1, 201 b 31; Aristotle, *On the Soul,* III.7, 431 a 6 [Gracia's note].

22. Special or restricted relativity theory, dealing with uniform motion, is grounded on two postulates: that the same laws of physics apply for observers in all inertial frames of reference and that free-space light speed has the same value c in all directions and all inertial frames of reference. No motion exceeds c, mass increases with the increase in velocity, $E = mc^2$, and time depends on relative motion of the observer measuring it. Halliday and Resnick, *Fundamentals of Physics,* 971. Einstein regards all uniform motion as relative. For this reason a passenger in a northbound train at rest, facing a southbound train on a nearby track, may experience surprise if the southbound train slowly begins to move: he may infer that his own train is leaving ahead of schedule. Zubiri refers to this perplexity as to which train is in motion.

23. General relativity applies to gravity. It holds that the local effects of a gravitational field and of acceleration of an inertial system are identical. Therefore astronauts in uniform circular motion accelerating toward earth cannot discern this acceleration from gravity-free space. Einstein concludes that gravitation is "not a force, but a curvature in space and time." Halliday and Resnick, *Fundamentals of Physics,* 349. See also note 18.

24. This is Newton's second law of motion; see chap. 5, note 17.

25. Quantity leads the list of Aristotle's nine accidents in *Categories,* 4, 25. For Thomas de Sutton in *De natura accidens* (chap. 1, "De accidente naturalis"), quantity is the first and closest accident to natural substance and, while foreign to the constitution of substance, measures things from within, while time and place measure them from without. In the *Summa theologica,* III, Ques. 77, Art. 2, St. Thomas Aquinas goes further, viewing all accidents as related to their subject and grounded through dimensive quantity, that is, a claim to their own relative quantified positions. Zubiri wishes to privilege local motion in the same way among variations.

26. "In India, ancient Jainism held an atomistic conception of time. Time would be constituted by small units or indivisible instants of time . . . of minimum duration. Time, then, would not be continuous. They thought that this was necessary to explain the interaction of two atoms of matter or the intervention of human freedom in the course of time." Zubiri, *Espacio, tiempo, materia,* 219–20.

27. "According to Heisenberg, in a temporal enclosure of the order of elementary particles the concepts of *before* and *after* cannot be adequately defined. As a result,

certain processes would unfold in time in a reverse direction from the one that the causal series would demand. But in this suggestion of Heisenberg two different issues are clearly glimpsed: one, the seriation of physical phenomena according to antecedents and consequences; two, the seriation of temporal moments. It is plain that the possible reversal in the succession of physical phenomena . . . leaves the irreversibility of time intact and presupposes it. . . . There has been a reversal in the series of phenomena unfolding in time, but not in time itself." Ibid., 227.

28. "Circumscriptively" means "by spatial limitation," as Christ's body is limited to the consecrated Host, or wafer, though wherever located. Latham, *Dictionary of Medieval Latin from British Sources,* 2C:344. In Latin, *circumscriptive.* In many sources this adverb is paired with *diffinitive,* also written *definitive* [definitively], and meaning "by spatial determination," in such a way that Christ's body is present as a whole and at the same time in every visible part of the Host. Hardt, *On the Sacrament of the Altar,* 47.

29. On *vis activa,* see chap. 4, note 28.

30. On constitutive and constitutional notes, see chap. 6, note 1.

31. On modes of inherence of accidents, see chap. 6, note 3.

Chapter 7: The Dynamism of Alteration

1. In Spanish, the word *emergencia* has two meanings: "emergency" and "emergence." Zubiri uses the word in the second sense.

2. Aristotle's prime matter is "the primary underlying subject in a thing, from which . . . something else is generated." *Physics,* I.9, 192 a 32–34 (Apostle trans., p. 24).

3. Ibid., I.2, 185 a 13–15.

4. Ibid., I.2, 185 a 27–33.

5. Ibid., I.7, 190 b 9–11.

6. Ibid., I.7, 190 b 23.

7. On prime matter, see note 2.

8. Production from nothing is creation. Production from something is eduction of the potency from matter. Forms educed are contained in the potency of matter but are moved out of that potency through the action of the agent. Suárez, *Disputaciones metafísicas,* 15, §2, 14 (2, 664–65).

9. Aristotle, *Physics,* I.6, 189 b 5.

10. Suárez, *Disputaciones metafísicas,* 13, §5, 9 (2, 432–33); and cf. §5, 13 (2, 435).

11. Bergson, *Creative Evolution,* 203.

12. In *Disputaciones metafísicas,* 15, §10, 40 (2, 754), Suárez observes the coexistence of the two views.

13. In drawing the bowstring, the archer generates potential energy; in releasing it to shoot an arrow, the archer produces kinetic energy. Potential energy deserves the name "configuration energy:" "The system on which the work is done—the bow, in our example—stores potential energy by changing its configuration in some sense or other." Halliday and Resnick, *Fundamentals of Physics,* 149–50.

14. Aristotle, *Metaphysics,* V.2, 1013 b 29–32.

15. On eduction, see note 8.

16. $E = mc^2$; see chap. 4, note 24.

17. Work done on a system (like drawing a bow) stores *potential* energy; see note 13. In addition, total work done on a particle is equivalent to its change of *kinetic* energy (the work-energy theory of physics). Halliday and Resnick, *Fundamentals of Physics,* 134.

18. Energy is convertible from potential to kinetic or from kinetic to potential in an isolated system, but it is not subject to creation or destruction. By special relativity theory, with its mass-energy equivalency formula $E = mc^2$, mass is recognizable as a type of energy, measurable either in energy units (ergs, calories) or in mass units (kilograms, tonnes). Ibid., 187.

19. In the 1968 article "Three Spectroscopies," 15–27, Victor F. Weisskopf (1908–), an Austrian American physicist, examines quantum mechanics as it had been applied to the decay of elementary particles. Those particles are bombarded with other high-energy particles. Atomic and molecular matter release energy as quanta or "packets of energy," most familiarly, photons (15). Weisskopf examines three types of spectra of energy states discussed: atomic, nuclear, and subnuclear (16). On the atomic level, "each quantum state corresponds to a certain vibrational pattern of electron waves, confined to the immediate neighborhood of the nucleus by the attractive coulomb force, or electric force, between the nucleus and the electrons" (16). Within the nucleus lies a "binding force" produced by the interaction between protons and neutrons, whose "confined waves" presumably produce patterns of vibration like electron wave patterns (20). Physicists also seek evidence of a strong binding force between hypothetical subnuclear particles such as quarks (27). These attractions on the atomic, nuclear, and subnuclear levels must be the "states of resonance of [vibrating] elementary particles" which, according to Zubiri, keep particles from being independent qua realities. In private conversations, Diego Gracia informs me that Zubiri assiduously read *Scientific American.*

20. Weisskopf, "Three Spectroscopies," 15.

21. Ibid., 19.

22. Derived from the Greek φῦλον [tribe or race], "phylum" denotes a broad category of biological grouping higher than species, genus, family, order, and class. Campbell, *Biology,* 485. Zubiri broadens the meaning of the word to embrace any dynamic, metaphysical class of beings capable of generating others of the same species, whether animal, vegetable, or mineral.

23. On prime matter, see note 8.

24. But cf. Zubiri, *Sobre la esencia,* 244, 310–14, 317, referring "constitutive scheme" [*esquema constitutivo*] to the phylum and species, instead of the "constituent scheme."

25. On potentialities of constitution, see ibid., 256–57, in which Zubiri discusses "evolutionary potentiality," which he also calls "potentiality for meta-speciation."

26. Zubiri's denial of evolution as actualization of virtualities refutes Neoscholastic thinkers of his time who try to reconcile religion with evolution theory. See chap. 8, note 2.

27. On the élan vital, see Bergson, *Creative Evolution,* 250.

28. Zubiri more fully analyzes Bergson in *Cinco lecciones de filosofía,* 200–201.

29. On the Aristotelian world order, or τάξις, see chap. 4, note 15.

30. "Secondary matter" here refers to matter as it normally reaches our senses. It presupposes prime matter (see note 2) and adds some form or accidental disposition to it. Suárez, *Disputaciones metafísicas*, 13, §I, 3 (2, 385–86).

31. A tensor is a mathematical quantity with "components in each of a given set of coordinate systems" and with a "prescribed law" that relates components belonging to one system to components of any other. Affleck, "Tensor," 172. The laws may stem from general relativity theory, relating the energy of a body to its momentum in four-dimensional space-time. (Relativity theory, rejecting absolute frames of reference, treats only relative motion of two systems, space and time. Space and time, no longer viewed as separate, form a four-dimensional continuum known as space-time.) Ricci tensors, named for the Italian mathematician Gregorio Ricci-Curbastro (1853–1925), serve to measure gravitation over vast curved surfaces. "Curvature" equals energy minus momentum. If, as Zubiri puts it, the tensor is zero, the curvature does not exist, the surface is plane, and geodesic lines obtain to measure it, that is, the shortest distances between two points. But if the tensor is unequal to zero, non-Euclidean geometry applies to the space in question. Allendoerfer, "Differential Geometry," 215. Space-time is flat only locally.

32. Einstein eventually discovered that the path of any free body (not submitted to the impact of another body) describes a geodesic, the shortest possible curve between two points in curvilinear geometry. Just as an elevator in free fall behaves in this fashion—as Einstein first saw—so does a planet moving freely in orbit. Einstein applied to gravitation tensor analysis, refined by Ricci-Curbastro (see note 31). According to this view, the universe has four space-time dimensions, and with curvature allowed, the amount of curvature depends on distribution of masses in the universe and varies from place to place. Woollard, "Gravitation," 327–29.

33. As evidence for an expanding universe, Edwin Hubble discovered that light from remote galaxies is displaced toward red (longer wavelengths) as galaxies recede from one another with ever-increasing velocity. Laín Entralgo, *Cuerpo y alma*, 33.

34. On gravity as curvature of the universe, see note 32.

35. Planck's constant, written h, is 6.626×10^{-34} joules per second; light-speed, c, is 299,792,458 meters per second, or 186,300 miles per second; the constant of the electric charge on an element is 1.6×10^{-19} coulombs. The British astrophysicist Arthur Eddington (1882–1944) has listed the fundamental constants as e the charge of an electron, m the mass of an electron, M the mass of a proton, h Planck's constant, c light-speed, G the constant of gravitation, and L the cosmological constant. To these may be added N_A the Avogadro constant, the number of "elementary entities" (atoms or molecules, for instance), or "moles," in any substance, equal to the number of atoms in a 12-gram sample of carbon 12 (Halliday and Resnick, *Fundamentals of Physics*, 484–85); R or the gas constant in the ideal gas law, $pV = nRt$ (the product of pressure and volume equals the number of moles times temperature times a constant) (ibid., 486); and k Boltzmann's constant, or the ratio of gas constant R to N_A (ibid., 489).

36. Eddington and the physicist Paul Dirac hypothesize that some universal constants

vary in time. Dirac reasons that G, the constant of gravitation, is diminishing as the universe expands. Sheldrake, "Variability of the 'Fundamental Constants.'"

37. See Aristotle, *Physics*, III.1, 201 a 10–11, criticized by Zubiri for distinguishing potency from substance; see chap. 4, note 12.

Chapter 8: The Dynamism of Selfhood

1. Among Greek philosophers, the pre-Socratic Heraclitus (536?-470? B.C.) first puts forth the theory of the *logos*, equating it to fire, the universal principle dominating the world. Fishler, "Heraclitus," 124–25. In the fourth century B.C., the Stoics develop the doctrine of the *logos*, the rational order of all nature. Stoics like Cleanthes of Assium (331–232 B.C.) call it *logos spermatikos*, the germ from which all else develops, an intelligible form with a single cosmic purpose. Church Fathers attach great significance to St. John's *logos* and make it the second person of the Trinity, identified with Christ the Redeemer. Morrow, "Logos," 183–84.

2. Neoscholasticism refers to renewal of interest in Scholasticism at the end of the nineteenth century. This tendency received direction in an 1879 encyclical in which Leo XIII (1810–1903) called for study of Scholastic philosophers, especially Aquinas. Guthrie, "Scholasticism," 284. Zubiri may refer to the leading French Neoscholastic Jacques Maritain's revival of St. Thomas's theory on the ascent of form to human generation: the vegetative soul cedes to the sensitive soul, and this in turn to the human or spiritual soul. With the appearance of the human soul, the vegetative and sensitive souls have descended from formal presence to mere virtual presence. "Virtue" acts as a transitive form or movement regulating a being in time. Maritain, "Vers une Idée Thomiste de l'Évolution," 95–104.

3. Cf. Weisskopf, "Three Spectroscopies," 17.

4. Zubiri poses an odd question. Amino acids, or the components of proteins, can and do constitute molecules in themselves. McMurry, *Organic Chemistry*, 974.

5. The German anatomist Wilhelm Roux (1850–1924), a pioneer in experimental embryology, in linking embryology to evolution devised research techniques he termed "developmental mechanics." Laín Entralgo, *El cuerpo humano*, 48.

6. On affine structures, see chap. 6, note 13. Affine geometry deals with affine transformations, that is, transformations plotting parallel lines to parallel lines and finite points to finite points.

7. Usually called a Möbius strip, a Möbius band, invented by A. F. Möbius (1790–1868), consists of a one-sided, continuous surface produced by taking a rectangle strip and twisting one of its ends 180° around the longitudinal axis, then attaching this end to the other. Möbius transformations, applied to the complex projective line, preserve angles and orientation in geometry.

8. Bacteria and blue algae fossil traces evince the existence of life on earth at least by 3.5 billion years ago. Campbell, *Biology*, 512–13.

9. The noun ἕξις, used in Aristotle's *Categories* VIII, 8 b 25–11 a 38, is distinguished as one of four qualities and is usually translated as "characteristic." Martin Ostwald,

in his translation of Aristotle's *Nicomachean Ethics,* offers alternatives: "trained ability, characteristic condition, characteristic attitude." He relates the word to the verb ἔχειν [to have, hold, keep, as a possession], "designating a firmly fixed possession of the mind, established by repeated and habitual action. Once attained, it is ever present, at least in a potential form." Aristotle, *Nicomachean Ethics,* 308–9.

10. Liddell and Scott, *Greek-English Lexicon,* 656. The expression refers to holding one's ground.

11. On kinetic and potential energy, see chap. 7, note 17.

12. The French philosopher and mathematician René Descartes (1596–1650) regarded all nature as merely matter in motion according to mathematical laws, with every organism a *bête machine* [mechanical beast]. *Discours de la méthode* (1637), Pt. V, 56.

13. In the 1920s, the Russian biochemist Alexander Oparin (1894–1980) and the English geneticist J. B. S. Haldane (1892–1964) independently revived the doctrine of spontaneous generation of life on earth. They hypothesized that chemical molecules needed for life spontaneously emerged in the atmosphere of the newly formed earth, then combined into ever more complex combinations until living cells came about. In support of this theory, the American chemists Stanley Miller (1930–) and Harold Urey (1893–1981) in 1953 synthesized amino acids from ammonia, methane, carbon dioxide, and water submitted to electrical sparks. Campbell, *Biology,* 514.

14. The Schrödinger wave equation (1926) allows development of probability functions for electron orbits around nuclei. Electron shells (probability densities) indicate where the electron may or may not be located. The controversial Klein-Gordon wave equation (1926), contrary to the Schrödinger one, takes relativity into account while describing the motion of a charged particle with no spin in an electromagnetic field. Fanchi, *Parametrized Relativistic Quantum Theory,* 2–3.

15. The cytoplasm includes cell contents between the nucleus and the membrane. The nucleus, lying within the cytoplasm, houses chromosomes. The Oxford geneticist C. D. Darlington (1903–81) based a theory of evolution on the behavior of chromosomes during meiosis wherein, as he discovered, mainly the exchange of chromosomal parts (crossing over) determines inherited traits. Sturdevant, *History of Genetics,* 78.

16. Pierre Teilhard de Chardin (1881–1955), geologist, paleontologist, and Jesuit priest, author of *The Phenomenon of Man* (*Le Phénomene humain,* 1955), conceived all evolution as a process leading humankind toward the creation of a vast collective consciousness. Laín Entralgo, *Cuerpo y alma,* 279.

17. Meiosis is that part of the process of gamete production in which the chromosomes fuse and undergo two cell divisions, halving the number of chromosomes in each resulting cell. Also see note 15. Campbell, *Biology,* 251.

18. Homeostasis, discovered by Claude Bernard (1813–1878) and named by Walter Bradford Cannon (1871–1945), is the physiological demand for self-regulation to maintain stable conditions while the inner body adapts to outer change. Laín Entralgo, *Antropología médica para clínicos,* 19; Young, "Drives," 392.

19. In his book *The Integrative Action of the Nervous System,* the British physiologist Charles Scott Sherrington (1857–1952) maintained that the spinal reflex serves as the

unit reaction of the nervous system, which configures the particular animal by correlating all body cells.

20. The Spanish original of the present translation contains the name "Brinkner" where I have substituted "Broca." Having noted a number of misprints in the original—doubtlessly due to oral transmission—and having unsuccessfully searched for a Brinkner in the history of medicine, I hypothesize that Zubiri means Sherrington's contemporary Pierre Paul Broca (1824–80), with a stature comparable to Sherrington's in physiology. In 1871 Broca localized the center of human speech in the third circumvolution of the prefrontal cortex, today called Broca's Area. See Laín Entralgo, *El cuerpo humano*, 138.

21. David Katz (1884–1953), a German-born experimental psychologist and educator associated with Husserlian phenomenology and early Gestalt psychology, applies such psychology to the crab in his book *Gestaltpsychologie* (Basel, 1944), translated as *Psicología de la forma* (Madrid, 1945) and circulated widely among Spanish intellectuals in Francoist Spain. On page 107 of the Spanish translation, Katz offers the example of the crab.

22. The "eleven nuances of sensibility" refer to the eleven senses: sight, hearing, smell, taste, localized touch (contact and pressure), coenestesia (visceral sensitivity), warmth and coldness, laberynthic and vestibular sensitivity (for balance), pain and pleasure, and kinesthesia or proprioception (sensations emerging from muscles, ligaments, and joints affecting perception of the body position). Zubiri, *Inteligencia sentiente*, 101–3; Laín Entralgo, *El cuerpo humano*, 134–35.

23. For the quotation from Bergson, see *Creative Evolution*, 128.

24. Pedro Laín Entralgo (1908–2001), Spain's foremost historian of medicine, was an intimate friend of Zubiri and considered himself Zubiri's student.

25. The German physiologist and chemist Georg Ernst Stahl (1660–1734) used the word "animism" to denote his conception of the soul as a vital principle causing organic development. Stahl, a professor of medicine in Montpellier, France, found adherents in his French students de Sauvages, Bordeu, Barthez, and Pinel. Vitalism teaches that the final basis of all processes in the organism is the vital principle (for Bordeu, nature; for Barthez, vital force). On Montpellier's vitalism in diagnostics, see Laín Entralgo, *El diagnóstico médico*, 40.

26. Here Zubiri parodies Aristotle's definition of potency, δύναμις, in *Metaphysics*, IX.6, 1048 a 28–29.

27. Aristotle, *On the Soul*, II.4, 415 b 13.

28. In ibid., II.4, 415 b 10–11, Aristotle identifies the soul as the source of movement. Zubiri's text lends itself to misreading: he is not saying that Aristotle defines life as locomotion. After all, in ibid., II.4, 415 b 23–24, Aristotle writes, "The power of locomotion is not found, however, in all living things." What Zubiri *is* saying is that Aristotle defines life as a mere property of the living being (i.e., soul, an underlying substance). Aristotelian substantialism once more comes under fire here.

29. Hylomorphism, seen in Aristotle, is the view of every physical object as composed of two principles, an immutable prime matter and a substantial form. Bourke, "Hylo-

morphism," 133. In *The Degrees of Knowledge,* 220–23, Maritain maintains that hylomorphism, notwithstanding its outdated concepts and examples, is as valid today as in antiquity. Both physicomathematical science and metaphysics rely on myths, with the scientific ones more problematic, more difficult to imagine.

30. The German biologist Hans Spemann (1869–1941) distinguished himself in experimental embryology for discovering the "organizer" in embryo parts. In amphibian eggs, he found in 1921 that if parts of one embryo are transplanted into another, there arise almost complete, though smaller, embryos. Those particular transplanted parts he called "organizers" for organizing the development of the embryonic area surrounding them. Laín Entralgo, *El cuerpo humano,* 55.

31. The German American geneticist Richard Goldschmidt (1878–1958), in the well-known book *The Material Basis of Evolution* (1940), hypothesized macroevolution through systemic mutations. He researched aspects of heredity and evolution like sex determination and gene theory as independent regulators of complex systems. Goldschmidt, *In and Out of the Ivory Tower,* 323–24.

In 1932, Spemann and his closest collaborators (H. Bautzmann, J. Holtfreter, and O. Mangold) published a brief article detailing experiments on dead inducers of new embryo parts: a normal inducer killed by overheating, desiccation, or freezing retains its capacity for induction to a degree. The active matter is absorbed by the agar, which can then be implanted in the other embryo. Laín Entralgo, *El cuerpo humano,* 56. In 1933 J. Holtfreter found that noninducing areas of an embryo can become inducers when killed. "Nachweis der Induktionsfähigkeit abgetäteter Keimteile," 584–633.

32. Maritain's teacher, the German zoologist and vitalist philosopher Hans Driesch (1867–1941), while experimenting with sea urchin eggs, discovered that part of an early embryo could grow into a complete adult, though smaller than usual. As against mechanismic theories, Driesch explained organic systems in terms of an autonomous principle of vitality. Laín Entralgo, *El cuerpo humano,* 49–50, 53.

33. On Fichte's *Wissenschaftslehre,* see chap. 3, note 6.

34. On Hegel, see "Foreword," notes 1 and 7.

35. In "The Three Spectroscopies" (22), Weisskopf's term "baryon" denotes "the nucleon in all its different states of excitation"; "nucleon" designates a particle from an atomic nucleus when that particle, before or after bombardment, is in its "ground state in the form of a proton or a neutron"; when hit by a high-energy particle, the nucleon may emit a "meson," a particle of "medium mass."

Chapter 9: The Dynamism of Self-Possession

1. On Katz's experiment with crabs, see chap. 8, note 21.

2. On open essence in response to Heidegger, see chap. 5, note 72.

3. According to Zubiri's *Sobre la esencia,* 486, "every reality 'in its own right' is 'its own,' but 'in its own mode.'" Modally, the human being is "its own" reality, whereas its structure makes it an "animal of realities," one open to the character of reality as such.

4. In *Summa contra Gentiles,* 1st Pt., Ques. 47, Art. 2:60:1 Aquinas views reasoning as the single activity proper to humans over other animals. "Potential intellect" distinguishes humans from others. 1st Pt., Ques. 47, Art. 2:60:4. The *form* of bodily beings gives them specificity and unity. But many individuals exist in the same species. The specific form furnishes the common basis for the universal idea. The form cannot individualize on its own, but needs a principle to make the individual: matter. *Summa theologica,* 1st Pt., Ques. 47, Art. 2. The doctrine of educated intelligence appears in Aquinas's treatise *De magistro* [*On the Teacher*], Art. 1 (see Aquinas, *Über den Lehrer*), where he finds that an active predisposition to know is necessary for learning.

5. The earliest known hominid fossils (*Ardipithecus ramidus*) date to 4.4 million B.C. and were found in Aramis, Ethiopia, in 1994. T. D. White et al., "New Discoveries," 306–12.

6. Australopithecines belonged to the genus *Australopithecus,* African hominids with small brains, upright posture, and apelike curved toes. Campbell, *Biology,* 668.

7. In 1972 in Tanzania Louis Leaky and Mary Leaky discovered *Homo habilis* [skillful man], who lived 1.75 million years ago.

8. "Half a million years ago, the hominized hominids (whether *Australopithecus* or *Homo habilis*) produced by evolution a clearly human type: *Archanthropus.*" Of him Zubiri has written that he has "dentition of the same type as that of *Australopithecus.* He has a very rudimentary trace of chin, very strong jaws, very large supraorbital ridges, a very thick skull with a strong crest at the occipital foramen, and a less pronounced occipital curvature than that of earlier types. "The Origin of Man," 49.

9. In 1891, in Java, Eugene Dubois discovered *Pithecanthropus erectus* [upright apeman], today known as *Homo erectus.* Fried, "Anthropology," 300.

10. The bones of a *Homo erectus* called *Sinanthropus pekinensis,* or "Beijing man," appeared in China near that city in the 1920s. Fried, "Asian Peoples," 57.

11. Zubiri dates *Paleoanthropus* to about two hundred thousand years ago. He finds this hominid different in body and mental development. "This human type evolved in different phases. The oldest type is that represented by the pre-Neanderthal men (Steinheim, Ehringsdorf, Saccopastore) and the pre-sapiens (Swanscombe and, much later, the Fontchévade man). Then come the classical Neanderthal men, distributed throughout Europe, Asia, and Africa. Those from Palestine are, perhaps, pre-*sapiens.* Lastly come those which mark the transition to a later type: the Rhodesian man and the Solo man (a descendent of Pithecanthropus)." Zubiri, "The Origin of Man," 49.

12. Neanderthal Man, first found in the Neander Valley near Düsseldorf, Germany, dates back to the Ice Age (200,000 to 30,000 years ago). In 1968 Zubiri did not consider Neanderthal a member of the human species, *Homo sapiens,* but scientific opinion is divided, with the majority today classifying Neanderthal as forming a subspecies of our own species.

13. Dating to around half a million years ago, Mauer's jaw, found in southwestern Germany, may have belonged to a *Homo erectus.* This human mandible is large, with about twelve teeth. Ibid., 48.

14. In Grimaldi, near the Italian border with France, the first prehistoric skeletons

with Negroid features were unearthed, but the racial distinction, not disputed by Zubiri (ibid., 48), is unclear.

15. Echinoderms are marine invertebrates covered with hard spines, supported by a calcite skeleton, and displaying five-rayed radial symmetry. They belong to the phylum Echinodermata, sharing an evolutionary line with the phylum Chordata, which includes birds and mammals. Both phyla have a similar embryonic development from the formation of the zygote to the development of the body cavities. But did human beings evolve from echinoderms? They may have had a common ancestor before diverging in their evolutions. Campbell, *Biology,* 606, 634.

16. Again Zubiri does not employ "phylum" in its strict biological sense, but in the sense of a paradigmatic unit of substantivities acting to conserve their paradigm. See chap. 7, note 22.

17. On *natura naturans,* see chap. 5, note 59.

18. For Zubiri, animals experience realities as stimuli, something affecting them, not as realities qua realities, the way human beings experience them. *Sobre la esencia,* 393.

19. For Hegel on evolution, see "Foreword," note 7.

20. Zubiri responds to Hegel's *Phenomenology of the Spirit:* in its evolution, reality (not Hegel's Spirit) becomes "self" (not *it*self). It constitutes itself in its selfhood precisely as a form of reality. If the self-constitution as *form* progresses and becomes hyper*form*alized, then reality becomes "hyper-self," in Zubiri's words. The human being takes possession of itself, unlike other substantivities.

21. In geometry, a chord subtends or intercepts the arc of a circle: the chord depends on the arc while asserting its being. The "I" grounds itself on the "to Me" to sustain its being. This is a *dynamic* subtension because in sustaining its being by grounding itself on the "to Me," the "I" is giving of itself, unfolding its essential notes.

22. The expression "second act" comes from Scholastic philosophy. Guthrie, "Act," *Dictionary of Philosophy,* 4. The second act is often in a complementary relation with the first act. In Zubiri, the "I," the "to Me," and the "Me" form a primary unit, calling for a second act to complement it. This second act is a "reactualization of my own reality qua mine." The primary unity is my reality; the second act, merely my being. My being is the translation into kinetic energy of what I am in potential.

23. Personhood is my substantivity, my reality, while personality is merely my being, which is grounded on it.

24. I use the word "insistence" to translate Zubiri's *instancia,* a noun made over from the verb *instar,* "to ask for insistently."

25. On constructs, see chap. 3, notes 7 and 10.

26. Aristotle, *Metaphysics,* IX.6, 1048 a 28–29.

27. Ibid., IX.6, 1048 a 32–35.

28. The Precambrian era is the first period of the earth's existence, ending 540,000,000 years ago. On fossil finds in that era, see chap. 8, note 8.

29. Voluntary muscles contract when two sets of interlocking filaments slide together: one thick set comprised of the protein myosin, and one thin set composed of the protein actin. The myosin filaments project outward as "cross bridges," interacting in

cyclical form with the thin filaments, carried in a rowing motion. Energy for this operation comes from the decomposition of adenosine triphosphate (ATP) through its interaction with water. The Hungarian American biochemist Albert von Szent-Györgyi (1893–1986) discovered actin, paving the way for research on contraction of the filaments and on the biochemical and molecular structure of muscle. Campbell, *Biology*, 1035–38.

30. For Aristotle, prime matter is in union with substantial form; see hylomorphism, chap. 8, note 29.

31. On the two Aristotelian conceptions of potency, see notes 26 and 27.

32. An efficient cause is "that from which the change comes." Aristotle, *Metaphysics*, V.2, 1013 a 29–32.

33. German uses *Kraft* to denote "force" in physics. However, general relativity makes Newtonian force problematic for Zubiri (chap. 7, note 32). Therefore he puts this concept out of play for the purposes of his own metaphysics.

34. Leave open the idea of power as predominance of a cause over its effect or [the idea] of the rank of a reality [Zubiri's note].

35. For Zubiri, life as such is the successful or failed realization of certain possibilities offered by the reality of things, other human beings, and of oneself, or discovered and even created by the person. Realization of such possibilities depends on accepting or appropriating them. This active or passive self-surrender to reality qua capacitating reality of my own reality constitutes for Zubiri the essence of will. *Sobre el sentimiento y la volición*, 399.

36. Recall that "condition" signifies capacity of a reality to be constituted into meaning for a human being.

37. Zubiri conceives human invention as "quasi-creation." He disagrees with Hegel regarding history as the mere development of potencies already present in the human being. The first human being possessed all potencies of the species, but not all possibilities of human history. In history are produced acts as well as, and previously, possibilities conditioning their reality. Therefore the "structure of spirit, as producer of history," is a "quasi-creation": "creation" because it affects its own possibilities, but "quasi" because it is not (divine) creation out of nothingness. *Naturaleza, Historia, Dios*, 380.

38. Here Zubiri is rejecting two previously considered formulas from Aristotle on motion; see chap. 4, pp. 28–29.

39. Neoplatonism is Platonic philosophy from Plotinus (A.D. 205?–270?) to Proclus (410?-85). Bourke, "Neo-Platonism," 209. Proclus's *Elements of Theology*, filtered through an unknown Arabic translator with ideas of his own, affected St. Thomas Aquinas. Zubiri's quotation "prima rerum creatarum est esse" appears in Aquinas's *Quaestiones disputatae de veritate*, Ques. I, Art. 1, and in *Summa theologica*, 1st Pt., Ques. V, Art 2.4. Here St. Thomas mentions as his source the *Liber de causis* [Book of causes] and erroneously attributes it to Aristotle before reinterpreting the quote for his own purposes. In his commentary to the *Liber de causis*, Aquinas recognizes the work as a considerably altered fragment from Proclus. Smith, "Membership or Transcendence?"

40. "Epagogically" means "inductively, starting from a particular proposition and moving to a general one."

41. *Dynamic Structure of Reality* (1968) is almost contemporaneous with *Sobre la esencia* (1962), equating metaphysics to first philosophy and to "intramundane" cognition of reality as actualized in apprehension. Gracia, *Voluntad de verdad,* 112; *Sobre la esencia,* 210. According to Gracia, 112, *Sobre la esencia* deems it possible to perform "transmundane" research, but this research would remain methodically up in the air without grounding on metaphysics. "Intramundane" denotes focused on the transcendental order, that is, the order of real structures qua real, something determined by the particularity of each object.

42. The distinction between "general metaphysics" and "specific metaphysics" stems from Christian von Wolff (1679–1754), for whom "real philosophy" divides into general metaphysics and special metaphysics, with "general" synonymous with "ontology," and "special" encompassing cosmology, psychology, and theology. F. P. Siegfried, "Ontology," in *The Catholic Encyclopedia.* Causality, mentioned by Zubiri, belongs to ontology.

Chapter 10: The Dynamism of Living Together

1. In *Nature, History, God,* 195, invoking St. Thomas, for whom true being is the cause of itself (equals God), Zubiri contrasts human freedom with divine freedom. Divine freedom creates things; human freedom only chooses from among possibilities offered to it. Hence the human being is merely a second (efficient) cause, referred to God, the first efficient cause. Suárez, *Disputaciones metafísicas,* 31, §14 (V, 211).

2. In chap. 2, Zubiri has distinguished being from reality. Reality [*realitas*] precedes being [*esse*], its second act or complement. Being is *realitas in essendo,* or reality in the act of being.

3. Every molecule of sulphuric acid, written H_2SO_4, contains two atoms of hydrogen, one of sulphur, and four of oxygen.

4. In his best-known work *Lois de l'imitation* (*The Laws of Imitation*) (1890), Gabriel de Tarde (1843–1904) posits multiple dynamic relations between individuals and among groups. As against evolutionary theories of society, Tarde finds imitation the constant of the social fact. He links imitation to processes of identification, propagated through domination, influence by example, resistance, and counterimitation. Imitation brings about innovation—invention and elementary social adaptation available to all, expanding and strengthening through repetition and opposition.

5. In *The Rules of the Sociological Method* (*Les Regles de la méthode sociologique,* 1895), 50–59, Émile Durkheim (1858–1917) counters Tarde's thesis of imitation by taking as his own point of departure the "social fact." While agreeing with the imitation of each social fact and with its ability to spread to others, he finds its propagation the consequence, not the cause, of its sociological character. Moreover, given the coercive element peculiar to each social fact, Durkheim questions the appropriateness of the term "imitation" for what is often an individual, not a social, phenomenon.

As for social mimesis in Hegel, the individual develops from subjective to objective rational consciousness through ever more rational institutions of family, civil society, and state. To the ethical powers regulating individual lives, according to Hegel, individuals belong the way accidents do to substance. The ethical powers are "represented" in those individuals. A kind of mirroring or imitation is implied. In individuals, Hegel says, those ethical institutions "have the shape of appearance, and become actualized." *Philosophy of Right*, 55.

6. On social institutions as substance in Hegel, see note 5. Zubiri reverses Hegel and makes society merely a moment of the individual's reality.

7. On habitudes, see chap. 8, note 9.

8. On the world as reality in respectivity as such, see chap. 2, notes 5 and 6.

9. On Zubiri's philosophy of history, cf. "La dimensión histórica del ser humano," [The historical dimension of the human being], *Realitas*, 1:11–69 [Gracia's note].

10. Here Zubiri plays on words in a way difficult to capture in English. The social body constitutes a system of possibilities situated outside the person and capable of being assigned a place—in Greek a τόπος. Now, *topicidad*, Zubiri's word for "place," has originated in the Spanish *tópico*, meaning a "commonplace," something trite—related to a topos, a literary convention in English. Someone who does nothing but refer to this trite social world dwells by constitution in the commonplace as such. He or she is nothing but a tourist in every situation.

11. The expression "the present state of fortune," παρούσα τύχη, appears in Aeschylus's *Prometheus Bound*, 375; Liddell and Scott, *Greek-English Lexicon*, 1673. Zubiri simply inserts before the adjective παρούσα [present] the phrase in the genitive, τῆς πόλεως [of the city].

12. "Tychistic" is a word in the philosophy of the American sage Charles Sanders Peirce (1839–1914), referring to the doctrine of chance as an objective reality. See "The Doctrine of Chances," 604–15.

13. Again Zubiri plays with the roots of Spanish words in a way not apparent in English. Each inhabitant of a social body, by becoming depersonalized, "incorporates" himself or herself into that body, becomes imbedded in it. The word for "body" in Spanish is *cuerpo*, derived from the Latin *corpus* (genitive, *corporis*). The same root, *corpor-*, appears in the verb *incorporar* [to incorporate].

14. John 17:15 [Gracia's note].

15. Wordplay identical to that discussed in note 13 is going on here: the depersonalized human being is incorporated [*incorporado*, literally, "em-bodied"] into what the community has of a body [*cuerpo*].

16. The Greek παράδοσις stems from the verb παραδίδωμι [to give or hand over]. Liddell and Scott, *Greek-English Lexicon*, 1180. Likewise, Latin *traditio* comes from *tradere* [to give over or impart], derived, in turn, from *trans-* [across] and *-ditus*, a combined form of *datus* [given]: thus the word "tradition." The verb forms of both nouns refer to giving. The tradition, or object handed over, "gives" of itself. It displays its essential notes, or reactivates itself. This giving of itself is the dynamism of tradition as such.

17. The Bauhaus (literally, "house of building"), a school of design founded by Walter Gropius (1883–1969) in Weimar in 1919, revolutionized architecture: it integrated technology, craftsmanship, and art into severely elegant structures. Seeing mass production as the requirement for design in a mechanized age, Bauhaus members criticized Victorian stress on individual embellishment. Hence, the protest against the repetition of the Parthenon, the jewel of Doric architecture (designed by Ictinus and Callicrates between 447 and 432 B.C. and situated on the peak of the Acropolis, the highest place in Athens). Loewy, "Industrial Design," 732–33; Stillwell, "Parthenon," 463–64.

18. In Spanish, the word for "conspiracy" is *conspiración,* which resembles the Spanish word for "aspiration," *aspiración. Con-* means "with" or "together." *Ad-* means "toward."

19. On society as product of history, or as the unfolding of universal spirit, see note 5, above, and "Foreword," note 7.

20. Zubiri refutes Bergson, *Creative Evolution,* ix, on the uninterrupted evolution from lower vertebrates to the formation of intelligence as an appendage to the faculty of acting.

21. In the second paragraph of chap. 1, Zubiri offers two usual acceptances of becoming: coming to be something by ceasing to be what one was or adding something that one was *not* to what one already was.

22. Zubiri is evidently refuting the following notion from the introduction, §III, to Hegel's *Philosophy of History,* 46: "And as the germ bears in itself the whole nature of the tree, and the taste and form of its fruits, so do the first traces of Spirit virtually contain the whole of that History."

23. On Hegelian dialectic, see chap. 1, note 8.

24. Hegel's introduction, §III to the *Philosophy of History,* 179, with its substantialist vision of history, likens historical *possibility* to Aristotelian δύναμις [potency]. For Zubiri's concept of possibilities, see chap. 9, note 35.

25. Zubiri refers to his concept of human being as open essence (see chap. 5, note 72), something wholly different from history as open structure. Openness of essence implies modification of something in itself endowed with intelligence and will to choose among possibilities, and this is not the case of history.

26. Alcibiades (450?–404? B.C.) was an Athenian general and politician, a student of Socrates (469–399 B.C.), and a nephew of the great leader Pericles (495?–429? B.C.). Plato, *Alcibiades,* I, 104 a 6–b c 1.

27. Hegel, introduction, §I, *Philosophy of History,* 161: "It may be said of universal history that it is the exhibition of Spirit in the process of working out the knowledge of that which it is potentially."

28. Ibid., 171: "All the worth which the human being possesses, all spiritual reality, he possesses only through the state. For his spiritual reality consists in this, that his own essence—reason—is objectively present to him. . . . Thus only is he fully conscious."

29. Ibid.: "But morality [i.e., objective spirit] is duty—substantial right—a 'second

nature,' as it has been justly called; for the *first* nature of man is his primarily merely animal existence."

30. Ibid., 176: "Morality [i.e., objective spirit] is the identity of the subjective or personal with the universal will."

31. Ibid., 181: "Family memorials, patriarchal traditions, have an interest confined to the family and the clan. The uniform course of events, which such a condition implies, is no subject of serious remembrance."

Chapter 11: Dynamism as a Mode of Being in the World

1. On Aristotle's idea of τάξις, see chap. 4, note 15.

2. The inapplicable sense would be form in hylomorphism; see chap. 8, note 29.

3. Kant, *Critique of Pure Reason,* B 47, p. 31.

4. Ibid., B 50, p. 31.

5. Aristotle, *Physics,* IV.13, 222 a 10–11 (Apostle trans., 85).

6. Ibid., Bk. IV.10, 218 a 4–6 (Apostle trans., 78).

7. Ibid., Bk. IV.10, 218 b 14–15 (Apostle trans., 88).

8. On time in Jainism, see chap. 6, note 26. The Antwerp-born logician and metaphysician Arnold Geulincx (1624–69) led the occasionalist movement, which has interested Zubiri (see chap. 5, note 42). In "El concepto descriptivo del tiempo," 14, Zubiri writes, "For Geulincx, irreducible occasionalist, God creates every instant of time and annihilates it to create the following one. The continuity of time and of movement would be an illusion."

9. Zubiri refers to the Spanish psychologist Mariano Yela Granizo (1921–94).

10. In "El concepto descriptivo del tiempo," 21, Zubiri relates minimum duration to Heisenberg. Let δE equal the energy of a light signal and δt the time duration of that signal (δ being the spread of possible values for each). According to Heisenberg, we can observe or measure an event in time only to an accuracy limited by the uncertainty principle, whereby the product of δE and δt must be equal to or greater than h, Planck's constant. Hence, an event in time is not measurable with accuracy greater than δt. Minimum metrizable duration is equal to h divided by δE times two. Topsoe, "Notes on Programming Neural Systems."

11. Cf. Aristotle, *Physics,* IV.12, 220 b 15–17.

12. Zubiri, "El concepto descriptivo del tiempo," 15, and Zubiri, "Zurvanismo," *Gran enciclopedia del mundo* 19 (Bilbao: Durvan, 1964), 485 [Gracia's note].

13. Ibid. [Gracia's note].

14. Aristotle, *Physics,* IV.10, 218 a 1–2 [Gracia's note].

15. In "El concepto descriptivo del tiempo," 15, and in *Espacio, tiempo, materia,* 221, Zubiri uses the figure of twelve thousand years for the cosmic time of long duration of the Persians. The Spanish version of *Dynamic Structure of Reality* uses six thousand years, which I must infer is a misprint. *Estructura dinámica de la realidad,* 284.

16. Aristotle, *Physics,* IV.10, 218 b 2–10 (Apostle trans., 79).

17. The Hebrew word *'olam* [forever] covers natural phenomena and also the course

of history. Hence it applies to the eternal God, a being without beginning or end. Zubiri, "El concepto descriptivo del tiempo," 17.

18. The Spanish festival of the burial of the sardine was celebrated on Ash Wednesday with a grotesque burial ceremony to symbolize the passage from Carnival to Lent. Moliner, *Diccionario de uso del español,* 1:1142.

19. In set theory, the German mathematician Ernst Friedrich Ferdinand Zermelo (1871–1953) attempted to resolve Cantor's continuum hypothesis by theorizing in 1902 on the addition of transfinite cardinals and, in 1904, by proving that every set can be well ordered. The continuum hypothesis proposed the countability of every continuum (its possible 1-to-1 correspondence with the natural numbers) or the cardinality of the continuum (possible 1-to-1 correspondence with real numbers). Transfinite numbers surpass the finite ones. Yet many set theorists of Zermelo's time vehemently opposed Zermelo's type of proofs. Grattan-Guiness, *The Search for Mathematical Roots,* 115, 216–17; Zubiri, "El concepto descriptivo del tiempo," 17.

20. Zubiri synthesizes Aristotle (on non-existence of past and future) with St. Augustine (on the existence of the present alone). See Aristotle, *Physics,* IV.10, 217 b 10–218 a 1 (Apostle trans., 78); and St. Augustine, *Confessions,* XI.18.

21. Concerning the time needed to pronounce verses, a shorter verse, pronounced more fully, may take longer to utter than a lengthier verse, said quickly; "Hence . . . time is nothing else than protraction; but of what, I do not know; and I would be surprised if it may not be of the mind itself" ["inde mihi visum est nihil esse aliud tempus quam distentionem: sed cuius rei, nescio, et mirum, si non ipsius animi"]. Augustine, *Confessions,* XI.26. In other words, the mind extends the past to the present.

22. On affine geometry, see ch. 6, note 13.

23. See chap. 6, note 27.

24. Zubiri, "El concepto descriptivo del tiempo," 19. The second law of thermodynamics means that "it is not possible to change heat completely into work, with no other change taking place." Halliday and Resnick, *Fundamentals of Physics,* 510. Here, work equals the force applied to a system multiplied by the distance of its application, and it varies with pressure and change in volume of a gas. Ibid., 468–69.

25. Zubiri uses the Greek word in the sense of the right point of time or opportunity for action. Liddell and Scott, *Greek-English Lexicon,* 760.

26. Chronological age does not necessarily coincide with individual productivity. Laín Entralgo, *Antropología médica para clínicos,* 82.

27. Aristotle, *Physics,* IV.11, 219 b 2 [Gracia's note].

28. See note 20.

29. Aristotle, *Physics,* IV.11, 219 b 10–12: "But every simultaneous time is self-identical; for the 'now' as a subject is an identity, but it accepts different attributes. The 'now' measures time, insofar as time involves the 'before and after.'"

30. Cf. Bergson, *Creative Evolution,* 46: "Real duration is that duration which gnaws on things, and leaves on them the mark of its tooth."

31. See note 21.

32. Bergson refutes the intellectualization of problems on time and free will in spa-

tial terms. Our experience does not perceive real life as a succession of demarcated conscious states progressing along an imaginary line, but rather as a *durée,* a duration, a continuous flow. *Time and Free Will,* 100.

33. Bergson's image appears in "Introduction à la métaphysique," 1398; cf. a like image in *Time and Free Will,* 103.

34. *Zukunft,* the German word for "future," derives from *zukommen,* to come up to [*zu-kommen*] or to reach a point. In 1956, Laín Entralgo related Heidegger's word *Zukunft* to the Spanish word for "future," *porvenir,* and divided it into its components *porvenir* [*venir,* "come"; *por,* "for the sake or purpose of"]. *La espera y la esperanza,* 293.

35. For Heidegger the future enjoys primacy over the past and the present because time springs out of the projection of the future from the vantage point of the present. *Sein und Zeit,* §65, 327.

36. For Heidegger, temporality forms the ultimate meaning of our existence, because every endeavor to interpret existing must refer to temporality. Ibid., §5, 17, §45, 234; Laín Entralgo, *La espera y la esperanza,* 293.

37. For clarity, I translate *estar* as "being-there" whenever the verb refers to time. In Spanish, two verbs, *ser* and *estar,* are usually both translated "to be." But *ser* refers to being an essence, *estar* to being in a situation. Hence, in my translation, I always use "to be there" to translate *estar* as applied to temporality. Zubiri stresses the difference between being [*ser*] and time, and his present chapter concerns "being in the world," according to its title.

38. See chap. 2, note 4.

39. See chap. 4, note 28.

40. In Kant, *Critique of Pure Reason,* B 51, p. 33.

41. Ibid., B 50–51, p. 33.

42. According to Zubiri, *Sobre la esencia,* 440, Heidegger finds that through temporality we are as we are and can let entities be what they are, so as to enable us to understand being. Therefore our being and the being of all other entities are grounded on temporality. Being in Heidegger depends on time.

43. For the metaphor of the light related to being, see chap. 2, the subsection entitled "Being."

44. Zubiri uses "gerund," "gerundial," and "gerundive" interchangeably. "Gerund" in Latin and English is a verbal noun (for instance, *conversando doceo:* "by conversing, I teach"). "Gerundial" is an adjective meaning pertaining to the gerund. However, "gerundive" is a verbal adjective in Latin used as a future passive participle (for example, *res agenda,* "things to be done"). Modern Spanish does not use the gerundive but does use the gerund, often accompanying auxiliary verbs (as here) to express progressive action (*Estoy terminando:* "I am finishing little by little"). Ullman and Henry, *Latin for Americans,* 2:95.

45. In Hegelian dialectic, progressing from thesis to antithesis to synthesis, one stage follows the other through *Aufhebung,* a word that encompasses both negation and affirmation—the part useless for progress is denied, the useful part stored or con-

served—and here Zubiri expresses both the negative and the affirmative nuances with the word "absorption." See chap. 1, note 8.

46. On the openness to eternity through the synthesis, Hegel saw the world as the unfolding expression of one absolute Idea, a living Spirit evolving with the power of reason. Everything starts with the thesis, develops to an opposite antithesis, and both are unified by the synthesis. In this way the world reaches perfection and eternity. Hegel, *Science of Logic,* §1781.

47. On time as eternity in potential, see Hegel, *Philosophy of Nature,* §201. In *Encyclopedia of the Philosophical Sciences in Outline and Critical Writings.* On necessity as potential freedom, see Hegel, *Science of Logic,* §1788.

48. On unity by elevation, Hegel's *Philosophy of History* presents every national character as but a single individual in the process of universal history. That history shows the development of Spirit in its highest forms in a gradation whereby it reaches the consciousness of itself. See introduction to *Philosophy of History,* pp. 157–71.

49. X. Zubiri refers at this point [of his public course] to the Latin word *mora* [delay] in Ernout and Meillet, *Dictionnaire étymologique de la langue latine,* in which the history of the words *moror* [I delay], *moratio* [delay, impediment], *demorare* [to delay, stay, reside], etc., are analyzed [Gracia's note].

50. See *Sobre la esencia,* 495–97 [Gracia's note].

51. See note 33, above.

52. Kant, *Critique of Pure Reason,* B 47, pp. 29–31.

53. Ibid.

54. "Pure" refers to knowledge detached from experience and universal. Ibid., B 3–4, p. 4.

55. Bergson, *Time and Free Will,* 79.

56. This is Zubiri's formal definition of time: it is the actuality of the dynamic unity, the structure of self-givingness, characterizing respectivity in the world as such. Respectivity is referentiality of notes within and among realities, and all these references form the world. Hence the whole structure of self-givingness achieves its potential for displaying its notes in time. See chap. 2, note 6.

57. Zubiri uses the expression "the years of Buridan" to mean simply a long time ago. The French nominalist philosopher Jean Buridan was born between 1295 and 1305 and died between 1358 and 1361.

58. On "circumscriptively" and "diffinitively," see chap. 6, note 28.

59. The Russian-born mathematical physicist Hermann Minkowski (1864–1909) proposed the use of non-Euclidean space for understanding the physics of Lorentz and Einstein. He conceived space and time as being linked together in a four-dimensional "space-time continuum," including the three dimensions of space (length, width, depth) and the one of time. Geometrical representation of space-time is the chronotope (from the Greek for time, χρόνος, and place, τόπος). Pirani, "Relativity," 710.

60. Synoptical in the sense of containing a synopsis of the totality of a lifetime.

61. Heidegger writes that the wholeness of the surroundings unveils itself as a cate-

gorical totality of possibilities for our existence, that is, of possibilities for linking instruments into a project (*Sein und Zeit,* §31, 144–45). Projectedness, we have already seen (note 35) depends for Heidegger on the future, and it redefines the past and present as well (§65, p. 327).

62. On sentient intelligence, see "Foreword," note 5.

63. Cf. Zubiri, "El concepto descriptivo del tiempo," 36 [Gracia's note].

64. Cf. ibid., 15.

65. On *realitas in essendo,* see chap. 10, note 2.

Chapter 12: Reality in Its Dynamism

1. The Dutch philosopher Benedict (Baruch) Spinoza (1632–77) explained his pantheism in his posthumously published *Ethics* (1677), holding that God is the Only Substance, besides which no other substance is arguable or conceivable. Spinoza's pantheism identifies God with the universe. Since two different substances cannot possess the same qualities, and since God, the perfect being, has every possible and actual attribute, no other substance exists. *Ethics,* 355–72.

On the Spirit in Hegel, see "Foreword," note 7.

2. Zubiri uses the pair of opposites "actions and passions" in the sense in which the contrast appears in Aristotle's *Categories,* chap. 4, 2 a: it is the active-passive antithesis, nothing more.

3. In all this, distinguish: 1. Reality is respective [referential]. 2. Reality is active by itself. 3. And this respectivity [referentiality] is what makes reality be there *in activity.* Respectivity is not dynamism, but the basis of the activity of things, which are active in themselves [Zubiri's note].

4. The Greek philosopher Anaximander (b. 610–11?) founded with Thales and Anaximenes the Milesian school of philosophy. He searched for the basis of the multiple natural processes in a single cosmic principle, which he termed the "boundless." Fishler, "Anaximander," 12. Gracia documents the fragment cited by Zubiri as D.-K., 12 B 1, 1–2.

5. Gracia documents the text cited by Zubiri from Heraclitus as D.-K., 22 B 54. Heraclitus held that nothing abides, everything flows, order in nature lies hidden. Fishler, "Heraclitus," 124–25.

6. On the universe as *taxis* [ordering] in Aristotle, see chap. 4, note 15.

Bibliography

Affleck, George B. "Tensor." In *Collier's Encyclopedia.* 17th ed. Ed. Louis Shores. New York: Crowell, Collier, and Macmillan, 1967. 22:172–73.

Allendoerfer, Carl B. "Differential Geometry." In *Collier's Encyclopedia.* 17th ed. Ed. Louis Shores. New York: Crowell, Collier, and Macmillan, 1967. 8:214–16.

Aquinas, St. Thomas. *Quaestiones disputatae de veritate.* Bonn: Peter Hanstein, 1918.

———. *The Summa contra Gentiles.* 5 vols. Trans. English Dominican Fathers. London: Burnes, Oates, and Washbourne, 1923.

———. *Summa theologica.* 5 vols. Ed. Ottawan Institute of Medieval Studies. Ottawa, Ontario: Commissio Piana, 1955.

———. *Truth.* 3 vols. Trans. R. W. Mulligan, J. V. McGlynn, and R. W. Schneider. Chicago: H. Regnery, 1952–54.

———. *Über den Lehrer = De magistro: Quaestiones disputatae de veritate, quaestio 11.* Trans. and ed. G. Jüssen, G. Krieger, and J. H. J. Schneider. Hamburg: Meiner, 1988. 11.

Aristotle. *Aristotle's Physics.* Trans. Hippocrates G. Apostle. Bloomington: Indiana University Press, 1969.

———. *Categories.* Trans. E. M. Edgehill. In *Great Books of the Western World.* Ed. Robert Maynard Hutchins. Vol. 8. *Aristotle.* Chicago: Encyclopaedia Britannica, 1952. 1:3–21.

———. *Metafísica de Aristóteles.* 2d rev. ed. Trans. and ed. Valentín García Yebra. Madrid: Editorial Gredos, 1982.

———. *Metaphysics.* Books I–IX. 10th ed. Trans. Hugh Tredennick. Cambridge, Mass.: Harvard University Press, 1996.

———. *Nicomachean Ethics.* Trans. and ed. Martin Ostwald. Indianapolis: Bobbs-Merrill, 1962.

———. *On Generation and Corruption (De generatione et corruptione).* Trans. H. H. Joachim. In *Great Books of the Western World.* Ed. Robert Maynard Hutchins. Vol. 8, *Aristotle.* Chicago: Encyclopaedia Britannica, 1952. 1:409–41.

————. *On the Soul* (*De anima*). Trans. J. A. Smith. In *Great Books of the Western World.* Ed. Robert Maynard Hutchins. Vol. 8, *Aristotle.* Chicago: Encyclopaedia Britannica, 1952. 1:631–68.

————. *Physics* (*Physica*). Trans. R. P. Hardie and R. K. Gaye. In *Great Books of the Western World.* Ed. Robert Maynard Hutchins. Vol. 8, *Aristotle.* Chicago: Encyclopaedia Britannica, 1952. 1:259–355.

————. *Topics* (*Topica*). Trans. W. A. Pickard-Cambridge. In *Great Books of the Western World.* Ed. Robert Maynard Hutchins. Vol. 8, *Aristotle.* Chicago: Encyclopaedia Britannica, 1952. 1:143–223.

Augustine, St. *Confessions.* 3 vols. Ed. James J. O'Donnell. Oxford: Oxford University Press, 1992.

Baylis, Charles A. "Neorealism." In *Collier's Encyclopedia.* 17th ed. Ed. Louis Shores. New York: Crowell, Collier, and Macmillan, 1967. 17:299.

Bergson, Henri. *Creative Evolution.* Trans. Arthur Mitchell. New York: Henry Holt, 1911.

————. "Introduction à la métaphysique." In *Oeuvres.* Ed. André Robinet. Paris: Presses Universitaires de France, 1970. 1392–1432.

————. *Time and Free Will: An Essay on the Immediate Data of Consciousness.* 1889. Trans. F. L. Pogson. London: George Allen and Unwin, 1910.

Bourke, Vernon J. "Hylomorphism." In *Dictionary of Philosophy.* 11th ed. Ed. Dagobert D. Runes. Towota, N.J.: Littlefield, Adams, 1962. 133.

————. "Maritain, Jacques." In *Dictionary of Philosophy.* 11th ed. Ed. Dagobert D. Runes. Towota, N.J.: Littlefield, Adams, 1962. 188.

————. "Neo-Platonism." In *Dictionary of Philosophy.* 11th ed. Ed. Dagobert D. Runes. Towota, New Jersey: Littlefield, Adams, 1962. 209.

————. "Plato." In *Dictionary of Philosophy.* 11th ed. Ed. Dagobert D. Runes. Towota, N.J.: Littlefield, Adams, 1962. 236–37.

Campbell, Neil. *Biology.* 2d ed. Reading, Mass: Benjamin/Cummings, 1990.

Church, Alonzo. "Uncertainty Principle." *Dictionary of Philosophy.* 11th ed. Ed. Dagobert D. Runes. 325. Towota, N.J.: Littlefield, Adams, 1962.

Descartes, René. *Discours de la méthode.* Paris: Didier, 1971.

Detlefsen, Michael. "Hilbert's Programme and Formalism." *Routledge Encyclopedia of Philosophy.* Ed. Edward Craig. New York: Routledge, 1998. 4:422–29.

Diels, Hermann, and Walter Kranz, eds. *Die Fragmente der Vorsokratiker, griechisch und deutsch.* 3 vols. 6th ed. Berlin: Weidmann, 1951–52.

Durkheim, Émile. *The Rules of the Sociological Method.* Ed. Steven Lukes. Trans. W. D. Halls. New York: Free Press, 1982.

Engels, Friedrich. *Dialectics of Nature.* Trans. and ed. Clemens Dutt. New York: International Publishers, c1940.

Ernout, A., and A. Meillet. *Dictionnaire étymologique de la langue latine, histoire des mots.* 4th ed. Paris: C. Klincksieck, 1967.

Fanchi, John R. *Parametrized Relativistic Quantum Theory.* London: Kleuwer, 1993.

Fichte, Johann Gottlieb. *Wissenschaftslehre 1804.* Stuttgart: W. Kohlhammer, 1969.

Bibliography

Fishler, Max. "Anaximander." In *Dictionary of Philosophy*. 11th ed. Ed. Dagobert D. Runes. Towota, N.J.: Littlefield, Adams, 1962. 12.

———. "Heraclitus." In *Dictionary of Philosophy*. 11th ed. Ed. Dagobert D. Runes. Towota, N.J.: Littlefield, Adams, 1962. 124–25.

———. "Parmenides." In *Dictionary of Philosophy*. 11th ed. Ed. Dagobert D. Runes. Towota, N.J.: Littlefield, Adams, 1962. 225.

Fowler, Thomas B., Jr. "The Formality of Reality: Xavier Zubiri's Critique of Hume's Analysis of Causality." *Xavier Zubiri Review* 1 (1998): 57–66.

Galilei, Galileo. *Dialogues concerning the Two New Sciences (Dialoghi delle scienze nuove)*. Trans. Henry Crew and Alfonso de Salvio. In *Great Books of the Western World*. Ed. Robert Maynard Hutchins. Vol. 28, *Gilbert, Galileo, Harvey*. Chicago: Encyclopaedia Britannica, 1952. 129–260.

Goldschmidt, Richard B. *In and Out of the Ivory Tower: The Autobiography of Richard B. Goldschmidt*. Seattle: University of Washington Press, 1960.

———. *The Material Basis of Evolution*. New Haven: Yale University Press, 1940.

Gracia, Diego. *Voluntad de verdad: Para leer a Zubiri*. Barcelona: Labor Universitaria, 1986.

Grattan-Guiness, I. *The Search for Mathematical Roots, 1870–1940*. Princeton: Princeton University Press, 2000.

Greenwood, Thomas. "Principle of Sufficient Reason." In *Dictionary of Philosophy*. 11th ed. Ed. Dagobert D. Runes. Towota, N.J.: Littlefield, Adams, 1962. 250.

Guthrie, Hunter. "Act." In *Dictionary of Philosophy*. 11th ed. Ed. Dagobert D. Runes. Towota, N.J.: Littlefield, Adams, 1962. 4.

———. "Scholasticism." In *Dictionary of Philosophy*. 11th ed. Ed. Dagobert D. Runes. Towota, N.J.: Littlefield, Adams, 1962. 280–84.

Halliday, David, and Robert Resnick. *Fundamentals of Physics*. 3d ed. New York: Wiley, 1988.

Hardt, Tom G. *The Sacrament of the Altar: A Book on the Lutheran Doctrine of the Lord's Supper*. Fort Wayne, Ind.: Concordia Theological Seminary Press, 1984.

Hegel, G. W. F. *Encyclopedia of the Philosophical Sciences in Outline and Critical Writings*. Ed. Ernst Behler. Trans. Steven A. Taubeneck. New York: Continuum, 1990.

———. *Phänomenologie des Geistes*. Ed. Dietmar Köhler and Otto Pöggeler. Berlin: Akademie Verlag, 1998.

———. *Phenomenology of Spirit*. Trans. A. v. Miller. Oxford: Clarendon Press, 1977.

———. *The Philosophy of Hegel*. 2d ed. Ed. Carl J. Friedrich. New York: Modern Library, 1954.

———. *Philosophy of History*. Trans. J. Sibree. In *Great Books of the Western World*. Ed. Robert Maynard Hutchins. Vol. 46, *Hegel*. Chicago: Encyclopaedia Britannica, 1952. 153–369.

———. *Philosophy of Right*. Trans. T. M. Knox. In *Great Books of the Western World*. Ed. Robert Maynard Hutchins. Vol. 46, *Hegel*. Chicago: Encyclopaedia Britannica, 1952. 1–150.

————. *The Science of Logic.* Trans. A. V. Miller. London: George Allen and Unwin, 1969.

Heidegger, Martin. *Sein und Zeit.* In *Gesamtausgabe.* Vol. 2. Frankfurt: Vittorio Klostermann, 1977. 1–583.

Holtfreter, J. "Nachweis der Induktionsfähigkeit abgetäteter Keimteile." *Wilhelm Roux' Archiv für Entwicklungsmechanik der Organismen* 128 (1933): 584–633.

Kant, Immanuel. *Critique of Pure Reason.* Trans. F. Max Müller. Garden City, N.Y.: Anchor Books, 1966.

————. *Kritik der reinen Vernunft.* Hamburg: Felix Meiner, 1930.

Katz, David. *Psicología de la forma.* Trans. José M. Sacristán. Madrid: Espasa-Calpe, 1945.

Laín Entralgo, Pedro. *Antropología médica para clínicos.* 3d ed. Barcelona: Salvat, 1986.

————. *Cuerpo y alma: Estructura dinámica del cuerpo humano.* Madrid: Espasa-Universidad, 1991.

————. *El cuerpo humano: Teoría actual.* Madrid: Espasa-Calpe, 1989.

————. *El diagnóstico médico: Historia y teoría.* Barcelona: Salvat, 1982.

————. *La espera y la esperanza.* 3d ed. Madrid: Alianza Universidad, 1984.

————. *Teoría y realidad del otro.* 4th ed. Madrid: Alianza, 1983.

Latham, R. E. *Dictionary of Medieval Latin from British Sources.* Fascicule 2C. London: Oxford University Press, 1981.

Leibniz, G. W. *Gesammelte Werke.* Vol. 4. Ed. Georg Heinrich Pertz. Hildesheim: Gg. Olms, 1966.

————. *La Monadologie.* Ed. Émile Boutroux. Paris: Delagrave, 1968.

Liddell, George, and Robert Scott. *A Greek-English Lexicon.* 6th rev. ed. New York: Harper, 1878.

Loewy, Raymond. "Industrial Design." In *Collier's Encyclopedia.* 17th ed. Ed. Louis Shores. New York: Crowell, Collier, and Macmillan, 1967. 12:732–38.

Marías, Julián. *Historia de la filosofía.* 21st ed. Madrid: Revista de Occidente, 1968.

Maritain, Jacques. *The Degrees of Knowledge.* Trans. Bernard Wall and Margot R. Adamson. London: Geoffrey Bles, Centenary Press, 1937.

————. "Vers une Idee Thomiste de l'Évolution: Première approche." *Nova et Vetera* 42, no. 2 (Apr.–June 1967): 87–136.

McClintock, Robert. *Man and His Circumstance: Ortega as Educator.* New York: Teachers College, Columbia University, 1971.

McMurray, John. *Organic Chemistry.* 2d ed. Pacific Grove, Calif.: Brooks/Cole, 1988.

Moliner, María. *Diccionario de uso del español.* 2 vols. 2d ed. Madrid: Gredos, 1967.

Moody, Ernest A. "Medieval Philosophy." In *Collier's Encyclopedia.* 17th ed. Ed. Louis Shores. New York: Crowell, Collier, and Macmillan, 1967. 18:707–12.

Morrow, Glenn R. "Logos." In *Dictionary of Philosophy.* 11th ed. Ed. Dagobert D. Runes. Towota, N.J.: Littlefield, Adams, 1962. 183–84.

Nagata, Jun-Iti. *Modern General Topology.* New York: American Elsevier, 1968.

Orringer, Nelson R. *La aventura de curar: La antropología médica de Pedro Laín Entralgo.* Barcelona: Galaxia Gutenberg, Círculo de Lectores, 1997.

Ortega y Gasset, José. *El hombre y la gente.* In *Obras completas.* 2d ed. Madrid: Revista de Occidente, 1965. 7:73–272.

Bibliography

——. *La idea de principio en Leibniz y la evolución de la teoría deductiva.* In *Obras completas.* 2d ed. Madrid: Revista de Occidente, 1965. 8:63–356.

——. *El tema de nuestro tiempo.* In *Obras completas.* 5th ed. Madrid: Revista de Occidente, 1965. 3:145–242.

Peirce, Charles S. "The Doctrine of Chances." *Popular Science Monthly* 12 (March 1878): 604–15.

Pintor Ramos, Antonio. "El magisterio intelectual de Ortega y la filosofía de Zubiri." *Cuadernos Salmantinos de Filosofía* 10 (1983): 55–78.

——. *Zubiri (1898–1983).* Madrid: Ediciones del Orto, 1996.

Pirani, F. A. E. "Relativity." In *Collier's Encyclopedia.* 17th ed. Ed. Louis Shores. New York: Crowell, Collier, and Macmillan, 1967. 19:709–19.

Plato. *Alcibiades I.* In *Charmides. Alcibiades I and II. Hipparchus—The Lovers. Theages. Minos. Epinomis.* 6th ed. Trans. W. R. M. Lamb. Cambridge, Mass.: Harvard University Press, 1999. 95–223.

——. *Republic.* 2 vols. Vol. 1: Books 1–5, 10th ed. Vol. 2: Books 6–10, 9th ed. Trans. Paul Shorey. Cambridge, Mass.: Harvard University Press, 1994.

——. *Theaetetus, Sophist.* 9th ed. Trans. Harold North Fowler. Cambridge, Mass.: Harvard University Press, 1996.

Rodríguez de Lecea, Teresa. "En la muerte de Pedro Laín Entralgo." *Revista de Hispanismo Filosófico,* 6 (October 2001): 75–78.

Scott, J. F. "René Descartes." In *Collier's Encylopedia.* 17th ed. Ed. Louis Shores. New York: Crowell, Collier, and Macmillan, 1967. 8:128–34.

Sheldrake, Rupert. "The Variability of the 'Fundamental Constants.'" *Seven Experiments That Could Change the World.* 1995. The Edge of Science, at Transaction.net: <http://www.transaction.net/science/seven/constant.html#top>.

Sherrington, Charles. *The Integrative Action of the Nervous System.* New York: Scribner's, 1906.

Siegfried, F. P. "Ontology." In *The Catholic Encyclopedia.* Ed. Kevin Knight. New York: Appleton, 1999. Vol. 11. New Advent Web site: <http://www.newadvent.org/cathen/11258a.htm>.

Smith, Anne Collins. "Membership or Transcendence?: Being, Life, and Intelligence in Thomas Aquinas' Commentary on the *Liber de causis.*" Abstract. 1999. Susquehanna University, Department of Philosophy, Religion, and Classical Studies Web site: <http://www.susqu.edu/prcs/facpages/acsmith/kalam.htm>.

Smith-Rose, R. L. "Maxwell, James Clerk." In *Collier's Encyclopedia.* 17th ed. Ed. Louis Shores. New York: Crowell, Collier, and Macmillan, 1967. 15:573–75.

Spinoza, Benedict de (Baruch). *Ethics.* Trans. W. H. White. In *Great Books of the Western World.* Ed. Robert Maynard Hutchins. Vol. 31, *Descartes, Spinoza.* Chicago: Encyclopaedia Britannica, 1952. 355–463.

Stillwell, Richard. "Parthenon." *Collier's Encyclopedia.* 17th ed. Ed. Louis Shores. New York: Crowell, Collier, and Macmillan, 1967. 18:463–64.

Stroke, George W. "Light." *McGraw Hill Encyclopedia of Science and Technology.* 8th ed. New York: McGraw-Hill, 1997. 10:55–64.

Bibliography

Sturdevant, A. H. *A History of Genetics.* 2d ed. Cold Spring Harbor, N.Y.: Cold Spring Press, 2001.

Suárez, Francisco. *Disputaciones metafísicas.* 7 vols. Trans. and ed. Sergio Rábade Romeo, Salvador Caballero Sánchez, and Antonio Puigcerver Zanón. Madrid: Gredos, Biblioteca Hispánica de Filosofía, 1960–66.

Sutton, Thomas de. *De natura accidens.* In *Corpus Thomisticum.* Ed. Enrique Alarcón. Corpus Thomisticum, Thomae de Sutton, De natura accidentis, Web site: <http://sophia.unav.es/alarcon/amicis/xpa.html>.

Tarde, Gabriel de. *Les Lois de l'imitation; étude sociologique.* Paris: Alcan, 1890.

Teilhard de Chardin, Pierre. *Le Phénomène humain.* Paris: Éditions du Seuil, 1955.

Topsoe, Fleming. "Notes on Programming Neural Systems." Nov. 20, 2001. Web site: <http://www.neuralmachines.com/notes/time2html>.

Uffink, Jos, and Jan Hilgevoord. "The Uncertainty Principle." In *Stanford Encyclopedia of Philosophy.* 2001. Web site: <http://plato.stanford.edu/entries/qt-uncertainty/index.htm/#note-1>.

Ullman, B. L., and N. E. Henry. *Latin for Americans.* 2 vols. Rev. ed. New York: Macmillan, 1950.

Weisskopf, Victor F. "The Three Spectroscopies." *Scientific American* 218, no. 5 (May 1968): 15–27.

White, T. D., G. Suwa, W. K. Hart, R. C. Walter, G. Wolde Gabriel, J. de Heinzelin, J. D. Clark, B. Asfaw, and E. Vrba. "New Discoveries of Australopithecus at Maka in Ethiopia." *Nature* 371 (1994): 306–12.

Woollard, G. P. "Gravitation." In *Collier's Encyclopedia.* 17th ed. Ed. Louis Shores. New York: Crowell, Collier, and Macmillan, 1967. 11:324–36.

Young, Paul T. "Drives." In *Collier's Encyclopedia.* 17th ed. Ed. Louis Shores. New York: Crowell, Collier, and Macmillan, 1967. 8:392–93.

Zettili, Nouredine. *Quantum Mechanics.* Chichester, N.Y.: Wiley, 2001.

Zubiri, Xavier. *Cinco lecciones de filosofía.* 3d. ed. Madrid: Alianza Editorial, 1980.

———. "El concepto descriptivo del tiempo." *Realitas* 2:7–47. Madrid: Sociedad de Estudios y Publicaciones—Editorial Labor, 1976.

———. "La dimensión histórica del ser humano." *Realitas* 1:11–69. Madrid: Sociedad de Estudios y Publicaciones, 1980–83.

———. *Espacio, tiempo, materia.* Madrid: Alianza Editorial, Fundación Xavier Zubiri, 1996.

———. *Estructura dinámica de la realidad.* Madrid: Alianza Editorial, Fundación Xavier Zubiri, 1989.

———. *El hombre y Dios.* Madrid: Alianza Editorial, Sociedad de Estudios y Publicaciones, 1984.

———. *Inteligencia sentiente.* 3 vols. Vol. 1, *Inteligencia sentiente,* 2d ed. Vol. 2, *Inteligencia y logos.* Vol. 3, *Inteligencia y razón.* Madrid: Alianza Editorial. Sociedad de Estudios y Publicaciones. 1980–83.

———. *Naturaleza, Historia, Dios.* 9th ed. Madrid: Alianza Editorial, Sociedad de Estudios y Publicaciones, 1987.

————. *Nature, History, God.* Trans. Thomas B. Fowler Jr. Washington, D.C.: University Press of America, 1981.

————. *On Essence.* Trans. A. Robert Caponigri. Washington, D.C.: Catholic University of America Press, 1980.

————. "The Origin of Man." In *Contemporary Spanish Philosophy.* Trans. and ed. A. R. Caponigri. 42–75. Notre Dame, Ind.: University of Notre Dame Press, 1967.

————. "Ortega, maestro de filosofía." *El Sol* (March 8, 1936): 8.

————. "Respectividad de lo real." *Realitas* 3–4:13–43. Madrid: Sociedad de Estudios y Publicaciones, 1976–79.

————. *Sentient Intelligence.* Trans. Thomas B. Fowler. Washington, D.C.: Xavier Zubiri Foundation of North America, 1999.

————. *Sobre la esencia.* 5th ed. Madrid: Alianza Editorial, Sociedad de Estudios y Publicaciones, 1985.

————. *Sobre el sentimiento y la volición.* Madrid: Alianza Editorial, Fundación Xavier Zubiri, 1992.

————. "Zurvanismo." In *Gran enciclopedia del mundo.* Ed. Francisco M. Biosca. Bilbao: Durván, 1964. 19:485–86.

Index

Accident: as adherent, 69–70, 83; as inherent (by tradition), 21–22, 28, 83, 223n1 (chap. 4); life as, 124

Act, 22, 29–31

Action: in dynamism, 43, 85, 104, 207; in physical respectivity, 39–40, 85; and possibility, 163

Activity, 29–30, 32; and causality, 58, 62, 64; as different from reality, 57; and giving of itself, 58; grounding of, 64, 82; of personality in open essence, 159; and potency, 163; and structural stability, 108

Adherent notes, 69; and dynamism, 84; prearranged by substantivity, 71, 158–59; and respectivity, 70; and variation, 204

Affinity, mathematical, 75, 81, 188, 233n13

All, the, 61–62, 141, 206, 213

Aristotle, vii, 1–2; on activity, 29–30; on becoming, 12–13, 223n7 (chap. 4); on being, 218n1, 221n21; on causality, xiv, 47–49, 51–53, 211; on change, 87–88, 90, 221n23, 221n24; Christianized by Scholasticism, 217n11; on living, 124; on motion, 77; physicists' vision of things reversed by, 34, 36, 43; place absolutized by, 74; on potency, xii, 12–13; on prime matter, 88, 94; on subjectivity, xiii, 21, 124–25, 221n26; on substance, 21, 88, 125; on time, 185–86, 188–90; on variation, 71, 73; on world order, 183

Arousal: and animal behavior, 120; and formalization in life, 135; and habitude-respect structure, 114; and response, 111–13, 133; and surrounding medium, 118

Becoming: and act, 30; as "becoming in another," 200; and being, xiii, 9, 12–13, 20–27; and

degrees of reality, 97; as different from change, 26–32, 43, 158, 206–7; as different from changing and occupying place, 159; as different from élan vital, 98; in *Dynamic Structure of Reality,* xii–xiii, 1; dynamism as, 206; and motion, 30, 80; and non-being, 9; and process, 36; and reality, 5, 26–27, 43; two senses of, 9; as unity of being and non-being, 9, 12, 15, 20

Being: active character of, 193; as actuality of reality, 16–17, 193, 203; as copula, 15; and non-being, 10–12; as not respectivity, 16; and potency, 29; and reality, 15–17; as second act of reality, 17–18, 20, 193; substantive, 15–16; and time, 203

Bergson, Henri, 218n10; on becoming as creation, xii; on evolution, 98; on existence of atoms, 89; on life as élan vital, 122; on time, 190, 196–98

Causality: and activity, 61; as appropriation, 155; of dynamism, xv, 44, 59; and ecstasy, 209; and effect, 62–68, 209; as functionality of the real qua real, xiv, 54–61, 104, 154, 208, 229n39; as immediately perceived, 208; implying predominance, 209; of intelligence, 141; and possibility, 155; as processive dynamism, 64

Cause: in Aristotle's works, 47–53, 67; as different from causality, 55–56, 59–62, 208; as different from force, 79; as different from physical law, 52, 62; and ecstasy, 209; in Galileo's works, 49–52; of motion, 79

Change: and cause, 48; as different from becoming, xiii, 13–14, 27, 41, 158; as different

Index

from dynamism, xiv, 207; as different from personality formation, 158; and dynamism of alteration, 87–91, 204; as identified with becoming (Aristotle), 12–13; kinds (Aristotle), 87; and mutations, 95; and process, 35; and repetition, 91–92, 103; as structure of dynamic self-giving, 41; and structure of real, 89

Cognizance of reality, 135; as changing medium into world, 136; as different from being stimulated, 135, 143; and subsistence, 140

Condition: as capacitation for meaning, 150, 163, 170; as ground of instances and resources, 150; as ground of meaning, 150; and naked reality, 163; and possibility, 157

Constitution, 26, 37; in constitutional and constitutive notes, 82, 204, 232n1; of possibility, 159

Construct state of notes: and meaning, 150; and person, 205, 209; and respectivity, 37–38, 57, 62; and structure, 24–27

Corticalization, cerebral, 120, 133

Determinism, scientific, 52; and causality, 53, 58, 62–65, 209

Dynamism: of alteration, xiv, xv, 84–105, 116; as becoming, constituting reality, xv, 26, 41, 206; causal, 47–68, 92–94; and change, xv, 26–44, 91; degrees in, 42; of depersonalization, 168–69; as different from consequent actuation, 207; as formally constitutive of world, 42, 207; as giving of itself, 41–43, 56, 203, 207; and history, 171; of incorporation, 173; of living beings, 116; of living together, xv, 162–80; as making possible, 148–59; organization of, 211; overview of types of, 104–5, 204–5; of personalization, 148, 168, 205; of potentiation, 212; and process, 42; of producing species, 93–94; of repetition, 92; of selfhood, xiv–xv, 104–34, 205; of self-possession, xv, xxi, 135–61, 205–6; as stratified, 86; as structural moment of things in the world, 183; and structure, 26, 42; three strata of, 124; of transformation, xv; of variation, xiv–xv, 68–69, 85–86, 104, 116, 211; of world-making (history), xv, 172–80

Einstein, Albert: on gravity, 77–79, 100–101; indeterminism of, 53; on mass-energy equivalency, 35, 90–91, 224–25n24, 236n18; structuralism in, xvi; on time as measure, 199; and Zubiri, ix–x

Electromagnetic field: charges as points of application of, 59; as closed essence, 66; Cou-

lomb's error about, 224n20; as different from biological medium, 111; discovered by Maxwell, 224n21; as irreducible to mechanical forces, 72; laws of, 224n22; as real for Einstein, 78; as undulating structure, 34–35; unprivileged as structure, 42

Energy: as capacity to produce work, 90; change of matter into, 90–91; exchange of, 107; potential and kinetic, 90, 115

Engels, Friedrich, 2, 219–20n7

Essence: and biological phylum, 166; constituent scheme of, 94; as constitutive system, 23–24, 65, 82–84; and dynamism, 207; as ecstatic, 209; and genesis, 93–94, 202; and giving of itself, 208; as not admitting distinction from existence, 61, 231n63; potentialities of, 99; and quiddity, 94, 105, 169; as reifier of the real, 70; of time, 190–96. *See also* Open essence

Evolution, 95–96; appearance of meiosis in, 118, 133; and becoming, 96; cascades of configurations in, 99; and change in universal constants, 101–2; as constitutive potentiation, 159; as different from course of open essence, 158; as different from élan vital, 98; as different from generation, 105; dynamism of, 33; and ecostructure, 112; and giving of itself, 96, 105, 121; human, xv, 139, 175; and individuation, 99; and in-its-own-right, 106; as integration of alterations, 102, 105, 204; and intelligence, 137; internalization of cellular nucleus in, 117, 120; and life, 115–18; of matter, 100; and mutation, 96, 105–6; origin of open essence in, 138; potentialities of, 98, 105; problem of modification of, 140; as production of virtualities, 212; and reality, 97; of space in universe, 100–101; and speciation, 100; and transformation, 139; and virtual powers, 96, 105

Extruct, 25, 27, 57, 65

Fichte, Johann Gottlieb, 23, 222–23n6

Formalization: and animal psychic makeup, 139; described in particular terms, 133; and hyperformalization, 135; of life, xv, 120, 133, 135

Form of dynamism, 184–85

Fowler, Thomas R., vii, 218n10, 227n18, 229n39

Freedom, 60–61, 164, 209

From, the: and the "to myself," 148, 162, 165–66

Giving of oneself: and activity, 58; adequately in living beings, 131; and adherent notes, 70; and

Index

alteration, 86; and causality, 64, 65, 67, 68; and change, 91, 158; and constitution of the self, 121; as divine property, 102; and dynamic frailty of reality, 214; in *Dynamic Structure of Reality,* xiv, 2; as dynamism and reality, 40–41; and ecstasy, 208; of every dynamism, 124; and evolutionary potentialities, 98; and generation, 94–95; as innovation in transcendental order, 213; and motion, 78–80; and prearranging, 70–71; as response of living being, 112–16; and selfhood, 131; and time, 192–97, 201; and variation, 83

God: and causality, 56, 160–61; in *Dynamic Structure of Reality,* xi; and eternity, 197; and giving of oneself, xvi, 41; the in-its-own-right of, 102; and motion, 14, 77–78; and multiplication, 93

Gracia Guillén, Diego, vii, xi, 219n3
Gurtler, Gary M., vii, xx

Habitude, 113–14; and formal respect, 133; of nutriment and stimulation, 114; society as, 167–68, 205

Hegel, Georg Wilhelm Friedrich: on being as becoming, 218–19n1; compared with Parmenides, 220n8; compared with Zubiri, 218–19n1, 219–20n7; on freedom and necessity, 195; on history as dialectical development, 175; on individual as servant to history, xv, 178; on the self, 126; on social imitation, 167; on society as result of history, 174; on society as substantive, 167; on synthesis in dialectical movement, 195; on universal spirit as becoming reality, 1–2, 142, 177–79, 206

Heidegger, Martin, 218n10; on being, xii; on open essence, xv, 67; on projects, 200; on time, 191; and Zubiri, ix–x, xvi

Heisenberg, Werner, ix–xi, 76, 81, 248n10
Heraclitus, xvi–xvii, 13, 210

History: as constituted by events, 176; defined, 175–76; and de-realization, 177; and dynamism of incorporation, 172–74; as dynamism of possibilities of social body, 171, 174, 176, 205; Hegel on, xv, 177–78; as lacking in selfhood, 177; of medicine, xi–xii, 240n24, 240n25; as mounted on possibility, 176; as open structure, 177; of philosophy, xii; as quasi-creation, 157–58; social body as subject and principle of, 174; and society, 169–74, 205; strata of life and universal, 133; as time lapse, 176; and tradition, 173–74; and world, 178

Homeostasis, 119, 133

Human being: as animal of realities, 136, 139, 143; as evolution, 138; evolved from echinoderms, 140; and hyperformalization, 135; and the "in order to," 127; and *natura naturans,* 141; as open essence, 136–37; and other human beings, 166; as person, 136; and possibilities, 151–56, 163; and power of the real qua real, 154; as rational animal, 139; and self-possession, 146; and stimuli, 136, 141; types of, 138–39

Hume, David, 50–55, 227n18
Husserl, Edmund, 218n10; method of, xii; Ortega and, ix–x; Zubiri and, xvi, 2, 219n5

"I": in Fichte's works, 23; grounded on the "to Me," 147; as resource for future living, 158; as second act of human reality, 18, 156

In-itself: intelligence as mode of, 137; and living with others, 166; and openness, 136

In-its-own-right, xiv, xxi, 219n2; and causality, 64; as constitutional system of notes, 23, 26; as different from essence and existence, 134; evolution of, 102; and genesis, 97; and giving of itself, 2, 134, 225–26n30; of living being, 127; and person, 146; and reality, 19–20, 22–27, 38–40, 124; as respective, 38; and selfhood, 106; as structural, 26; and taking cognizance, 135

Intelligence: arising out of animality, 142; as capacity to face things as real, 143; as having stabilizing function, 140–41; as hyperformalization, 141–43; and living with others, 166; as modification of evolution, 137, 140; and open essence, 137, 145, 166; produced by intrinsic causality, 142; and projects, 201; and rationality, 139; Saint Thomas on, 137

Kant, Immanuel, 218n10; on causality, xii, xiv, 51–55; and Fichte, 222–23n6; in *On Essence,* 2, 219n5; on time and space, 61, 184–85, 194, 198

Katz, David, ix, 120

Laín Entralgo, Pedro, xi–xii, xv–xvi
Laws in physics, 34–36, 43, 50, 54; and evolution, 101; as "hows," 52, 62–63; as related to causality, 59–60, 62; as unrelated to reality, 63

Leibniz, Gottfried Wilhelm: on causality, 47, 51, 54; dynamic viewpoint of, 49; infinite analysis in, 60; on motion originated by subject, 77; on possibility, 29, 223n6; on reality as activity, 225n28; refuted by Zubiri, 39–40, 57–58, 64, 82

XAVIER ZUBIRI (1898–1983) is largely considered the last great Spanish philosopher of the twentieth century. His works include *Sentient Intelligence, On Essence,* and *Nature, History, God.*

NELSON R. ORRINGER is a professor of Spanish and comparative literature at the University of Connecticut. His works include *Ortega and His Germanic Sources* and *Unamuno and the Liberal Protestants.*

The University of Illinois Press
is a founding member of the
Association of American University Presses.

———————————————————————

Composed in 10.5/13 Minion
with Caflisch and Arabesque display
by Jim Proefrock
at the University of Illinois Press
Designed by Dennis Roberts
Manufactured by Thomson-Shore, Inc.

University of Illinois Press
1325 South Oak Street
Champaign, IL 61820-6903
www.press.uillinois.edu